AGING AND CAREGIVING

OTHER RECENT VOLUMES IN THE
SAGE FOCUS EDITIONS

AGING AND CAREGIVING

Theory, Research, and Policy

Edited by

David E. Biegel
Arthur Blum

SAGE Publications
International Educational and Professional Publisher
Newbury Park   London   New Delhi

11- 8 -95

For information address:

SAGE Publications, Inc.
2455 Teller Road
Newbury Park, California 91320

SAGE Publications Ltd.
6 Bonhill Street
London EC2A 4PU
United Kingdom

SAGE Publications India Pvt. Ltd.
M-32 Market
Greater Kailash I
New Delhi 110 048 India

Printed in the United States of America

Library of Congress Cataloging-in-Publication Data

Main entry under title:

Aging and caregiving : theory, research, and policy /
    editors, David E. Biegel, Arthur Blum.
        p.   cm. — (Sage focus editions ; v. 110)
    Includes bibliographical references.
    ISBN 0-8039-3566-8. — ISBN 0-8039-3567-6 (pbk.)
    1. Aged—Care—United States.   2. Caregivers—United States.
I. Biegel, David E.   II. Blum, Arthur.
HV1461.A49   1990
362.6'0973—dc20   89-27848
                                                         CIP

93 94 15 14 13 12 11 10 9 8 7 6 5 4 3 2

Contents

Acknowledgments

The idea for this volume grew out of the efforts of the Practice Demonstration Program, Mandel School of Applied Social Sciences. This program engages in research and demonstration activities that seek to increase knowledge about human service needs and to test the effectiveness of alternative human service delivery approaches to meet those needs. A major program component is the Family Caregiving Project funded by The George Gund Foundation, whose goal is to improve the ability of human service agencies to better address the needs of family caregivers and to assist families more fully in their caregiving tasks.

Chapters in this volume by Raveis, Hanks, Chiriboga , Montgomery, and colleagues are expanded versions of papers originally published in the Special Issue: Aging and Family Caregivers, *The Journal of Applied Social Sciences, 13* (1), Fall/Winter, 1988–89, edited by David Biegel and Arthur Blum. *The Journal of Applied Social Sciences* is thanked for permission to utilize these papers in this book.

The development and publication of this volume would not have been possible without the combined assistance of a number of individuals. Judy Simpson, Project Officer, The George Gund Foundation, provided continued encouragement for our work and helped secure the financial resources necessary to make this project a reality. Richard L. Edwards, Dean, Mandel School of Applied Social Sciences, is thanked for his support of this project and for his commitment of resources which aided our efforts. Administrative and technical support were provided by Jackie Goodin, Ellen Durand, Kathleen Fant, and Linda Wykoff.

Introduction

DAVID E. BIEGEL
ARTHUR BLUM

In the past decade, there has been an increasing awareness of the significant role that families provide in caring for dependent family members. Informal service providers have always been the dominant source of human service care to most individuals in need. In fact, if the informal network was unavailable, professional agencies would become so inundated with service demands that they would be unable to function.

More recently, researchers have recognized that family caregiving, though having positive aspects for the caregiver, is often stressful as well. This knowledge has led to the development of a number of service and policy initiatives designed to reduce caregiver burden and provide supportive assistance to enable families to continue their caregiving roles. There is now a growing body of literature pertaining to family caregiving with a variety of dependent population groups, such as the mentally ill, Alzheimer's patients, stroke victims, the mentally retarded, cancer patients, and the frail elderly.

This volume focuses on a particular population group for whom family caregiving is an extremely important issue—the elderly. The majority of disabled older persons lives in the community and is cared for by families. As many researchers have shown, it is a myth that the elderly are abandoned by

AUTHORS' NOTE

Kathleen Farkas, Eva Kahana and Richard Schulz are thanked for their helpful comments on an earlier draft of this paper.

their families (Brody, 1982; Cantor, 1975; Select Committee on Aging, 1987; Shanas, 1979; Sussman, 1976). Rather, family members provide extensive support and represent the elderly's most significant resource. In 1977, the U.S. General Accounting Office estimated that 70–80% of supportive care to older persons was provided by family members (U.S. General Accounting Office, 1977). More recent research has substantiated the significant levels of care being provided by families, friends, and neighbors. It is estimated that approximately 75% of noninstitutionalized disabled elderly persons in the community rely solely on care from the informal support system (Select Committee on Aging, 1987). The more frail the elderly family member, the greater likelihood that children will assume more responsibility for care. The family is also the source of care most preferred by the elderly.

Trends and Issues in Caregiving

Caregiving needs of the elderly are heightened by a number of recent (and anticipated) demographic, economic, and social changes that help explain the growing interest in family caregiving as a research, practice, and policy issue. Key trends include:

• Life expectancy and the percentage of the elderly population has increased dramatically during this century.

Life expectancy has increased substantially since 1900, regardless of race or sex. Between 1900 and 1985 this increase ranged from 25 years for white males to 40 years for black females (National Center for Health Statistics, 1987). In 1986, the average life expectancy for women was 78.5 years, and 71.5 years for men. By 2005, life expectancy will increase to 81 years for women and 74.1 for men (Older Women's League, 1989). The death rate for the elderly has been falling steadily over the past 40 years, with the age-adjusted death rate for individuals 65 years of age or over falling 29% from 1950 to 1982. The death rate for women fell considerably faster than that of men. During this period the death rate for the aged from heart disease decreased by over one-third (34%) and from cerebrovascular diseases by over one-half (56%) (Waldo & Lazenby, 1984). A consequence of the decreases in mortality has been an increase in elderly persons with chronic impairments and functional disabilities.

The increase in life expectancy of the elderly coupled with other demographic and social trends has led to a large increase in the elderly population.

The number of elderly persons in the United States is growing faster in proportion to the total population than younger age groups. In 1900, only 4% of the population was aged 65 and over; by 1980 the percentage of elderly had risen to 11%. It is estimated that by the year 2000, 13% of the population in the United States will be 65 years and over and by the year 2050, one out of every five persons in the United States will be elderly (Select Committee on Aging, 1987). In the 30 year period from 1950 to 1980, there was a doubling of the elderly population from 12.3 million in 1950 to 25.5 million in 1980 (Taeuber, 1983).

The oldest cohort, those aged 85 years and over, who are at greatest risk for chronic illness, who have the most functional dependency, and who have the greatest needs for health and social services, are growing the fastest. Between 1950 and 1980, the population 85 years and older rose 165%. Between 1980 and 2050, this sub-group of the elderly is expected to increase from 2.2 million persons, 1% of the population, to 16.1 million persons, 5.2% of the total population (Taeuber, 1983).

There are more elderly women than elderly men that require caregiving assistance. Women live significantly longer than men. In 1980, there were 10.2 million men aged 65 years and over, and 15.2 million elderly women, a ratio of 68 men to 100 women. This ratio declines rapidly with age. Whereas for the elderly 65–69 years, there are 80 males to every 100 females, there are only 44 males to every 100 females aged 85 years and older. Elderly women are also more likely to have lower incomes than elderly males, to live alone, and to experience multiple chronic health problems (Biegel, Shore, & Gordon, 1984; Rix, 1984).

- There has been an increase in multigenerational families, resulting in a growing number of elderly caregivers.

One consequence of the above-noted increase in life expectancy and growth in the number and percentage of the elderly population is a shift toward multigenerational families. One-fifth of the elderly in their early sixties have a surviving parent, as do 10% in their late sixties and 3% in their seventies (Hooyman and Lustbader, 1986; Select Committee on Aging, 1987). Thus, the elderly are caregivers as well as care-recipients. Data from the Informal Caregivers Study of the 1982 National Long Term Care Survey indicate that over one-third of the caregiver sample was age 65 and older (25.4% age 65–74 years and 10.1% 75 years and older). In a 1988 nationwide telephone survey of caregivers who provide care to a family member aged 50 years and older, the American Association of Retired Persons (AARP) found that 15% of all caregivers were age 65 and older. Of those who identified themselves as primary caregivers, 20% were age 65 and older (AARP, 1989; Stone, Cafferata & Sangl, 1987).

• Family structures are changing due to declining fertility rates and increases in the divorce rate.

Fertility rates declined 44% between 1955 and 1975 (National Center for Health Statistics, 1987). During the 1990s while the total number of births will decrease by 9.2%, the elderly population will increase by over 10% (Older Women's League, 1989). Reduced fertility rates mean there will be fewer children and siblings to share the burden of care for the future generation of elderly persons (Treas, 1977, 1981). The combination of declining fertility rates and increasing life expectancy has led to a reversal in traditional caregiving patterns. The average woman now spends 18 years of her life helping an elderly parent as compared to 17 years of her adult life caring for a dependent child. Married couples now have more parents than children (Preston, 1984; Select Committee on Aging, 1987).

Divorce rates have also increased over the past 25 years. From 1960 to 1984, the percentage of divorced males increased from 2% to 6.1% while the percentage of divorced females increased from 2.9% to 8.3% (Rosen, Fanshel, & Lutz, 1987). This increase in divorces together with an increase in remarriages has led to a growing number of "reconstituted families." As Hooyman and Lustbader (1986) point out, these developments have had a significant impact on caregiving. One consequence is that adult children now may be providing care for former parents-in-law in addition to current parents and parents-in-law. An additional consequence is that adult children who become divorced may have less time or emotional energy left for caregiving to an elder.

• Greater numbers of women, the traditional caregivers, are in the labor force.

It is estimated that almost three-quarters (72%) of caregivers to the functionally impaired elderly are women (Select Committee on Aging, 1987). Whether by choice or economic necessity, females (wives, daughters or daughters-in-law), the traditional caregivers, are working in increasing numbers. Concern has been expressed about the impact of this trend on the ability of these caregivers to continue to be able to meet the needs of their dependent elderly relatives in the future (Biegel et al., 1984; Doty, 1986; Select Committee on Aging, 1987). In 1960, slightly over one-third (37.7%) of women were members of the civilian labor force; by 1986, this percentage had increased to 55.3% (U.S. Bureau of the Census, 1987). Three-quarters of all women who work outside the home do so on a full-time basis (U.S. Department of Labor, 1984). The largest category of working women are middle-aged married women. Sixty percent of married women between the ages of 45 and 54 are in the labor force, while 42% of married women between the ages of 55 and 64 are in the labor force (U.S. Department of Labor, 1984).

Doty's (1986) review of studies that examined caregiving and work indicates conflicting evidence on the actual impact of female employment on family caregiving. Some studies find diminished ability to provide home care for elderly relatives because of caregiver employment, while other studies find no difference in the likelihood of providing care or in the amounts of hours of care provided by working and nonworking caregivers. Data collected in 1982 from the Informal Caregivers Survey indicate that one-fifth of the employed caregivers reported conflicts between work and caregiving that required some alterations in caregiving schedules (Stone et al., 1987). In a recent nationwide telephone survey of caregivers who provide care to a family member aged 50 years and older, one-third (33%) of caregivers who work full time report losing time from work due to caregiving, while 9% report having to take a leave of absence (AARP, 1989).

There has been concern expressed by Brody (1981), Hooyman and Lustbader (1986), and others about the so-called "sandwich generation," that is, women in the middle generation with multiple role responsibilities of wife, mother, and caregiver to an elderly parent or in-law. If the caregiver is employed, work becomes another responsibility that needs to be managed at the same time. Unresolved issues include how women manage work and caregiving, the impact of work on the purchase of caregiving services, and the impact of an increase in the percentage of women caregivers who work on the roles and responsibilities of male caregivers.

- Concern about the increasing costs of institutional care for the elderly has led to the development of a number of state level initiatives to support caregivers, which are aimed at delaying or preventing institutionalization.

Public and private expenditures for nursing home care have been increasing at a rapid rate. For example, in 1970 total expenditures for nursing home care were $4.7 billion; by 1984 this total had risen 581% to $32 billion. Four years later, in 1988, this figure had grown by an additional 47% to $47 billion. This latter figure represents 10.9% of all health care expenditures. It is anticipated that total expenditures for nursing home care will grow to $56 billion by 1990. During the period from 1970 to 1985, Medicare costs for nursing home care doubled from $300 million to $600 million, while Medicaid costs increased by 950% from $1.4 billion to $14.7 billion (Arnett, McKusick, Sonnefeld, & Cowell, 1986; Marcus, 1987; Waldo, Levit, & Lazenby, 1986).

Historically, there has been little public support for long-term care services in the home. Home care especially has been episodic, short-term, and responsive to acute conditions and not chronic diseases (Berkman, 1978; Shanas & Maddox, 1976). Traditionally, government has not supported families' caregiving efforts or functions. Indeed, families who care for the functionally dependent aged are often penalized, as the state has traditionally withheld services and income benefits when the family retains the caregiving role (Moroney, 1976; Oktay & Palley, 1981). It is only when the family is perceived as being unable to provide care or when family resources are nonexistent, that the government has stepped in to make up the deficit. Now, because of the rising costs of institutional care, some states have responded with policies to address support for home health care as well as direct support for family caregivers.

Findings from a national survey of State Departments of Aging show that 34 states offer some type of economic supports for family caregivers: 14 states have tax supports only, 10 states have direct payment programs only (payments to caregivers for services rendered), and 10 states have both tax and direct payment programs. Despite the rapid growth of state programs, which differ considerably from each other, few state level evaluations have been conducted (Biegel, Schulz, Shore, & Morycz, 1989; Linsk, Keigher, & Osterbusch, 1988).

- Changes in health care reimbursement and medical technology have increased the responsibilities of family caregivers.

Economic pressures have led to a number of changes in the health and social services system which have put additional pressure on family caregivers. The prospective payment system (PPS) for hospital care under Medicare has led to shorter hospital stays, resulting in families having to provide more care than in the past. At the same time, advances in medical technology have increased the number of patients who are being sent home to family caregivers, who must administer drugs and monitor the patient's medical regime. Although there have been no definitive studies of the impacts of the above trends on family caregivers, Coulton (1988) identifies several problems, such as the inability to identify patient needs correctly and the difficulty in assessing caregivers' abilities to provide care, that make it difficult for hospitals to provide adequate support to patients and caregivers upon hospital discharge. In addition, as Coulton points out, the very nature of PPS creates incentives for hospitals to presume that family members can manage care at discharge since the alternative presumption may delay discharge and mean additional costs for the hospital.

The Status of Caregiving Research

These trends make clear the increasing and complex demands being placed on family caregivers of the elderly. Over the past decade, the needs of caregivers have become a prominent focus of gerontologists. In recent years, there has been a large increase in the number of papers on this subject presented at each Annual Meeting of the Gerontological Society of America and published in the gerontological literature. There has also been a concomitant increase in funding of caregiver research by the National Institute on Aging and the National Institute of Mental Health, as well as support of caregiver research by numerous private foundations.

Caregiving research has developed along two major streams. The first has focused on the caregiving process itself, with major emphasis on the effects of caregiving on the caregiver, while the second stream of research has focused on interventions to address caregiver and patient needs.

Research on the effects of caregiving on the caregiver show very clearly that caregiving is not without costs to the caregiver. Many families report caregiving is an emotional and at times financial burden, and this burden may be a major factor in the decision to institutionalize an elderly parent (Krause et al., 1976; Morycz, 1985; Ross & Kedward, 1977; Tobin & Kulys, 1981). Significant caregiving problems identified by researchers include: coping with increased needs of the elderly caused by physical and/or mental illnesses; coping with disruptive behaviors, especially those associated with dementia; physical demands; restrictions on social and leisure activities; infringement of privacy; disruption of household and work routines; conflicting multiple role demands (wife, mother, worker, and caregiver of spouse, parent, or in-laws); lack of support and assistance from other family members; disruption of family relationships; and lack of sufficient assistance from agencies and agency professionals.

Research on the effects of caregiving on the caregiver has gone through a predictable pattern, common to new research in the social sciences. Early caregiver research studies were action and advocacy oriented. They attempted to describe the roles, needs, and burdens of family caregivers, often in the words of the caregivers themselves and often without the utilization of any theoretical frameworks. These studies served an important role in helping to focus attention on the nature of the problem—the needs of family caregivers.

There was then an attempt to develop better conceptualizations and quantitative measures of the concept of burden itself. Various burden scales were developed, and burden was correlated with a variety of caregiver and care-recipient demographic and socioeconomic characteristics and also with such caregiver variables as personality, coping style, social support, health, and mental health outcomes. These studies also began to utilize various theoretical frameworks to guide the analysis. The major limitation was that these studies were cross-sectional in nature, so researchers were not able to make causal inferences, and study samples were small and not representative. At the same time period in which the above studies were being conducted, there were also several large national studies undertaken to help determine the extent, nature, and scope of family caregiving. Thus, for example, a major national study of caregivers of the elderly who were at risk for institutionalization was undertaken that provided data on caregiver and care-recipient characteristics, the nature and extent of caregiving roles, caregiver satisfaction, and emotional, financial and physical strain (Stephens & Christianson, 1986). These studies helped bring national attention to caregiving as a public policy issue and helped place caregiving research in the limelight.

Later studies, based primarily on stress/coping theoretical frameworks, used more sophisticated longitudinal designs, variable measurements, and multivariate data analysis techniques. To address a concern that caregiving research in aging was proceeding in isolation from caregiving research with other populations, several years ago the federal government organized a conference of researchers from various disciplines who were principal investigators on federal research grants studying caregiving with a variety of particular populations. Soon after this conference, the first federal grants were funded that examined caregiving across various dependent population groups in order to begin to identify the similarities and differences of caregiving needs, processes, and outcomes across dependent populations. A number of such studies are currently in progress.

Most recently, caregiver research has begun to shift the focus of caregiver outcomes from caregiver stress or burden to the "harder" outcomes of caregiver morbidity, both psychiatric and physical. Part of this shift has also included a focus on the search for mediating mechanisms, both physical and psychosocial, that affect caregiver morbidity outcomes.

Caregiver intervention research developed as a parallel stream to the above research on the effects of caregiving on the caregiver. This stream of research, which began through government and agency funded examination of program outcomes, developed entirely separately from the research on caregiver burden and morbidity. More recently, the two research streams have begun to merge, with intervention research focusing on an examination of process as well as outcome issues. Intervention research is extremely important because it provides a mechanism for testing causal hypotheses of caregiver outcomes.

Caregiving research is continuing to undergo further development, refinement, and expansion. As this volume makes clear, caregiving research has now broadened considerably to include the examination of the relationship between formal and informal caregiving, contextual factors in caregiving situations, the relationships between caregivers and care-recipients, ethical decision-making, and other related issues.

Organization and Content of This Volume

Despite the advances in the state of the art of caregiving research, there are many gaps remaining in our understanding of caregiving. Our intent in planning the organization of this volume, and in selecting the chapters included here, was to try to respond to omissions in theory, research, and policy rather than to develop a comprehensive reader. In so doing, this volume addresses issues both technical as well as conceptual. The former is addressed by the examination of issues pertaining to needed advancements in sampling, study design, and measurement, while the latter addresses appropriate theoretical frameworks, frames of reference and paradigms for caregiving research utilized to carry out research studies, research questions that need to be asked, and the variables which need to be conceptualized and analyzed in these studies.

The first two chapters of the book provide a review and assessment of the current state of theory and research with an emphasis on gaps in the current literature. The following chapters present new theoretical approaches, research studies, and policy analyses which we think are responsive to the current gaps in knowledge and serve to move the state of knowledge, research methodology, and policy development forward. Our goal is to provide new insight and to give direction for future developments. Thus, each of the chapters provides not only new information, but, in addition, the authors attempt to make explicit the implications of their work for future research, knowledge, and policy development. In order to achieve the widest possible perspectives in examining these issues and in order to move toward a truly interdisciplinary approach to caregiving, we have purposely made this volume interdisciplinary in nature, with contributions by anthropologists, economists, psychologists, sociologists, social workers, and researchers in other related disciplines.

Part 1, *Theory, Conceptual Framework, and Methodology,* presents a series of four chapters. The first two look at the state of current knowledge and research approaches and identify gaps in theory and methodological shortcomings of current research. These chapters are followed by two chapters which suggest new paradigms and theoretical approaches which can broaden our understanding of caregiving and provide direction for future developments.

Schulz, in Chapter 1, reviews the theoretical frameworks which have given direction to caregiver research and finds that there have been a limited number utilized. Rather, the tendency has been to base research on particular variables or outcomes which are not necessarily derived from a theoretical base. Much of the research is an attempt to describe the caregiving situation and its consequences using a limited number of variables and theories. The result often is a negation of the complexity of the interactive processes and the multiplicity of variables which affect it.

The focus in the Raveis, Siegel, and Sudit chapter is on the limits of the research methodologies which have been utilized in the study of psychological variables. Although the paper limits the analysis to psychological impact, the research critique and the issues raised are valid concerns across the wide range of caregiver studies. Concerns are raised, for example, about sample selection, sample size, the adequacy and validity of measurement instruments, and the need for multivariate analysis, comparative studies, longitudinal studies, and more appropriate outcome criteria. Solutions to these methodological issues will require both more sophisticated research methodology and, as indicated by Schulz, the development of more adequate theoretical frameworks for the study of caregiving.

Chapter three, the Kahana and Young chapter, represents one response to trying to fill the gaps in theory and research identified in the first two chapters. The authors analyze the current paradigms which have been used in caregiver research and, using the dyadic relationship as an example, present the need to expand current paradigms to include the interaction between caregiver and care-recipient. Variables which could give direction to interactive studies are identified as well as the need to develop paradigms which go beyond the dyad. The chapter is an excellent example of the care and thought which must be given to conceptualizing the phenomena to be studied and the implications for theory and research which emerge from careful analysis of the complex interactions which characterize the caregiving situation.

Hanks and Settles bring a new perspective to our concerns about caregiving as they add ethical considerations to our understanding. Using a case study approach, the chapter weds social science theory with ethical theory and a feminist ideology within a historical analysis of the nature of the relationship between caregiver and receiver leading up to the current caregiving situation. Although the case represents an extreme example of an ethical dilemma, ethical considerations related to the quality of life, rather than only survival, will play an increasing role in caregiving decisions as medical technologies make it possible to prolong life. Issues such as the degree of family responsibility for caregiving carry with them powerful ethical considerations which must be recognized in the caregiving process and in policy development.

Part 2, *Research—Cognitive and Physical Impairment,* not only presents new data on caregiving, but also represents studies which are responsive to the earlier critical reviews of theory and of research methodology and provide examples of a new wave of research efforts. Each chapter addresses a critical issue in caregiving utilizing expanded sets of variables, more sophisticated research methodologies, and, together, reflect the thinking of persons representing different disciplines.

Chiriboga, Weiler, and Nielsen utilize a stress psychological well-being framework to explore a wide variety of potential stressors related to stress both in the caregiving interaction and in the environment of adult children who care for an elderly parent afflicted with Alzheimer's disease. A series of regression analyses indicates that stressors not directly associated with caregiving, particularly work stress and stresses involving social relationships, play a more important role than caregiver-related stressors. The study emphasizes the importance of environmental stressors and the need to broaden our analyses and program intervention to include factors outside the dyadic caregiver–care-recipient relationship.

Responding to the need for comparative studies and the examination of caregiving over time, Montgomery, Kosloski, and Borgatta studied three groups of caregivers and receivers: those presumed to be suffering from Alzheimer's disease, those with cognitive impairment but for whom Alzheimer's disease was not the suspected cause, and those with no cognitive impairment. Controlling for differences in background characteristics, the results produced few meaningful differences among the three groups in the caregiving experience or in use of formal services. The authors raise important questions about policies and programs which assume uniqueness among diagnostic categories of the elderly.

The impact on employee performance (absenteeism and work interruption) and the stress of caregiving responsibility is examined by Neal, Chapman, Ingersoll-Dayton, Emlen, and Boise in a comparative study of four groups: caregivers of the elderly, disabled adults, children, and employees with no caregiving responsibility. Differences were found between caregivers and noncaregivers and within caregiver groups, with caregivers of children experiencing the greatest amount of work interruption. Implications are drawn as to the need and potential adjustments which are necessary in the workplace to support the care responsibilities of these different caregiving groups.

The importance of intensive study of a particular variable over time is exemplified by the work of Kashner, Magaziner, and Pruitt, who examine the association of household size and family size with informal caregiving, use of formal caregivers, and use of institutional placement for aged patients with hip fractures, at three points in time: prefracture, two month postfracture, and six month postfracture. Findings suggest that characteristics of the entire family, not only the designated caregiver, are important determinants of the amount of time devoted to caregiving, as are an optimal family size of two to four members and the duration of the period of dysfunction related to the hip fracture. In addition to overall informal caregiving time, the study examines the amount of time devoted to eight categories of informal caregiving and provides a data base which could be used to compare caregiver time for the physically and cognitively impaired elderly. Most important for research and practice, the study draws our attention to the need to consider the entire family constellation and not only the designated or self-appointed caregiver.

In the last chapter in this section, Chelst, Tait, and Gallagher draw our attention to what has been reported as one of the most frustrating aspects of caregiving—a breakdown in communication between the caregiver and care-recipient. Utilizing a laboratory-based experimental design, the authors study the linguistic strategies used by normally hearing caregivers in conversations with simulated elderly hearing-impaired spouses. Using linguistic and communication theory previously used to explain speech development in young children, the research suggests commonalities in communication patterns which are effective with hearing impaired elderly.

The study represents an excellent example of the need to include a variety of disciplines in our quest to understand the caregiving process. It also demonstrates the relevance of theories which explain development processes of other age cohorts in giving us better insight into the aging processes and appropriate responses to these processes.

Part 3 of the book, *Public Policy Perspectives,* is not intended to represent a comprehensive analysis of public policy. Rather, it is an attempt to identify a limited set of issues which we think should be added to the general debate on public policy for the elderly and to provide insights which could enrich that debate. The first two chapters focus on analyses specific to American social policy, while the latter two chapters examine social policies in two countries at very different stages of development. They serve to provide different perspectives on caregiving which may help us frame the questions in the U.S. debate in different ways and alert us to additional issues and alternatives for consideration.

Women represent the overwhelming majority of caregivers. Hooyman's analysis focuses on the changing role of women in American society, the shifts in the role of women in the workplace, the inequities in role expectations of women as caregivers, and the consequences of these changes for caregiving. The paper suggests a series of implications for social policy which result from these changes in role and role expectations of women as a means of providing more adequate care, but on a more equitable basis in relation to the female caregiver.

In a democratic society, one assumes that public opinion is the driving force behind decisions on public policy made by lawmakers. Gilliland and Havir explore this assumption through an analysis of public opinion polls and the consistency and inconsistency of congressional response to long-term care policy for the elderly. Following an exploration of some myths held by lawmakers concerning responsibility for elderly care, the authors utilize political economy theory to explain the lag in responsiveness and the incongruence between current legislation on long-term care and public opinion as reflected in pubic opinion polls.

Hokenstad and Johansson present in their analysis of family caregiving policy and program development in Sweden a stark contrast to U.S. policy, based on a major difference in ideology. In Sweden, elderly care policy is based on a societal commitment to support the formal caregiving system. The government is responsible for funding the care needs of all elderly, and the informal care system is supplementary or is a substitute for formal care only by choice of the elderly or the caregivers. In contrast, U.S. policy derives from an ideology that believes that elderly care is the responsibility of the family and the informal care system, and that formal care, supported by public policy, is to be available only in instances in which it is impossible for the family and the informal care system to meet the needs of the elderly. The development of policy and programs in Sweden represent an exciting example of community commitment to elderly care. The current policy issues related to direct support for family care and the need and approaches to integrate more effectively the formal and informal care systems provide important insight and potential alternatives which might give direction to greater unification of the fragmented system of elderly care in the U.S. Recognizing that ideological differences will result in different systems of care, this chapter provides examples of creative attempts to deal with the needs of the elderly which might be adapted and utilized in the policy debate in the U.S.

In addition to providing a fascinating look at the cultural changes occurring in mainland China, Ikels's chapter draws our attention to the unintended consequences of economic policy, labor policy, and the demands of modern technological change for family caregivers. In a culture in which the total responsibility for elderly care has for centuries been assigned to the family, current responses to the demands of modernity have made it difficult for families to fulfill this responsibility and has required a governmental policy response to assist in meeting the needs of the elderly. The chapter underlines the need in the U.S., as well as in China, to examine carefully the consequences of economic and labor policy and the shifts in patterns of production on systems of care for the elderly. Social policy must be developed in the context of changes occuring in the total society and the consequences of these broader developments for the elderly care system.

Given the anticipated increased demands on family caregivers of the elderly in the future, it is critical that service delivery and policy initiatives to address the needs of family caregivers be based upon careful consideration of research findings from well conceptualized and implemented research studies. The issues raised by this volume are complex and not easily addressed. The contribution of this volume, we hope, will be to stimulate new ways of looking and thinking about these issues and to encourage the continued development and expansion of caregiving research.

References

American Association of Retired Persons. (1989). *Working caregivers report, March 1989.* Washington, DC: AARP.

Arnett, R.H., McKusick, D.R., Sonnefeld, S.T., & Cowell, C.S. (1986). *Health Care Financing Review, 7*(3), 1-36.

Berkman, B. (1978). Mental health and aging: A review of the literature. *Clinical Social Work Journal, 6,* 230-245.

Biegel, D.E., Shore, B.K., & Gordon, E. (1984). *Building support networks for the elderly: Theory and applications.* Newbury Park, CA: Sage.

Biegel, D., Schulz, R., Shore, B., & Morycz, R. (1989). Economic supports for family caregivers of the elderly: Tax policies and direct payment programs. In M. Z. Goldstein (Ed.), *Family involvement in the treatment of the frail elderly.* Washington, DC: American Psychiatric Press.

Brody, E.M. (1981). Women in the middle and family help to older people. *The Gerontologist, 21*(5), 471-480.

Brody, E.M. (1982). Older people, their families and social welfare. *Social Welfare Forum, 1981.* New York: Columbia University Press.

Cantor, M. H. (1975). Life space and the support system of the inner city elderly of New York. *The Gerontologist, 15*(1), 23-27.

Coulton, C. (1988). Prospective payment requires increased attention to quality of post hospital care. *Social Work in Health Care, 13*(4), 19-31.

Doty, P. (1986). Family care of the elderly: The role of public policy. *The Milbank Quarterly, 64*(1), 34-75.

Hooyman, N.R., & Lustbader, W. (1986). *Taking care: Supporting older people and their families.* New York: Free Press.

Krause, A., Spasoff, R., Beattie, E., Holden, E., Lawson, J., Rodenberg, M., & Woodcock, G. (1976). Elderly applicants to long-term care institutions. *Journal of the American Geriatrics Society, 24,* 117-125.

Linsk, N.L., Keigher, S.M., & Osterbusch, S.E. (1988). State policies regarding paid family caregiving. *The Gerontologist, 28*(2), 204-212.

Marcus, L.J. (1987). Health care financing. In A. Minahan (Ed.), *Encyclopedia of Social Work* (18th ed., Vol. 1, pp. 697-709). Silver Spring, MD: National Association of Social Workers.

Moroney, R. (1976). *The family and the state: Considerations for social policy.* London: Longman Press.

Morycz, R.K. (1985). Caregiving strain and the desire to institutionalize family members with Alzheimer's Disease. *Research on Aging, 7*(3), 329-361.

National Center for Health Statistics. (1987). *Health/United States.* Washington, DC: U.S. Public Health Service, CDC, National Center for Health Statistics.

Oktay, J., & Palley, H. (1981). A national family policy for the chronically ill elderly. *Social Welfare Forum, 1980.* New York: Columbia University Press.

Older Women's League. (1989). *Failing America's caregivers: A status report on women who care.* Washington, DC: Author.

Preston, S.H. (1984). Children and the elderly. *Scientific American, 250*(6), 44-49.

Rix, S.E. (1984). *Older women: The economics of aging.* Washington, DC: Women's Research and Education Institute of the Congressional Caucus for Women's Issues.

Ross, H., & Kedward, H. (1977). Psychogeriatric hospital admissions from the community and institutions. *Journal of Gerontology, 32,* 420-427.

Rosen, S.M., Fanshel, D., & Lutz, M.E. (Eds.). (1987). *Face of the Nation, 1987. Statistical supplement to the 18th Edition of the Encyclopedia of Social Work.* Silver Spring, MD: National Association of Social Workers.

Select Committee on Aging, U.S. House of Representatives (Stone, R.). (1987). *Exploding the myths: Caregiving in America* (One hundredth Congress, First Session. Comm. Pub. No. 99-611). Washington, DC: U.S. Government Printing Office.

Shanas, E. (1979). The family as a social support system in old age. *The Gerontologist, 9*(2), 169-174.

Shanas, E., & Maddox, G. (1976). Aging, health and organization of health resources. In R. Binstock & E. Shanas (Eds.), *Handbook of aging and the social sciences.* New York: Van Nostrand Reinhold.

Stephens, S.A., & Christianson, J.B. (1986). *Informal care of the elderly.* Lexington, MA: D.C. Heath and Company.

Stone, R., Cafferata, G.L., & Sangl, J. (1987). Caregivers of the elderly: A national profile. *The Gerontologist, 27*(5), 616-626.

Sussman, M.B. (1976). The family life of old people. In R.H. Binstock & E. Shanas (Eds.), *Handbook of aging and the social sciences.* New York: Van Nostrand.

Taeuber, C. (1983). America in transition: An aging society. *Current population reports* (Special Studies Series, P-23, No. 128). Bureau of the Census. Washington, DC: U.S. Department of Commerce.

Tobin, S., & Kulys, R. (1981). The family and the institutionalization of the elderly. *Journal of Social Issues, 37,* 145-157.

Treas, J. (1977). Family support systems for the aged: Some social and demographic considerations. *The Gerontologist, 17,* 486-491.

Treas, J. (1981). The great American fertility debate: Generational balance and support of the aged. *The Gerontologist, 21,* 98-103.

U.S. Bureau of the Census. (1987). *Statistical abstract of the United States: 1988* (108th ed.). Washington, DC: U.S. Government Printing Office.

U.S. Department of Labor, Bureau of Labor Statistics (1984). *Employment and Earnings, 30*(1) Washington, DC: U.S. Government Printing Office.

U.S. General Accounting Office. (1977). *Report to the Congress: The well-being of older people in Cleveland, Ohio.* (Doc. No. HRD-77-70). Washington, DC: U.S. Government Printing Office.

Waldo, D.R., & Lazenby, H.C. (1984). Demographic characteristics and health care use and expenditures by the aged in the United States: 1977-1984. *Health Care Financing Review, 6*(1).

Waldo, D.R., Levit, K.R., & Lazenby, H. (1986). National health expenditures, 1985. *Health Care Financing Review, 8*(1), 1-21.

PART I

Theory, Conceptual Framework, and Methodology

1

Theoretical Perspectives on Caregiving

Concepts, Variables, and Methods

RICHARD SCHULZ

The central questions about caregiving are who provides what type of care to whom, and what are the costs and benefits of providing that care? These inter-related questions are the bases of much of the published literature on caregiving.

The major purpose of this chapter is to address these questions broadly and to raise a third, often overlooked, question, namely, why do people provide informal care, despite the often high costs associated with doing so? Diverse theoretical perspectives and a rich empirical data base are brought to bear to these issues. The question of "why" is addressed first, followed by a discussion of key conceptual and methodological issues relevant to evaluating the costs and benefits of caregiving. Finally, the question of "who" is addressed by examining issues of external validity in the caregiving literature.

Why Do People Help?

Much of the literature on caregiving is aimed at dispelling the "illusion of the Golden Past" (Brody, 1985; Kent, 1965), the myth of the idyllic three

AUTHOR'S NOTE

Preparation of this manuscript was in part supported by grants from the National Institute on Aging (AGO 5444) and the National Institute of Mental Health (MH 41887).

generation household in which, in contrast to current practice, the oldest generation was diligently cared for by younger generations. As Brody (1985) points out in her review of this literature, it is ironic that this myth persists despite the fact that "nowadays adult children provide more care and more difficult care to more parents over much longer periods of time than they did in the good old days" (p. 21).

Although there exist abundant data documenting the validity of Brody's analysis, few researchers have attempted to answer the appropriate follow-up question: why do people provide such large quantities of help, particularly in view of the apparent personal costs often associated with providing care? To some, the answer to this question may be self-evident. As the demand for care changes so does the amount of care provided since there exist strong normative expectations in our culture to help our kin. This explanation obviously tells us little of the psychological significance in understanding caregiving and invites further speculation about the motives of caregivers. The purpose of this section is to address this question from a psychological perspective.

For almost two decades, experimental social psychologists have been interested in developing theory and a data base to answer the questions: why and when do people help? Interest in these questions was kindled by the tragic stabbing death of Kitty Genovese in 1964, who was repeatedly attacked over a period of 37 minutes in the presence of 38 witnesses, none of whom helped, and only one of whom finally called the police. Many experts and members of the press blamed the onlookers for their failure to get involved, suggesting that they were cruel and selfish; others suggested they lacked moral compunction, or were cowards. Still other social scientists had no ready explanation for the behavior of the onlookers and decided to investigate systematically the giving and receiving of help as a form of social behavior.

Given the circumstances surrounding the murder of Kitty Genovese, it is not surprising that much of the early research in this area was focused on finding out why and when people are willing to help strangers in emergency situations. This is obviously far removed from a family caregiving situation, but some of the findings of this research may be relevant nevertheless. For example, one phenomenon documented in a series of studies (Latane & Darley, 1970) was the *bystander effect*: the more people present the less likely a given individual is to help. The presence of others may result in the *diffusion of responsibility* and cause an individual to feel that others will take care of the problem or it may make an individual feel apprehensive because others will be evaluating their performance as helpers. When applied to a family caregiving situation, the bystander effect raises some interesting questions which have not yet been addressed in the caregiver literature. For example, although we know that eldest daughters and wives are most often cast in the caregiving role, we know little about how caregiving responsibilities are negotiated and shared as a function of family size, how this process affects satisfaction with the caregiving role, and how caregiving behavior and satisfaction is affected by the caregivers' concerns regarding evaluations of their performance by others.

Another series of studies showed that the victims' personal attributes are powerful determinants of helping. Individuals are more willing to help people who need help if they are physically attractive (Harrell, 1978), dressed attractively (Kleinke, 1977), and if they possess no stigmatizing physical characteristics, such as unattractive birthmarks (Piliavin, Piliavin, & Rodin, 1975), eye patches, or scars (Samorette & Harris, 1976). People are also more willing to help others who are similar to themselves on such attributes as attitudes, political beliefs, nationality, race, and the way they dress (Dovidio, 1984). Applied to the family caregiving context, these findings point to another set of variables that have been neglected in the caregiving literature. To date, the patient characteristics most frequently studied include physical functioning, cognitive abilities, and perceived personality changes; little attention has been paid to physical appearance changes associated with a debilitating illness.

Motives for Helping

Attempts to identify specific motives for helping have yielded two types of explanations. One assumes that helping serves an *egoistic or self-serving motive*, while the other centers on *empathy and altruism* (Batson & Coke, 1983). The egoistic explanation argues that helping is motivated by the anticipation of rewards for helping and punishment for not helping. Individuals may help another for obvious reasons, such as the expectation of payment, gaining social approval (Baumann, Cialdini, & Kenrick, 1981), avoiding censure (Reis & Gruzen, 1976), receiving esteem in exchange for helping (Hatfield, Walster, & Piliavin, 1978), complying with social norms (Berkowitz, 1972), seeing oneself as a good person (Bandura, 1977), or avoiding guilt (Hoffman, 1982). For example, caring for a relative in order to prevent institutionalization can be interpreted in terms of avoiding censure, complying with social norms, and/or seeing oneself as a good person (Brody, Poulshock, & Masciocchi, 1978).

Guilt and indebtedness are the motives alluded to by the often heard comment made by caregivers, "I know I'm doing everything I can for my mother, but somehow I still feel guilty" (Brody, 1985, p. 26), or in the idea that providing care is a repayment in kind for care provided by the parent at an earlier age. Feelings of guilt may also be the motivating force for individuals who feel they must atone for past sins (e.g., neglect, bad treatment) against their spouse or parent. A theoretical basis for indebtedness as a motive is provided by Greenberg (1980), who states that feeling indebted has motivational properties, such that the greater its magnitude, the greater the resultant arousal and discomfort, and, hence, the stronger the ensuing attempts to deal with or reduce it. Feelings of indebtedness should be higher to the extent that an individual feels the help provided him or her was based on altruistic motives on the part of the helper, help was given in response to requests or pleas for help from the recipient, and the helper incurred costs in providing the help. All of these factors apply to spousal and parent–child relationships and may be factors worthy of attention in our efforts to understand who becomes the caregiver, the magnitude of the costs the caregiver is willing to incur in providing help to a relative, and the amount of residual guilt experienced by the caregiver.

A substantially different perspective on human nature is provided by a theory of helping that is based on purely *altruistic motivation*. According to this view, individuals help others because they are able to adopt the perspective of the other, experience an emotional response—*empathy*—congruent with the other's welfare. The empathic emotion then evokes a motivation aimed at reducing the other's needs. The magnitude of the altruistic motivation is assumed to be a direct function of the magnitude of the empathic emotion. Unlike the egoistic perspective described earlier, the primary goal of empathically evoked altruism is to benefit the other and not the self, even though benefits to oneself may be a consequence of helping (see Batson & Coke, 1983, for a review of the relevant literature). It seems reasonable to assume, although it has not been demonstrated empirically, that the ability to empathize may be based on such variables as kinship, similarity, prior interaction, attachment, or some combination of these variables, all of which are relevant to the intrafamilial caregiving situation. This suggests that higher levels of similarity, attachment, and prior positive interaction should result in greater levels of caregiving, although they may also lead to higher levels of distress among caregivers (Cantor, 1983; Horowitz, 1985).

Although helping an elderly relative is likely to be based on both altruistic and egoistic motivation, it would be interesting to know whether the two motives differentially affect caregiver well-being. Since emotions are a central feature of altruistically motivated helping, one might hypothesize that the emotional status of the patient plays an important role in determining the amount of help provided and the affect of the helper. Moreover, the nature of the cognitive declines associated with a disease such as Alzheimer's suggests that altruistic motivation may be more relevant to the early stages of the disease when cognitive function is still more or less intact and the caregiver can readily empathize with the patient, and that egoistically motivated helping is the driving force in later stages of the disease when cognitive function is debilitated.

Social Norms and Helping

Sociological explanations for why people help others frequently emphasize the role of social norms, such as the norm of *reciprocity*, *equity*, or *social responsibility*. The reciprocity norm enjoins us to pay back what others give to us, while the equity norm underscores the importance of costs and rewards in a relationship. Simply stated, a relationship is equitable if those involved receive from it a return that is proportional to what they have invested in it. According to the social responsibility norm, helping others in need—the sick, infirm, or very young—is a duty that should not be shirked, although the manner in which and how much we help another may depend on our beliefs about who or what is responsible for the cause and solution of the recipient's problem (see Brickman et al., 1982).

The notion of social norms is obviously relevant to understanding caregiver behavior. For example, they may be useful in predicting caregiving behavior among successive cohorts of caregivers, but the existence of norms do not in themselves explain why people adhere to them. We still need to answer the questions: why do these norms exist, or where do they come from? To address these questions, we need to examine some underlying characteristics about the nature of human beings.

Sociobiology of Helping

The social-psychological theories of helping, described above, are based on the notion that social behavior in humans is developed through experience and learning, rather than through instinct. A new theoretical approach that can have direct relevance for understanding the helping process, *sociobiology*, challenges this orthodoxy. Sociobiology suggests that the fundamental goal of the organism is not mere survival, or survival of its offspring, but "inclusive fitness," to pass on the maximum number of genes to the next generation (Hamilton, 1964). Sociobiology believes that human helping can only be understood in terms of the human evolutionary past—close relatives help each other, even at risk of their lives, in order to increase the chance that their genes will survive in their relatives (Forsyth, 1987). Thus sociobiology takes a positive view of human nature, believing that human beings are innately helpful to each other albeit for a "selfish" purpose, the preservation of the gene pool.

To date, tests of this theory, which have relied on research with nonhumans only, indicate that helping is much more common among close relatives than among strangers and in dense rather than dispersed communities (Barash, 1982). Applying this theory to family caregiving, it can be argued that, in general, intrafamilial helping behaviors enhance the survival of the familial gene pool. Thus, intrafamilial helping of all types is desirable—old helping young as well as the young helping the old. However, this general rule likely has at least one qualification: when resource constraints demand that priorities be set among those who can be helped, we would predict that resources will be allocated to the young rather than the old.

This discussion of why people help obviously raises more questions than it answers. Understanding peoples' motives for helping is at least as important as other questions that have been asked about caregiving, yet little research is available to enlighten us about this issue.

The significance of the "why" question is underscored by the large empirical literature showing that individuals frequently incur high personal costs in order to care for a disabled relative. This literature is examined next.

The Costs and Benefits of Providing Care

Much of the literature on caregiving can be characterized as an attempt to link some antecedent variables to outcomes assessing the well-being of individuals who provide support to elderly relatives. A typical independent variable in this conceptualization might be the functional or behavioral status of the patient and a representative dependent variable, any one of a number of measures assessing the psychosocial status or physical and mental health of the caregiver, such as morale, life-satisfaction, depression, or perceived strain or burden.

Sandwiched in between the independent and dependent variables are a large number of individual and situational conditioning variables characteristic of all stress-coping models, such as age, gender, socio-economic status, type and quality of the relationship between caregiver and patient, social support, and a number of individual characteristics of the caregiver, such as self-esteem, locus of control, and religiosity. The need for conditioning or intervening variables is justified by data demonstrating only moderate relationships between independent variables, such as patient impairment (e. g., ability to perform activities of daily living), and caregiver outcomes, such as mental health (Coppel, Burton, Becker, & Fiore, 1985; Pagel, Becker, & Coppel, 1985). This basic model has been elaborated by a number of researchers (e.g., Cohler, Groves, Borden, & Lazarus, 1989; Haley, Levine, Brown, & Bartolucci, 1987; Montgomery, Stull, & Borgatta, 1985; Schulz, Tompkins, & Rau, 1988; Schulz, Tompkins, Wood, & Decker, 1987). On the whole, these models provide a convenient framework for organizing the large number of variables relevant to understanding the caregiving process.

Given the basic similarity of caregiving outcome models, it should not surprise us that there exists considerable consensus regarding the central variables relevant to understanding caregiving outcomes. There are differences, to be sure, but they are primarily differences in emphasis, reflecting the disciplinary orientation of the investigator rather than fundamental disagreements about the nature of the phenomenon being studied. Presumably, a study incorporating measures of all of the variables we have identified, carried out prospectively with sufficiently large population, with appropriate analytic strategies applied, would provide us with a thorough understanding of the determinants of caregiving endpoints. Unfortunately, such a study doesn't exist. We can, however, examine the existing literature and assess the current status regarding the conceptualization and measurement of key components of these models.

Objective Stressors—Patient Characteristics

Our interest in and concern about caregiving is based on the underlying assumption that patient illness and disability represents an objective stressor to family members. The illness or disability is typically characterized on a number of dimensions including disability in self-care, cognitive impairment, behavior problems, and catastrophic emotional reactions. For example, among Alzheimer's patients, the most frequently identified stressors include memory problems, disability in self-care, and disruptive behaviors, such as night waking or daytime wandering. If the patient is an elderly spinal cord injured person, the emphasis is more likely to be on the level of disability in self-care.

On the whole, the existing literature on relationships between patient status or symptomatology and caregiver outcomes suggest that the two are moderately related. The one frequently cited exception to this generalization is the study by Zarit, Reever, and Bach-Peterson (1980) in which they found

OBJECTIVE STRESSORS
Type of Illness
Nature of onset
Prognosis
Visibility
Stage of disease
Disabilities in self-care
Cognitive impairment
Illness-related behavior problems
Patient coping

Figure 1.1 Objective Stressors

no relationship between reported burden and patient characteristics, such as frequency of memory and behavior problems, or the extent of function and cognitive impairment in a sample of 29 caregivers of Alzheimer's patients. In a substantially larger sample of caregivers, George and Gwyther (1986) found small but significant correlations (i.e., $r \leqslant .20$) between severity of the patients' symptoms and caregiver well-being; and Poulshock and Deimling (1984) reported a moderate to strong relationship between elder impairment and caregiver burden and caregiver depression.

In studies focused on other chronically disabled populations (e.g., stroke patients and elderly spinal cord injured persons), Schulz and colleagues (Schulz et al., 1987, 1988) also found moderate to strong relationships between level of disability and caregiver burden, as did Robinson (1983) with caregivers of recently hospitalized elderly hip surgery and heart patients. In sum, while patient status clearly plays a role in determining important caregiver outcomes, such as burden or institutionalization (Chenoweth & Spencer, 1986), it is obviously not the only factor contributing to these outcomes and, under some circumstances, may not even be the most important one.

In addition to patient disabilities, it seems important to us to consider, as well, other illness-related factors that are likely to play a role in caregiver response to disability. The *visibility* of patient disability may have large impacts on the social life of the caregiver. Patient behaviors that are disruptive and cause embarrassment may result in a constricted social network as the caregiver tries to limit contact with network members. Thus, illnesses such as dementia are likely to be more visible and may be perceived as more stigmatizing than illnesses such as heart disease.

Other factors likely to affect the caregiver are the *nature of illness onset* (sudden or insidious) and *prognosis* (recuperative, stable, degenerative, or terminal). In sum, it is important to assess not only the biological and behavioral consequences of a disease but also its perceived natural history and the stage of illness in which the patient is located; for example, prediagnostic, diagnostic and treatment, rehabilitation and control, recurrence, or terminal (Leventhal, Leventhal, & Nguyen, 1985). It seems likely that equivalent levels of functional disability will affect differently caregivers caring for a declining, as opposed to stable or recovering, patient. As Callahan (1988) eloquently puts it, "All things may be endurable if the demands are finite in depth and time. But a future that offers no exit at all, even if the burden on a daily basis is not utterly overwhelming, can be an obvious source of sadness and depression. . . . No burden can be greater than trying to imagine how one can cope with a future that promises no relief" (p. 325).

In order to study the symbolic significance or meaning attached to different illnesses, it is essential that we carry out comparative studies of illnesses. For example, if we wish to assess the role that the perceived prognosis of an illness plays in affecting caregiver outcomes, it is necessary that we have sufficient range on that variable in a given study population. This is frequently difficult to achieve in studies of single diseases, such as Alzheimer's disease, where the prognosis is always further decline with eventual death. What is needed is a comparative study of diseases that would allow the researcher to hold constant certain disease attributes, such as functional disability, and systematically vary others, such as prognosis.

One of the major shortcomings of the caregiving literature is that individuals in very different stages of a disease process are combined and treated as a homogeneous group. Since there are large individual differences in the rate of disease progression, this strategy is likely to create confusion regarding the underlying causes of caregiver distress as well as distort the consequences of caregiving. For example, in the immediate post-diagnostic phase of a terminal illness such as cancer or Alzheimer's disease, the primary stressor may be the anticipated loss of a loved relative; while in the late terminal stages of an illness, the primary stressors are more likely to include the sheer physical demands of providing care to an extremely disabled relative. Unless outcome measures are sensitive to both types of stressors and their unique consequences, the effects of caregiving are likely to be underestimated and/or distorted. We are not aware of any studies that directly attempt to distinguish between the effects of anticipatory bereavement, feelings of empathy and sympathy for the disabled relative, and the physical/behavioral demands of caregiving.

Perceived Stress/Burden

The central feature of virtually all caregiving studies is the measurement of burden. It is frequently treated as the primary outcome measure, while at other times it is used as a predictor of other outcomes, such as depression or institutionalization. Some researchers take a narrow perspective in conceptualizing burden, focusing on the tasks associated with taking care of a relative, while others view it broadly and assess burden in terms of general well-being or in terms of a number of multiple dimensions assessing the caregivers' status. Finally, researchers have also attempted to distinguish between objective and subjective measures of burden.

Since the concept of burden lies at the heart of caregiving, it is essential that we achieve some clarity on the notion of "burden" both at the conceptual and at the measurement level. Dictionary definitions of "burden" refer to the load borne or carried. Applied to caregiving, this translates to the time and effort required for one person to attend to the needs of another. Thus, a very rudimentary and relatively objective measure of burden might be a summary score reflecting the amount of time spent, types of services provided, and financial resources expended on behalf of the patient. Presumably, such a measure would be reliably related to objective measures of patient disability.

If we add to this rudimentary measure of burden questions regarding the inconvenience and discomfort associated with performing specific caregiving tasks, our measure becomes both more complex and more subjective. One may wish to assess burden even more broadly by asking questions about the extent to which caregiving causes strain with regard to work, finances, emotional and physical status (Cantor, 1983; Robinson, 1983), assess caregiving-related feelings about health, well-being, family relationships, and social life (Zarit et al., 1980), or measure emotional impact (Horowitz & Shindelman, 1983) or emotional distress (Gilleard, Belford, Gilleard, Wittick, & Gledhill, 1984) associated with caregiving. Poulshock and Deimling (1984) advocate one further refinement by suggesting that burden be viewed as a multidimensional concept in which specific burdens are linked to specific types of impairment. Finally, the literature contains one additional type of

PERCEIVED STRESS
Types of tasks performed
Amount of time spent caring for patient
Financial resources expended
Foregone opportunities: work, recreation,
   relationships, sleep
Inconvenience and discomfort
Burden
Role and work strain
Financial, emotional, and physical strain

Figure 1.2 Perceived Stress

burden measure, namely, general measures of psychological well-being, health status, or social activities.

Given the lack of consensus in the conceptualization and measurement of burden, it should not surprise us that the literature presents a confusing picture regarding the correlates and causes of burden. If we hope to achieve some clarity in this domain, it is essential that we develop a consensus regarding the conceptual status of burden as well as a consistent approach to its measurement.

First, most researchers would agree that burden is a subjective state reflecting perceptions of the individual caregiver. It follows, therefore, that the caregiver is the appropriate source of data concerning felt burden. We agree with others that it would be useful to measure both the tasks carried out by the caregiver to assist the disabled relative and the extent to which carrying out these tasks results in inconvenience and discomfort. However, we disagree with those researchers who claim that measures such as types of tasks performed and amount of time spent caregiving represent objective measures while measures of discomfort and strain are subjective. Both types of measures are subject to distortion and are therefore best viewed as caregivers' subjective perspective of their situation.

Second, measures of burden should assess specific problems experienced in relation to caring for an impaired relative. Researchers should attempt to distinguish care-related problems from the many other sources of distress that characterize the caregiving context. For example, being upset about the physical decline of a loved one is different from being upset about the time and effort expended to care for that relative. Yet, no existing burden scales attempt to make this distinction.

Third, as suggested by Poulshock and Deimling (1984), burden should be treated as an intervening measure between impairment and other indicators of caregiving effects. Thus, global measures of psychological well-being, physical health, or depression should be viewed as being affected by burden, as well as many other factors, but should not be viewed as measures of burden. Moreover, efforts should be made to achieve more specificity in linking patient status to particular aspects of felt burden and linking burden to specific outcomes.

Contextual Variables/Mediators

All models of caregiving recognize that contextual or situational variables contribute to caregiving outcomes. This category of variables is broadly defined to include the social network and support system of the caregiver; characteristics of the caregiver, including socioeconomic status, health, gender, and relationship to patient; as well as personality attributes, such as orientation toward control and attitudes about helping others. It also includes factors characterizing the environment, such as the availability and utilization of professional services.

The large number of studies focusing on these variables has paid off in a significant body of reliable findings (e.g., see Horowitz, 1985; Select Committee on Aging, 1987, for excellent reviews; Kashner, Magaziner, & Pruitt, Chapter 8 of this book). At the descriptive level, investigators have characterized the caregiving population in terms of gender, age, marital status, employment, economic status, health status, and living arrangements. Thus, for example, we know that: (a) most caregivers are female; (b) their average age is about 57 years of age; (c) about 70% of all caregivers are married, with female caregivers twice as likely to be widowed as their male counterparts; (d) one-third of informal caregivers are employed, although as a group both men and women caregivers are less likely to be employed than similarly aged counterparts; (e) compared to their age peers in the general population, male and female caregivers are more likely to report adjusted family incomes below the poverty line; (f) their self-assessed health is lower than their age peers; (g) approximately three-quarters of caregivers live with the disabled family member or friend; and (h) household size is related to the amount of care provided, with optimal size being between two and four members.

CONTEXTUAL VARIABLES
Demographic characteristics
Age
Gender
Education
Income
Relationship to patient
Household composition
Employment status
Personality attributes
Attitudes toward helping
Orientation toward control
Optimism
Social support/social network
Religiosity

Figure 1.3 Contextual Variables

A second body of research examines these variables in terms of their direct relationship to caregiving impact. As one would expect, the living arrangement between the caregiver and care-recipient is a major predictor of caregiver involvement, behavior, and burden. Caregivers who live with the impaired elder are more involved with the daily care of the patient and experience greater limitations on their personal lives. Employed caregivers frequently experience conflict between the demands of work and the needs of the patient. Caregivers with a great deal of social support cope better with the demands of caregiving than those with little support.

A third body of research, as yet relatively undeveloped, treats these variables as interactive conditioning factors that mediate the relationship between stressors and their impact on the caregiver. One example of this approach is the stress-buffering hypothesis applied to social support. According to this view, individuals exposed to high levels of caregiving stress benefit from support received from others, while individuals who are not stressed or who experience low levels of stress as a result of caregiving exhibit no beneficial effects attributable to social support.

One of the important contributions of research on social support is its emphasis on the search for mechanisms through which caregiving stressors exert their impact on caregiver outcomes. For example, support may play a role at two different points in the causal chain linking stress to illness. It may intervene between the stressor and a stress reaction by attenuating or preventing a stress appraisal response, or it may intervene after the stress is experienced and prevent the onset of pathological outcomes by reducing the emotional reaction, dampening physiologic processes, or by altering maladaptive behavior responses (Cohen, 1988). Thus, knowing that others will be available to help care for the patient when necessary, support may prevent a caregiver from feeling burdened or stressed. Alternatively, the availability of social support may dampen the impact of a perceived stressor by providing helpful information or assistance or by facilitating healthful behaviors. To date, we know relatively little about psychosocial and pathogenic processes through which social support exerts its positive impact. Not only should future research identify where in the stress-coping process support exerts its effects, it should also identify how this is accomplished. In order to achieve the latter, it will be necessary to assess the impact of support on behavior, psychological states, such as perceived control and self-esteem, as well as biological processes.

Enduring Outcomes—Psychiatric and Physical Health Effects of Caregiving

Generally, there exist two types of studies aimed at assessing the *mental health consequences* of caregiving. The majority of published studies use standardized self-report inventories to measure psychiatric symptomatology such as depression (Anthony-Bergstone, Zarit, & Gatz, 1988; Gilleard et al., 1984; Grad & Sainsbury, 1968; Haley, Levine, Brown, Berry, & Hughes, 1987; Schulz et al., 1988). A second and more recent type of study is based on clinical assessment of the caregiver and is aimed at identifying the prevalence of actual clinical cases (Cohen & Eisdorfer, 1988; Coppel et al., 1985; Gallagher, Rose, Rivera, Lovett, & Thompson, in press).

Overall, the literature on psychiatric morbidity is suggestive but not conclusive. There exists strong evidence for increased symptom reports for depression and demoralization among *some* caregivers, as well as support for increased clinical psychiatric illness among some caregivers. In addition, there exist anecdotal reports of increased health care utilization among

ENDURING OUTCOMES
Symptom reports
    Depression
    Anxiety
    Anger
    Fatigue
    Poor health
Pre-clinical disease
    Hypertension
    Blood Measures
        Clinical chemistries
        Lipids
    Atherosclorisis
    Pulmonary Function
    Compromised immune function
Clinical disease
    Depression
    Infectious disease
    Heart disease
Health Care Utilization
    Drugs
    Health care services

Figure 1.4 Enduring Outcomes

caregivers and one large survey study showing higher rates of psychotropic drug use among caregivers than noncaregivers (George & Gwyther, 1986). However, all of these studies combined provide little evidence about the prevalence or incidence of clinically significant psychiatric conditions attributable to caregiving. The samples in almost all studies are biased in favor of those caregivers who are likely to be more distressed. Moreover, few researchers (for an exception, see Gallagher et al., in press) report data regarding the reliability of their assessment procedures.

Given the large body of literature linking emotional and physical stress to physical illness such as respiratory diseases, hypertension, and cardiovascular disease, one could reasonably predict that caregivers should have higher rates of *physical illness* since they are chronically exposed to such stressors. Indeed, the caregiver has frequently been referred to as the "hidden patient" (Fengler & Goodrich, 1979).

Three types of outcomes have been examined as indicators of illness effects among caregivers. The most frequently used measures are self-reports of physical health status, illness, and illness-related symptoms (Chenoweth & Spencer, 1986; Haley, Levine, Brown, Berry, & Hughes, 1987; Snyder & Keefe, 1985; Stone, Cafferata, & Sangl, 1987). A few studies have examined health care utilization as an indicator of physical morbidity (George & Gwyther, 1986; Haley, Levine, Brown, & Bartolucci, 1987), and one study assessed immune function as an indicator of susceptibility to disease (Kiecolt-Glaser et al., 1987).

Taken together, all of the existing research on the physical health effects of caregiving are suggestive but not conclusive. First, these studies suffer from sample selection biases. In most studies, the samples are small and are recruited in ways that assure a relatively distressed group. Second, the pattern of results within studies is often inconsistent, raising questions about the adequacy of measurement. Third, without objective health status data, it is difficult to know how to interpret self-report data. The literature shows that the relationship between self-reports of physical health and objective measures of physical health are moderate at best (Maddox & Douglass, 1973), and that the rates of concordance decrease as the complexity of the diagnoses increase (Colditz et al., 1986). It is also well known that emotional distress can exert a significant influence on self-report of physical illness and use of health care facilities (Katon, 1985). Those suffering from mental distress are more likely initially to seek medical rather than mental health services and present with somatic complaints (Schulberg, McClelland, & Burns, 1987). This suggests that self-reports of physical symptoms, illnesses, and medical care utilization data must be viewed cautiously.

Why Caregiving Health Effects are Difficult to Obtain

Even if the definitive study assessing caregiving effects on illness were carried out, there are a number of reasons to expect that the observed effects might be small. First, health status is likely to be an important selection factor in determining who takes on the majority of the caregiving responsibilities (Horowitz, 1985). Thus, caregivers may be physically more robust to begin with. Moreover, the amount of help the primary caregivers receive from other relatives is likely to increase when the caregivers' health is threatened. Institutionalization of the patient, either permanently or temporarily, may serve as another safety valve for the caregiver.

Second, we may be looking for illness effects at the wrong point in time in the caregiving history of an individual. Since the caregiving role may limit or discourage access to professional health care services, it would be difficult to detect illness effects if the primary outcome measure is utilization among active caregivers. It may be easier to detect such effects after the caregiving role has been relinquished because caregivers feel they cannot attend to their own needs or because the effects of caregiving stress are *lagged*.

Finally, the negative effects of caregiving may be counteracted by the benefits of caregiving. While caregivers report a great deal of distress associated with caregiving, they also report a number of beneficial effects. National estimates show that almost three-quarters of caregivers report that it makes them feel useful (Stone et al., 1987). Caregiving may also improve the relationship between caregiver and care-recipient, and it may provide company for the caregiver (Schulz et al., 1988). The role of these factors has been relatively unexplored in the caregiving literature.

Recommendations

We have raised a number of questions and have made recommendations regarding the search for linkages between caregiving and morbidity. The recommendations that follow reiterate and elaborate on some of the major issues raised above.

The assessment of psychiatric illness has been limited primarily to responses to self-administered inventories. These instruments can provide estimates of emotional disturbance, but they rarely provide information regarding the frequency and duration of symptoms that is required for clinical diagnoses. It would be a valuable addition to the literature to assess the mental health of caregivers using the National Institute of Mental Health Diagnostic Interview Schedule (DIS) (Robins, Helzer, Croughan, & Ratcliff, 1981) and the Schedule for Affective Disorders and Schizophrenia (SADS) (Endicott & Spitzer, 1978), two structured interviews for assessing mental disorders. Population estimates are available for both DIS and SADS diagnoses which would serve as comparison rates for those derived from caregiving samples.

Self-report measures of physical health should also be complemented with more objective measures of verified clinical disease and pre-clincial disease (e.g., hypertension), health care utilization data, and medication use. Moreover, attempts should be made to assess whether illness effects are the result of existing conditions, defined in terms of prior illness or risk factors being exacerbated, or are new conditions unrelated to prior medical history or risk factors. It seems likely that illness effects are more likely to be found among individuals with increased risk factors for illness.

It would also be useful to determine whether the illness risk of caregivers varies by the predominant type of patient disability; in other words, find out whether there is a link between type of stressor (e.g., physical disability versus cognitive disability in the patient) and type of health problem.

Finally, to the extent that illness effects are observed, it will be important to determine the mechanisms that account for those effects, keeping in mind that mechanisms accounting for symptom reporting, health care utilization, and disease processes may all be different from each other (Cohen, 1988).

Balancing Internal and External Validity

The primary emphasis of this chapter has been on issues of internal validity—the conceptualization and measurement of key concepts in the study of caregiving. In order to give equal time to issues of external validity, the remainder of this chapter will focus on a consideration of this topic as it applies to caregiving.

External validity is one of the cornerstones of social science research and is achieved through careful measurement and sample selection. Since scientists rarely have the opportunity to study a total population, it is essential that data collected from study populations be representative of the group we wish to generalize to or, alternatively, that the group being studied has a clearly identifiable external referent. Judged by this criterion, the existing caregiving literature would receive only fair marks.

In general, three approaches have been taken to identify samples of caregivers. The first is characterized by direct recruitment of informal caregivers from support groups, businesses, professionals who work with caregivers or patients, or through a variety of media solicitations. The second approach is more indirect and involves, first, the identification of a disabled or ill population; and, second, the individuals who provide assistance to the disabled persons. The third approach is similar to the second in that caregivers are identified after first locating ill or disabled individuals, but differs in that the starting point for the search is a general probability sample of adults or specific age segments of the adult population. Examples of each of these approaches can be found in the literature; and, in practice, each has advantages and disadvantages.

Direct Recruitment Approaches

The direct recruitment approaches are the most widely used, but also are one of the most problematic because it is likely to yield biased samples. A typical example of this recruiting method is to solicit subjects from support groups for caregivers of Alzheimer's, stroke, or cancer patients. Since only a small percentage of caregivers participate in such groups, it is likely that membership is determined by important selection factors such as level of distress, social competence, socioeconomic status, the desire for help, and expectations regarding the impact of self-help groups. Participants are likely to be highly distressed, have the means (e.g., transportation, time) to attend group meetings, be confident in their social skills regarding group participation, and expect that participation will be helpful. However, since we are rarely able to collect data from nonparticipants, the conjectures about the biasing characteristics of participants are just that. The dilemma is that we know that support group samples are biased but can't be sure in exactly which way.

Media solicitations directed at caregivers (e.g., newsletter, newspaper, or television ads) also present problems, primarily because they will result in the recruitment of subjects who are more likely to be distressed (Anthony-Bergstone et al., 1988), and depending on the specific wording of an ad may miss some caregivers altogether. For example, many informal caregivers would not identify themselves as such (Scannell, 1988). Thus, an ad that used the term "caregiver" would likely miss a substantial portion of the eligible population.

Researchers have been sensitive to these biasing problems, and one approach to dealing with them has been to include a matched control group of noncaregivers in studies designed to assess the effects of caregiving (e.g., Haley, Levine, Brown, Berry, & Hughes, 1987; Kiecolt-Glaser et al., 1987). This strategy has yielded mixed results because there is no strong consensus on what the matching variables should be. Minimally, one would want to match on such variables as income, education, age, gender, and marital status since these variables are often correlated with outcome examined in caregiving studies. It would also be desirable to match on health status at entry in longitudinal studies, and it could be argued that one should include a second control group that is matched on the level of psychological distress present at intake. If the goal of an investigator is to identify the unique psychiatric and physical morbidity effects of caregiving, then a strong case can be made for the inclusion of the latter control group. The pragmatic difficulty of identifying and recruiting appropriate control groups might appropriately cause some researchers to abandon this approach.

An easier approach to the biasing problem is to compare the sample data with population norms on key independent and dependent variables. Of course, this strategy is limited to studies using variables for which standardized data are available. In addition, caution is advised in pursuing this strategy since national profiles of caregivers indicate that they are nonnormative on a number of dimensions: they are less likely to be employed, have incomes below the poverty line, and perceive themselves to be in poorer health (Stone et al., 1987).

Finally, it should be pointed out that the problem of nonrepresentative study populations can be eliminated altogether by acknowledging the scope and limited generalizability of the results of a study. For example, it would be perfectly appropriate and useful to recruit subjects from a caregiver support group if the goal of the study is to develop intervention strategies to be used by caregiver support groups. Ideally, such a study would recruit subjects from a common source and then randomly assign them to treatment and nontreatment conditions.

Indirect Recruitment Approaches

The hallmark of this approach is that caregivers are identified indirectly through the disabled or ill elderly person. As a result, the representativeness of the caregiving sample is largely determined by the sampling procedures used to select the patient population.

A number of variations on this basic theme can be found in the literature (e.g., Cantor, 1983; Schulz et al., 1987, 1988; Soldo & Myllyluoma, 1983; Stephens & Christianson, 1986; Stoller, 1983; Stone et al., 1987).

Probably the most frequently cited study within this genre is the work of Stone and others who used probability sampling techniques to generate a national profile of informal caregivers. The data for this study were drawn from the Informal Caregivers Survey (ICS), a component of the 1982 National Long-Term Care Survey (LTC) conducted by the Bureau of the Census. Initially, a random sample of 36,000 persons was drawn from the Medicare

Health Insurance Files and screened by telephone to determine if the respondent had a long-term problem with at least one Activity of Daily Living (ADL) or one Instrumental Activity of Daily Living. The yield from this screen was a sample of 6,393 persons representing a population of 5.1 million. A subsample representing 2 million elderly individuals who had a problem with one or more ADLs was used to identify the caregiving sample. Eligibility criteria for caregivers included being 14 years of age or over and providing assistance with at least one ADL. A total of 2,089 eligible caregivers were identified and 92% of them were interviewed. The sample interviewed represented 2.2 million persons caring for 1.6 million disabled elders.

A similar approach to identifying caregivers was used by Stephens and Christianson (1986). They first identified elderly community residents who had at least three functional disabilities and who had two or more unmet service needs. These respondents were then asked to identify their primary informal caregivers, who then had to meet the criterion of providing some form of care to the disabled individual. A total of 1,940 persons were interviewed in this study.

The advantages of both the Stone et al. (1987) and Stephens and Christianson (1986) studies are that the investigators were able to generate relatively large samples of caregivers who were representative of specific segments of the caregiving population. One disadvantage is that, because the samples were large, the range of questions asked was relatively limited. A second concern in studies such as these is that the samples generated are determined by the criteria used to define the patient and caregiver. If the goal is to generate a national profile of informal caregivers, the outcome will vary substantially if the criterion is inability to carry out one ADL or opposed two ADLs. Similarly, whomever will be identified as a caregiver will vary as a function of the criteria used for type and amount of help provided.

Another indirect approach to the identification of caregivers is exemplified by the work of Schulz and his colleagues (Schulz et al., 1987, 1988). In these studies, specific patient populations were identified first (e.g., stroke patients), who then identified their primary support persons. Studies like these have limited generalizability defined by the type of patient being cared for. Even so, recruiting a representative sample is still challenging. For example, in our study of caregivers of stroke patients, we identified all first strokes by monitoring stroke admissions in all hospitals in a designated geographic area. Since virtually all completed strokes result in a hospital admission, we could be reasonably sure that our sample was representative of first stroke caregivers nationally. Moreover, we were able to compare our stroke sample with national profiles of first stroke patients to determine the comparability of the two groups. The advantage of this approach to sample selection is that relatively small samples (150–200) can be usefully studied. The obvious limitation is that the results are generalizable only to a specific subgroup of the caregiving population.

Secondary Analyses of
Existing National Probability Samples

The study by Soldo and Myllyluoma (1983) represents another variation of the indirect approach. It is based on secondary analysis of an existing nationally representative data base. Soldo and Myllyluoma used data from the 1976 Survey of Income and Education, a stratified, multistage, cluster sample of 151,170 households. The first step in defining the sample was to identify homecare households. Eligible households had to contain two or more persons, one of whom had to be at least 65 years of age or older and who required at least moderate assistance with either ADLs or mobility. These selection criteria yielded a sample of 2,338 eligible cases. Next, an algorithm was applied to assign individuals within the household the role of "care-recipient" and "caregiver." To be classified as a care-recipient, individuals had to require moderate to extensive assistance, as measured by the Need for Assistance Scale, and had to be the most impaired older person in the household. The algorithm for identifying caregivers was more complex. In two-person households, the primary caregiver was by default the "other adult." For households with three or more persons, an assignment rule was developed that involved examination of sex, age, impairment level, and relationship of each eligible household member to the designated care-receiver.

The strength of this study lies in the large sample size and the external validity afforded by the careful selection strategy. It provides a good descriptive account of caregivers who live with the dependent elderly, but is severely limited in the range of information it provides. A second problem is the circularity of using a variable, such as gender, to select the sample in order to generate generalizable descriptive information on the same variable.

The pragmatics of research often demand compromises between external and internal validity. Such compromises are patently evident in the research on caregiving. Investigators concerned primarily with issues of external validity have carefully selected large representative samples but have been limited in the range of issues examined and the depth with which they are pursued. Investigators concerned with internal validity have identified the phenomenon to be studied, selected appropriate measurement strategies, and focused their efforts on detailed and thorough assessment, but have shown less concern with the generalizability of their findings. Good science and informed policy require a greater emphasis on both external and internal validity.

Conclusion

The primary goal of this chapter has been to address the questions, who provides what types of care to whom, and at what cost? We have raised a number of theoretical issues concerning why people help and have attempted to make useful distinctions between the major conceptual variables relevant to understanding caregiving. At the same time, we have identified both measurement and sampling problems that will need to be addressed in future research of this area. It is our hope that clarifying the current status of research in this area will help us prudently chart its future course.

References

Anthony-Bergstone, C. R., Zarit, S. H., & Gatz, M. (1988). Symptoms of psychological distress among caregivers of dementia patients. *Psychology and Aging, 3*, 245-248.

Bandura, A. (1977). *Social learning theory.* Englewood Cliffs, N.J.: Prentice-Hall.

Barash, D. P. (1982). *Sociobiology and behavior (2nd ed.).* New York: Elsevier North-Holland.

Batson, C. D., & Coke, J. S. (1983). Empathic motivation of helping behavior. In J. R. Cacioppo & R. E. Petty (Eds.), *Social psychophysiology: A sourcebook.* New York: Guilford Press.

Baumann, D. J., Cialdini, R. B., & Kendrick, D. T. (1981). Altruism as hedonism: Helping and self-gratification as equivalent responses. *Journal of Personality and Social Psychology, 40*, 1039-1046.

Berkowitz, L. (1972). Social norms, feelings, and other factors affecting helping and altruism. In L. Berkowitz (Ed.), *Advances in experimental social psychology, Vol. 6.* New York: Academic Press.

Brickman, P., Rabinowitz, V. C., Karuza, J., Coates, D., Cohn, E., & Kidder, L. (1982). Models of helping and coping. *American Psychologist, 37*, 368-384.

Brody, E. M. (1985). Parent care as a normative family stress. *The Gerontologist, 25*, 19-25.

Brody, S. J., Poulshock, S. W., & Masciocchi, C. F. (1978). The family caring unit: A major consideration in the long-term support system. *The Gerontologist, 18*, 556-561.

Callahan, D. (1988). Families as caregivers: The limits of morality. *Archives of Physical Medicine and Rehabilitation, 69*, 323-328.

Cantor, M. H. (1983). Strain among caregivers: A study of experience in the United States. *The Gerontologist, 23*(6), 597-604.

Chenoweth, B., & Spencer, B. (1986). Dementia: The experience of family caregivers. *The Gerontologist, 26*, 267-272.

Cohen, S. (1988). Psychosocial models of the role of social support in the etiology of physical disease. *Health Psychology, 7*, 269-297.

Cohen, D., & Eisdorfer, C. (1988). Depression in family members caring for a relative with Alzheimer's disease. *Journal of the American Geriatric Society, 36*, 885-889.

Cohler, B., Groves, L., Borden, L., & Lazarus, L. (1989). Caring for family members with Alzheimer's disease. In E. Light & B. Lebowitz (Eds.), *Alzheimer's disease treatment and family stress: Directions for research*. Washington, DC: National Institute of Mental Health.

Colditz, G. A., Martin, P., Stampfer, M. J., Willett, W. C., Sampson, L., Rosner, B., Hennekens, C. H., & Speizer, F. E. (1986). Validation of questionnaire information on risk factors and disease outcomes in a prospective cohort study of women. *American Journal of Epidemiology, 123*, 894-900.

Coppel, D. B., Burton, C., Becker, J., & Fiore, J. (1985). The relationships of cognitions associated with coping reactions to depression in spousal caregivers of Alzheimer's disease patients. *Cognitive Therapy and Research, 9*, 253-266.

Dovidio, J. F. (1984). Helping and altruism: An empirical and conceptual overview. In L. Berkowitz (Ed.), *Advances in experimental social psychology, Vol. 17*. New York: Academic Press.

Endicott, J., & Spitzer, R. L. (1978). A diagnostic interview: The Schedule for Affective Disorders and Schizophrenia. *Archives of General Psychiatry, 35*, 837-844.

Fengler, A. P., & Goodrich, N. (1979). Wives of elderly disabled men: The hidden patients. *The Gerontologist , 19*, 175-183.

Forsyth, D. R. (1987). *Social psychology*. Belmont, CA: Brooks/Cole.

Gallagher, D., Rose, J., Rivera, P., Lovett, S., & Thompson, L. W. (in press). Prevalence of depression in family caregivers. *The Gerontologist,*

George, L. K., & Gwyther, L. P. (1986). Caregiver well-being: A multidimensional examination of family caregivers of demented adults. *The Gerontologist, 26*, 253-259.

Gilleard, C. J., Belford, H., Gilleard, E., Wittick, J. E., & Gledhill, K. (1984). Emotional distress amongst the supporters of the elderly mentally infirm. *British Journal of Psychiatry, 141*, 1467-1468.

Grad, J., & Sainsbury, P. (1968). The effect that patients have on their families in a community care and a control psychiatric service: A two year follow-up. *British Journal of Psychiatry, 114*, 265-278.

Greenberg, M. S. (1980). A theory of indebtedness. In K. J. Gergen, M. S. Greenberg, & R. H. Willis (Eds.), *Social exchange: Advances in theory and research* (pp. 3-26). New York: Plenum.

Haley, W. E., Levine, E. G., Brown, S. L., & Bartolucci, A. A. (1987). Stress, appraisal, coping, and social support as predictors of adaptational outcome among dementia caregivers. *Psychology and Aging, 2*, 323-330.

Haley, W. E., Levine, E. G., Brown, S. L., Berry, J. W., & Hughes, G. H. (1987). Psychological, social, and health consequences of caring for a relative with senile dementia. *Journal of the American Geriatric Society, 35*, 405-411.

Hamilton, W. D. (1964). The genetical evolution of social behaviour, I and II. *Journal of Theoretical Biology, 7*, 1-52.

Harrell, A. W. (1978). Physical attractiveness, self-disclosure, and helping behavior. *Journal of Social Psychology, 104*, 15-17.

Hatfield, E., Walster, G. W., & Piliavin, J. A. (1978). Equity theory and helping relationships. In L. Wispe (Ed.), *Altruism, sympathy, and helping* (pp. 115-139). New York: Academic Press.

Hoffman, M. L. (1982). Development of prosocial motivation: Empathy and guilt. In N. Eisenberg (Ed.), *The development of prosocial behavior* (pp. 281-313). New York: Academic Press.

Horowitz, A. (1985). Family caregiving to the frail elderly. In M. P. Lawton & G. Maddox (Eds.), *Annual review of gerontology and geriatrics: Vol. 5* (pp. 194-246). New York: Springer.

Horowitz, A., & Shindelman, L. (1983). Reciprocity and affection: Past influences on current caregiving. *Journal of Gerontological Social Work, 5*, 5-20.

Katon, W. (1985). Somatization in primary care. *Journal of Family Practice, 21*, 257-258.

Kent, D. P. (1965). Aging—fact or fancy. *The Gerontologist, 5, 2.*

Kiecolt-Glaser, J. K., Glaser, R., Shuttleworth, E. E., Dyer, C. S., Ogrocki, P., & Speicher, C. E. (1987). Chronic stress and immunity in family caregivers of Alzheimer's disease patients. *Psychosomatic Medicine, 49*, 523-535.

Kleinke, C. (1977). Compliance to requests made by gazing and touching experimenters in field settings. *Journal of Experimental Social Psychology, 13*, 218-223.

Latane, B., & Darley, J. M. (1970). *The unresponsive bystander: Why doesn't he help?* New York: Appleton-Century-Crofts.

Leventhal, H., Leventhal, E. A., & Nguyen, T. V. (1985). Reactions of families to illness: Theoretical models and perspectives. In D. C. Turk & R. D. Kerns (Eds.), *Health, illness, and families: A life span perspective*. New York: John Wiley.

Maddox, G. L., & Douglass, E. B. (1973). Self-assessment of health: A longitudinal study of elderly subjects. *Journal of Health and Social Behavior, 14*, 87-93.

Montgomery, R. J. V., Stull, D. E., & Borgatta, E. F. (1985). Measurement and the analysis of burden. *Research on Aging, 7*, 137-152.

Pagel, M., Becker, J., & Coppel, D. (1985). Loss of control, self-blame, and depression: An investigation of spouse caretakers of Alzheimer's disease patients. *Journal of Abnormal Psychology, 94*, 169-182.

Piliavin, I. M., Piliavin, J. A., & Rodin, J. (1975). Costs, diffusion, and the stigmatized victim. *Journal of Personality and Social Psychology, 32*, 429-438.

Poulshock, S. W., & Deimling, G. T. (1984). Families caring for elders in residence: Issues in the measurement of burden. *Journal of Gerontology, 39*, 230-239.

Reis, H. T., & Gruzen, J. (1976). On mediating equity, equality, and self-interest: The role of self-presentation in social exchange. *Journal of Experimental Social Psychology, 12*, 487-503.

Robins, L. N., Helzer, J. E., Croughan, J., & Ratcliff, T. (1981). National Institute of Mental Health Diagnostic Interview Schedule. *Archives of General Psychiatry, 38*, 381-389.

Robinson, B. C. (1983). Validation of a caregiver strain index. *Journal of Gerontology, 38*, 344-348.

Samorette, G. C., & Harris, M. B. (1976). Some factors influencing helping: The effects of a handicap, responsibility, and requesting help. *Journal of Social Psychology, 98*, 39-45.

Schulberg, H. C., McClelland, M., & Burns, B. J. (1987). Depression and physical illness: The prevalence, causation, and diagnosis of comorbidity. *Clinical Psychology Review, 7*, 145-167.

Schulz, R., Tompkins, C. A., & Rau, M. T. (1988). A longitudinal study of the psychosocial impact of stroke on primary support persons. *Psychology and Aging, 3*, 131-141.

Schulz, R., Tompkins, C. A., Wood, D., & Decker, S. (1987). The social psychology of caregiving: Physical and psychological costs of providing support to the disabled. *Journal of Applied Social Psychology, 17*, 401-428.

Select Committee on Aging (U.S. House of Representatives). (1987). *Exploding the myths: Caregiving in America* (pp. 99-611). Washington, DC: U.S. Government Printing Office.

Scannell, A. (1988). Caregivers adaptation to stroke: Long-term effects. Unpublished doctoral dissertation, Portland State University, Portland, OR.

Snyder, B., & Keefe, K. (1985). The unmet needs of family caregivers for frail and disabled adults. *Social Work in Health Care, 10*, 1-14.

Soldo, B. J., & Myllyluoma, J. (1983). Caregivers who live with dependent elderly. *The Gerontologist, 23*, 605-611.

Stephens, S. A., & Christianson, J. B. (1986). *Informal care of the elderly.* Lexington, MA: D. C. Heath.

Stoller, E. P. (1983). Parental caregiving by adult children. *Journal of Marriage and the Family, 45*, 851-858.

Stone, R., Cafferata, G. L., & Sangl, J. (1987). Caregivers of the frail elderly: A national profile. *The Gerontologist, 27*, 616-626.

Zarit, S. H., Reever, K. E., & Bach-Peterson, J. (1980). Relatives of impaired elderly: Correlates of feelings of burden. *The Gerontologist, 20*(6), 649-655.

2

Psychological Impact of Caregiving on the Caregiver

A Critical Review of Research Methodologies

VICTORIA H. RAVEIS
KAROLYNN SIEGEL
MYRIAM SUDIT

Introduction

In recent years, several trends have coalesced to produce a significant growth in the noninstitutionalized dependent population. These include: the deinstitutionalization of mental patients; the dramatic expansion of the aged segment of the population; and the movement toward maintaining in the community a variety of patient groups with chronic and debilitating illnesses. As a consequence, there is a growing interest in those individuals who provide informal care to the infirm or aged population and who have been called upon to assume a variety of complex, time-consuming, and stressful tasks in that role. It is often these individuals' willingness and ability to be caregivers that determines whether a family member, friend, or neighbor will have to be institutionalized to receive treatment and/or supervision. While the practical and emotional benefits to the recipients of this informal support and care have been well investigated over the past two decades (Brody, Poulshock, & Masciocchi, 1978; Croog, Lipson, & Levine, 1972; DiMatteo & Hays, 1981; Shanas, 1979; Wortman, 1984), the consequences for the caregiver have until recently received considerably less research attention.

The early studies of informal care provision, which grew out of the deinstitutionalization of mental patients, focused on the burdens on the family of caring for a mentally ill relative, but generally did not examine the caregiver physical or mental health outcomes. In these early investigations, "caregiver burden" emerged as an empirical concept of interest (e.g., Grad & Sainsbury, 1963, 1968; Hoenig & Hamilton, 1966a, 1966b; Sainsbury & Grad de Alarcon, 1969; Test & Stein, 1980; see also review by Niederehe & Fruge, 1984). In more recent work, which has primarily focused on the provision of home care to the frail elderly and to dementia patients, the concept of caregiver burden has been refined and expanded (see, for example, Chenoweth & Spencer, 1986; Horowitz, 1985; Jones & Vetter, 1984; Noelker & Wallace, 1985; Zarit, Orr, & Zarit, 1985; Zarit, Reever, & Bach-Peterson, 1980; Zarit, Todd, & Zarit, 1986). These investigations have demonstrated that providing care can have far-reaching and diverse consequences for the caregiver, negatively affecting various aspects of his/her life.

Perhaps the most significant of these consequences lies in the psychological realm. Research has documented a variety of emotional consequences for caregivers, including increased levels of depression, anxiety, helplessness, hopelessness, emotional exhaustion, low morale, distress, feelings of isolation, guilt, and anger (Brody, 1985; Bywater, 1981; Cantor, 1983; Deimling & Bass, 1986; Fengler & Goodrich, 1979; George & Gwyther, 1986; Gilhooly, 1984; Gilleard, Belford, Gilleard, Whittick, & Gledhill, 1984; Holroyd & Guthrie, 1979, 1986; Jones & Vetter, 1984; Kazak, 1987; Morycz, 1985; Rabins, Mace, & Lucas, 1982; Robinson & Thurnher, 1979; Sheehan & Nuttall, 1988; Stetz, 1987; Thompson & Haran, 1985). While the evidence concerning the emotional impact of giving care to a physically, mentally, or cognitively impaired individual has been accumulating, much of this research suffers from serious conceptual or methodological problems. Not only have individual studies often been flawed, but there has been little consistency in the field in the conceptualization and measurement of psychological burdens or impact. This has prevented the comparison of findings across studies, and made it difficult to determine whether inconsistent findings are theoretically relevant or merely a function of the different conceptualizations and measures adopted.

The present chapter aims to provide a critical methodological review of the extant research on the psychological burdens and consequences of performing the caregiver role. We will examine limitations in existing research studies, assess the different measurement approaches employed to investigate the psychological impact of providing care, and describe the current state of theory in the field. Admittedly, there are many well designed and executed studies, but this review endeavors to highlight the limitations of previous studies so that directions for improving future research can be identified.[1]

Omitted from this review is the extensive body of research which has focused on the impact of an illness on family functioning (e.g., Allan, Townley, & Phelan, 1974; Anthony, 1970; Cassileth et al., 1985; Croog & Fitzgerald, 1978; Cummings, 1976; Fife, Norton, & Groom, 1987; Grandstaff, 1976; Hafstrom & Schram, 1984; Hinds, 1985; Lawler, Nakielny, & Wright, 1966; Lewis, Ellison, & Woods, 1985; Morrow, Carpenter, & Hoagland, 1984; Satterwhite, 1978; Venters, 1981; Wellisch, Landsverk, Guidera, Pasnau, & Fawzy, 1983; see also the review by Lewis, 1986). While these studies document the stress of a variety of illnesses on the family unit, they have not systematically examined the extent to which the responsibilities and tasks of caring for an ill family member contribute to the psychological distress observed in the caregivers.

Sample and Respondents

Sampling Methods

Most studies which examine the psychological consequences associated with caregiving are convenience samples drawn from only one or two sources, usually hospital, clinic or social agency records, or mailing lists of self-help or support organizations. For example, Chenoweth and Spencer (1986) randomly sampled families from the mailing list of a chapter of an Alzheimer's disease organization. George and Gwyther (1986) contacted everyone on the mailing list of a statewide technical assistance program for caregivers of Alzheimer's patients. Rakowski and Clark (1985) drew their sample from among the caregivers of elderly patients in a university-based ambulatory geriatric service. Stetz (1987) drew her sample of spouse caregivers of advanced cancer patients from home care agency lists. Holroyd and Guthrie (1979) selected their sample of parents of children with neuromuscular disease from a university-based muscle clinic and the membership lists of the local Muscular Dystrophy Association, and obtained a comparison group of parents of psychologically disturbed children from the university's psychiatry clinic.

Samples drawn from sources such as these are necessarily biased. Selection effects operate to yield samples not representative of the caregiver population at large. For example, characteristics of patients in varying kinds of treatment settings are likely to differ, and role demands placed on the caregiver will vary accordingly. Patients being treated on an outpatient basis are likely to be more functional, and, in the case of cognitively impaired patients, may be more socially appropriate in their behavior than those who require hospitalization or some other form of institutionalization. Yet at the same time, institutionalization may shift the burden of providing many kinds of practical assistance onto formal caregivers, thereby lowering the physical demands on informal caregivers.

Similarly, those who approach an agency or organization for information or support have already self-selected themselves out of the broader caregiver population on the basis of initiating a search for aid or assistance. The situational, personality, and cultural factors that lead to a caregiver's decision to seek assistance may influence how they cope with and are affected by the caregiving experience in general. Research on help-seeking behavior has illustrated that personality, cultural, and socioeconomic characteristics are associated with the decision to seek help, the sources approached, and the conditions under which assistance is sought (Booth & Babchuck, 1972; Burke & Weir, 1976; Croog et al., 1972; Gourash, 1978; Gurin, Veroff, & Feld, 1960; Kammeyer & Bolton, 1968; Levine & Preston, 1970; Neighbors & Jackson, 1984; Rosenblatt & Mayer, 1972).

Those who approach social agencies or mutual support groups for aid may be those caregivers with the greatest need, and samples drawn from these sources could provide the most extreme view of the consequences of caregiving. Conversely, the support and assistance received from these agencies and groups may mitigate the caregiving burden, resulting in less evidence of negative impact than would be observed in the absence of such support.

A further source of concern is the extremely small sample sizes of many of these studies. Often, investigations are based on less than one hundred cases. For example, Zarit et al. (1986) carried out a longitudinal study of subjective burden in a sample of 64 spouse caregivers to dementia patients. Similarly, Hooyman, Gonyea, & Montgomery (1985) examined the impact of in-home services termination on 80 family caregivers to impaired relatives. Brown et al.'s (1978) research on the physical, emotional, and social impact of home dialysis on the patient and his dialysis partner (i.e., spouse or other family member) consisted of a sample of 40 patients and their caregivers.

Small restricted samples not only reduce the number of background and situational variables that can be controlled for or simultaneously examined in a given model, but can also affect the power of statistical tests of significance and yield unreliable estimates of the prevalence of various psychological sequelae of caregiving.

Sample Characteristics

Another consequence of samples being drawn from only one or two sources (such as a hospital, clinic, or social service agency) is that they tend to be fairly homogenous in such sociodemographic characteristics as social class or geographic residence (rural, urban, or suburban). Lack of variability can seriously restrict the generalizability of the findings to other populations.

This is a particularly significant limitation when a specific group or status is consistently underrepresented across studies. For example, investigations of the psychological burdens of caregiving have largely been carried out on predominantly white samples; and the findings cannot be assumed to be generalizable to other racial groups. Even when researchers have tried to achieve more racially representative samples, the number of cases attained is frequently insufficient for subgroup analyses due to the initially small sample sizes. For example, in Morycz's (1985) research on informal caregivers of the impaired elderly, blacks composed 23% of the sample, but this represented only 18 cases. Thus, when the analysis suggested that caregiver burden was less likely to have an impact on black caregivers' decisions to institutionalize the patient than on white caregivers, further investigation was hampered by the small number of black caregivers in the sample.

Another group inadequately represented in studies of the psychological impact of caregiving is men. Horowitz (1985) has argued that in studies of careprovision to the elderly, sons are underrepresented in this research relative to the proportion that has been identified as providing care. Similarly, the caregiving experiences of fathers of chronically ill or handicapped children have been considerably less extensively studied than mothers' experiences (Sabbeth, 1984). Although most familial caregivers are women, usually the wife, mother, or daughter of the care-recipient (Brody, 1981, 1985; Bywater, 1981; Sabbeth, 1984; Shanas, 1979; Stone, Cafferata, & Sangl, 1987), analyses based on predominantly female samples may inadequately reflect the experiences of male caregivers. There are indications that the caregiving experience is different and less stressful for adult sons than daughters (Horowitz, 1985), husbands than wives (Gilhooly, 1984; Noelker & Wallace, 1985), and fathers than mothers of chronic or handicapped children (Cummings, 1976); and there appear to be sex-linked differences in the types of caregiving tasks performed. For example, Stoller (1983) reported that daughters of the dependent elderly provided more assistance with domestic tasks compared to sons, although they were equally as likely to attend to financial matters and personal business.

There is also a paucity of information in the field regarding less common kinds of caregiver–patient relationships, such as those between neighbors or friends.

A related issue concerns the diseases studied. While early research on caregiver burden was largely limited to examining the consequences for family members caring for mentally ill patients, most recent work on caregiving burden has primarily focused on those assisting the frail elderly or dementia patients. Other caregiving situations have not been as intensively examined, and it is not known to what extent the findings on the psychological consequences of caregiving to elderly, mentally ill, or cognitively impaired adult populations apply to other diseases and age groups. There is evidence that the stress of the caregiving situation is influenced by the types of tasks performed, the extent and nature of the patient's impairment, the unpredictability of the symptoms, and the extent of control the caregiver can exert over the disease course or symptoms (e.g., Deimling & Bass, 1986; Holroyd & Guthrie, 1979, 1986; Jessop & Stein, 1985; Vachon et al., 1977; Zarit & Zarit, 1986), factors which transcend disease categories.

In fact, Stein and Jessop (1982), in their research on the impact of caring for an ill child, have argued for a noncategorical approach. They have pointed out that research on the consequences of chronic illness has generally adopted a disease-specific model which uncritically assumes the significance of the diagnostic label. Along with Pless and Perrin (1985) and Hamburg, Elliott, and Parron (1982), they have questioned the relevance of this approach and emphasized that generic dimensions may be more central to understanding the impact of illness on the family. Examples of such dimensions would be the chronicity of the disease, whether it is life threatening, and the extent to which it is stable or characterized by unpredictable crises.

Because studies of caregivers of infirm or impaired adults have generally been limited to one category of disease (e.g., Alzheimer's) or one kind of disability (e.g., cognitive impairment or mental illness), it is difficult to assess the value of a noncategorical approach to the study of caretaker burden when adults are the care-recipients. Studies that have focused on the frail elderly with a variety of health conditions have generally not made any attempt to discern the generic dimensions of these varied conditions that might be associated with different levels of psychological burden beyond such gross factors as whether the patient is cognitively impaired or engages in socially disruptive behavior.

At the same time, it must be recognized that there may be caregiving stresses that are unique to a particular disease or impairments which are especially stressful, as illustrated by D'Afflitti and Swanson's (1975) research on the wives of kidney patients. In this study, the wives of kidney dialysis patients assumed the primary responsibility for their husbands' home dialysis, a task they found very stressful. These women were haunted by the fear that their husbands would die "on the machine" and that they would feel directly responsible for their deaths.

Respondent Selection

Investigators in the field of caregiver research have not adopted a consistent method of establishing who qualifies as a caregiver. In some studies, the caregiver is nominated by the care-recipient (e.g., Cantor, 1983; Jones & Vetter, 1984; Robinson, 1983) or self-identifies as caregiver (Montgomery, Gonyea, & Hooyman, 1985). In other studies, the researcher may establish a priori criteria for determining who is the appropriate person. For example, Worcester and Quayhagen (1983) required that past or current caregivers must have resided in the same household as the care-recipient at the time care was given, and the caregivers had to state that the care-recipient needed too much care to live alone.

Additionally, one may be ipso facto designated as a caregiver by virtue of membership in a caregiver support group or inclusion on a mailing list for a caregiver organization (e.g., Jenkins, Parham, & Jenkins, 1985). Or, finally, the researcher may rely on the primary caretaker self-identifying him/herself as such (e.g., Hooyman et al., 1985).

Most studies do not attempt to distinguish the primary caregiver from anyone else who might be assisting in the patient's care. Yet, whether a caregiver has primary responsibility or whether it is shared will affect the extent of caregiving burden and stress experienced. Researchers need to determine whether, in fact, the caregivers in their samples are the main providers of care. Frequently, the spouse of the ill or debilitated patient is assumed to have the main responsibility; however, in samples with an aged population, it may be the adult daughter living outside the household who provides most of the care and assistance, not the elderly spouse.

Further variability is introduced when the care setting is not limited to noninstitutionalized populations. While many of the studies of the psychological consequences of caregiving have focused on care to a noninstitutionalized population, in a number of investigations the familial caregivers of both the institutionalized and at home care-recipients are included in the sample. The caregiving situation for an institutionalized dependent population is potentially different from that of those living in the community, and this may affect the psychological consequences of caregiving. For example, the nature and scope of tasks that must be assumed by the informal caregivers can differ significantly in these two groups. Patients who must be institutionalized are more likely to require extensive and skilled care (although responsibility for this care is shared with formal caregivers). Further, the social networks of institutionalized patients and/or their caregivers may be more limited or overtaxed, which may have contributed to the families' decisions to institutionalize the patients. In addition, actually making the decision for institutionalization has been shown to have far-reaching consequences for the relatives of the patients, including the evocation of strong feelings of guilt and anxiety (Brody, 1977; Pratt, Schmall, Wright, & Cleland, 1985).

Clearly, differences in how a caregiver is defined or identified introduce considerable variability among studies in the universe that is being sampled. Furthermore, among the different populations represented by these alternative definitions, there is much heterogeneity in the caregivers' objective burdens (i.e., tasks and responsibilities and hours of care); and this is likely to have observable psychological consequences. Caregivers who spend several hours a week in caretaking activities or who live with the care-recipient are likely to experience greater burden than someone who might assist or visit the care-recipient less frequently.

Study Design

Comparison Groups

A central issue in investigations of the psychological impact of performing the caregiver role is the necessity to establish that the emotional distress experienced is associated with those individuals' caregiving responsibilities, and that their levels of observed distress are, in fact, higher than comparable groups who lack caregiving duties. One strategy for attempting to establish this evidence is to include comparison groups.

This approach has been applied frequently in studies of chronically ill or handicapped children. In these cases, the research design may involve comparing the patient sample (i.e., chronically ill children) with a healthy sample of children matched on a variety of sociodemographic characteristics, such as age, sex, and race. Thus, Kazak (1987) compared the distress levels of three samples of mothers and fathers of children with either mental retardation, phenylketonuria, or spina bifida with three separate comparison groups of healthy children *matched individually* on such variables as age of the child, geographic locale, and family income. Alternatively, some researchers have included comparison groups matched at the group, as opposed to individual level of characteristics. For example, Cummings and associates (Cummings, 1976; Cummings, Bayley, & Rie, 1966) included comparison samples of normal healthy children when they explored the psychological impact on parents of caring for chronically ill, mentally retarded, or neurotic children. Similarly, in another study of parental caregiving to dependent children, Holroyd and Guthrie (1979) compared the level of stress experienced by parents of children with neuromuscular disease to that of parents of children attending an outpatient psychiatric clinic.

Another strategy for interpreting the significance of findings is to include measures of psychological impact which have established norms for general population samples and clinical samples (i.e., inpatient or outpatient psychiatric samples). Investigators employing this strategy compare the distress levels in their samples of caregivers to general population or clinical population norms. Many of the studies on caregiving in adult chronic disease and aging use this type of approach (see, for example, Fiore, Becker, & Coppel, 1983; Gilhooly, 1984; Sheehan & Nuttall, 1988; Thompson & Haran, 1985). However, for these types of comparisons, the population norms are not necessarily broken down to match specific characteristics of the caregiver sample under investigation. For example, George and Gwyther (1986) compared the overall well-being scores of their sample of dementia patient caregivers, who ranged in age from 21 to 90 and had an average age of 57, with mean scores obtained from three different general population samples of adults with varying age ranges (18 + , 65 + , 45–75) without dividing their sample into the appropriate age ranges for comparison.

The limitations of simply employing general population norms in research on the psychological consequences of caregiving is self-evident. Stone et al. (1987), for example, reported that in a national sample of caregivers to disabled elders, the caregivers in their sample differed from national estimates of their age peers in the general population on a number of characteristics. Although it is not entirely clear what effect these characteristics may have had on their caregiving, caregivers were less likely to be employed, more likely to have adjusted incomes below the poverty line, and perceived themselves to be in poorer health; and the younger caregivers were less likely than their peers to be married, while the older caregivers were more likely to be married.

Cross-Sectional Designs

The majority of studies examining the plight of caregivers and the psychosocial consequences of the caregiver role have been cross-sectional (see, for example, Chenoweth & Spencer, 1986; Gilhooly, 1984; Jones & Vetter,

1984; Rakowski & Clark, 1985; Worcester & Quayhagen, 1983). Cross-sectional studies are limited in that they document conditions at only one point in time. Retrospective items can be used in which the respondent is asked to recall his/her value on some variable at an earlier time (e.g., to rate his or her health six months ago as excellent, good, fair, or poor), and this can then be compared to a current rating to determine whether some change has occurred (e.g., whether the quality of his or her relationship with the patient has gotten worse, stayed the same, or gotten better over some time period). The impact or change measures obtained by such strategies are subject to distortions in recall (e.g., forward and backward telescoping) and are highly subjective (Featherman, 1980; Field, 1981; Funch & Marshall, 1984; Miller, 1976; National Center for Health Statistics, 1968, 1977). Indeed, the reports themselves can be conditioned by how one is feeling at that present time (Montgomery, Stull, & Borgatta, 1985; Poulshock & Deimling, 1984).

Given the inherent limitations of cross-sectional designs, it is apparent that they are ill-suited to addressing some of the more pressing research issues. As Niederehe and Fruge (1984) point out, it is important to know what is most stressful to the caregiver over the course of illness. Additionally, we need to know whether the negative impact on the caregiver increases over time as he/she endures the burdens of that role, or whether coping skills are learned over time which alleviate the burden experienced. These issues can most effectively be addressed with longitudinal designs. With a single assessment point, it is not possible to examine adequately the changing level and nature of the psychological impact of the caregiver role throughout the course of an illness, or to examine the effect on the caregiver of these changes in the patient's illness.

Measures

There is a great variability across studies concerning how the psychological consequences of caregiving have been conceptualized and empirically measured. As discussed in greater detail below, some investigations have focused on how much distress caregivers attribute to their caregiving experiences. In other studies, the degree of satisfaction with being a caregiver is examined. Still others include the psychological consequences of caregiving as part of a global inventory of caregiving burden which is expressed as a single summary score. In a number of studies, the psychological impact of caregiving is conceptualized as having far-reaching consequences, and instead of measures of distress that are specifically tied to the stressors of caregiving, measures of more general psychopathology (e.g., depression, anxiety, or demoralization) are used.

In those investigations which assess distress specific to caregiving, psychological distress is generally conceptualized as subjective burden (or the perception of burden) as compared to other types of caregiving consequences which are classified as objective burdens. Thus, for example, Montgomery, Gonyea, & Hooyman (1985), in their sample of family caregivers of the frail elderly, included a 13-item inventory of subjective burden to measure the caregivers' attitudes and emotions concerning their caregiving experiences.

In addition to assessing the mental and physical health and social role functioning of dementia patients' caregivers, Niederehe and Fruge (1984) developed a 36-item measure of "Feelings about Caregiving" that focused on how distressed the caregivers felt in their role and how capable they felt about continuing in it. The investigators believed that their measure of "subjective strain" assessed the same phenomenon other investigators were attempting to measure with their respective indicators of subjective burden.

In another investigation, Jones and Vetter (1984) used a scale which assessed "subjective burden" in terms of the amount of distress the caregivers felt in response to the problems experienced in caring for the dependent elderly. They also included two measures of psychological morbidity: anxiety and depression. Both caregiver distress and psychological morbidity were regarded as consequences of caregiving.

Still other investigators appear to be measuring what various researchers have labeled subjective burden, even though they do not necessarily refer to it in such terms. For example, when Cantor (1983) examined how the provision of care to the frail elderly affected the lives of the caregivers, included in the inventory administered were items which assessed the extent to which the caregiver experienced emotional strain. Similarly, Rakowski and Clark (1985) asked caregivers to report experiences of feeling "upset" that were associated with providing care to ill or impaired elderly relatives and to indicate how frequently these feelings occurred.

In distinct contrast to approaches in which the emotional consequences of caregiving are examined separately from other potential consequences are scales of burden which calculate a summary score across a variety of dimensions. One of the more widely known and used measures is the Burden Scale developed by Zarit and his associates (Zarit et al., 1980, 1986) as part of their research on caregivers of dementia patients. This scale measures the extent to which caregivers perceive their emotional or physical health, social life, and financial status to be adversely affected by their caring for a family member with senile dementia. Unlike other burden measures which tend to have isolated use, the Burden Scale has been adopted by other investigators for use in their studies of caregivers of Alzheimer's patients (e.g., Pratt et al., 1985; Scott, Roberto, & Hutton, 1986).

Horowitz (Horowitz, 1985; Horowitz & Shindelman, 1983) devised a scale of "Caregiving Consequences" based on respondents' perceptions of their caregiving experiences with the frail elderly. Although the scale examines the problems encountered and the emotional strain experienced, and also assesses the adverse effects of caregiving on personal and family life, only a summary score is calculated.

Morycz (1985) also used an inventory of caregiver strain to examine whether the level of subjective burden experienced by caregivers to Alzheimer's patients influenced the decision to institutionalize the patient. Similar to other global burden measures, this one includes items which not only assess emotional states, but also examine perceived changes in household routines, social relationships, health, and free time.

A disadvantage to using the type of indicator which combines, in a global measure, indicators of emotional distress with other types of caregiving consequences, such as a change in financial status or available leisure time, is that such a summary burden measure may obscure theoretically significant findings concerning caregiving impact. For example, Montgomery, Gonyea, and Hooyman (1985), in their research on the frail elderly, found that subjective and objective burdens had distinct sets of correlates which were not equally amenable to intervention techniques and change.

As we have seen, many investigators, who examine psychological distress with measures specific to the caregiving situation, develop their own indicators of distress. This approach not only increases the variability in the measurement of distress in the field, but it also raises concerns regarding the reliability and validity of the measures. In many of the studies in which multi-item scales or indices are used, investigators have provided information on the reliability and to a lesser extent validity of their measures. These reports have generally indicated that the measures have reasonable psychometric properties in the sample under investigation (e.g., Gilleard et al., 1984; Horowitz & Shindelman, 1983; Niederehe & Fruge, 1984; Robinson, 1983; Thompson & Doll, 1982; Worcester & Quayhagen, 1983; Zarit et al., 1980). Other investigators, however, employ measures of distress composed of a small number of items (in some cases, just one item) which possess only face validity (e.g., Hooyman et al., 1985; Rakowski & Clark, 1985).

It would be desirable to extend the use of existing scales of caregiver burden, which have documented acceptable reliability and validity in some caregiver populations, to the study of other caregiver populations as well. However, the reliability and validity of the measures in these different populations would need to be assessed before these scales, many of which were developed for use with caregivers of elderly or mentally impaired adults, could be routinely used.

A third approach to the measurement of the psychological impact of caregiving is to utilize inventories or scales of general psychopathology. This type of approach moves the examination from situationally specific consequences to a focus on broader far-reaching changes in psychological status. One advantage, as George and Gwyther (1986) point out, is that by not utilizing scales that are anchored to the caregiving situation, the same measures can be applied to noncaregiving populations, making it possible to compare study findings with data from community populations and clinic samples. Another advantage of employing established measures is that their psychometric properties are known, having been previously investigated in a variety of population groups. Furthermore, these measures assess clinically defined mental states and usually possess a criterion value for determining clinically significant morbidity, a useful feature in studies in which the goal is to target for intervention caretakers at high risk for psychopathology.

Even when researchers use measures of general psychopathology to estimate caregiving impact, there is variability in the scales used and the dimensions of psychological functioning assessed. Gilhooly (1984) studied the psychological well-being of caregivers of dementia patients by using the Kutner Morale Scale (Kutner, Fanshel, Togo, & Langner, 1956) and the mental health scale of the OARS Multidimensional Functional Assessment Questionnaire (Duke University, Duke Center for the Study of Aging and Human Development, 1978), which contains items on anxiety, depression, worry, tension, and hypochondriasis.

George and Gwyther (1986) used the Short Psychiatric Evaluation Scale developed by Pfeiffer (1979) to measure psychiatric symptoms associated with stress, the Bradburn Affect Balance Scale (Bradburn, 1969) to measure the ratio of positive to negative affect, and a single-item measure of life satisfaction to assess the psychological consequences of caregiving in a sample of caretakers of dementia patients. The Langner Symptom Checklist (Langner, 1962), a measure of adjustment and psychological demoralization, was used along with a measure of marital satisfaction, the Dyadic Adjustment Scale (Spanier, 1976), to measure the stress related to caregiving in parents of handicapped/chronically ill children (Kazak, 1987). In their research on the familial caregivers of amputees, Thompson and Haran (1985) used a psychiatric screening inventory which was developed to identify psychiatric cases in community populations. Similarly, the Beck Depression Inventory

(Beck, 1967) was used by Fiore et al. (1983) in their research on caregivers of Alzheimer's patients. Others (e.g., Jones & Vetter, 1984; Niederehe & Fruge, 1984, who were discussed above; as well Sheehan & Nuttall, 1988) included measures of general psychopathology as well as situationally specific distress measures to evaluate the impact of caregiving.

Perhaps part of the reason for the variability in how the psychological impact is measured can be attributed to the absence of a widely accepted comprehensive model of the process and nature of the psychological impact of caregiving. In fact, much of the research carried out is atheoretical, with little justification given for the inclusion of specific variables in the analysis.

Models of Caregiving Impact

A number of researchers have begun to incorporate theoretical models in their analyses. These explanatory models of the experience of distress are characterized by considerable diversity that results from being derived from quite different social, cognitive, and behavioral orientations.

One of the major variants in these models is the process through which the demands of the caregiver role influence the psychological outcome. This is evident in the variations in the conceptualization and measurement of that impact adopted by different investigators, which imply different causal paths. Among the competing perspectives are: that distress is experienced as part of the burdens of caregiving; or that the burdens are antecedent to and impact on the caregiver's psychological well-being as indicated by increased levels of depression or anxiety; or that distress is experienced both situationally as well as globally. There are also variations in the role factors external to caregiving (such as environmental factors, past relationships, and personality and social factors) which are hypothesized as playing a part in accounting for psychological impact and the ways in which they enter into the causal sequence between caregiving and distress; that is, do they contribute directly to the experience of distress or perform a mediating role?

One type of explanatory model applied to examinations of distress among caregivers utilizes exchange theory. In this model, the caregiver relationship is really a reflection of the exchanges and bonds of affection that have their roots in the past (Adams, 1968). Thus, adult children now care for elderly parents in repayment for the nurturance and support they had received from their parents earlier. Reciprocity is based on the "'credits' earned by the older relative for past help given to the caregiver. It is an obligation which stems from gratitude and is manifested in the desire to repay the older relative for past services rendered" (Horowitz & Shindelman, 1983, p. 6). The wish to reciprocate is viewed as the underlying motivation for caregiving behavior, while the past and current levels of affection mediate the impact of the stresses associated with caregiving (Horowitz & Shindelman, 1983).

Another approach applies concepts from role theory to explain the processes whereby burden develops out of the caregiver situation (Morycz, 1985; Noelker & Wallace, 1985). Morycz (1980) conceptualizes subjective burden as role strain and objective burden as stress associated with role conflict (competing roles) and role overload (too many roles), thereby providing a framework for understanding caregiver burden. In his model, "stress is an external event, whereas strain represents cognitive, affective, and physiological changes induced by stress. The degree of strain therefore is moderated by the individuals' perception of the stressor" (p. 331).

Zarit and his associates (Zarit et al., 1985; Zarit & Zarit, 1986) utilize a stress management model in which stress arises out of the caregiver having to deal with major obstacles, such as disruptive, embarrassing, or irritating behaviors of the patient, coupled with the patient being unable to perform his or her role responsibilities, and drains on the caregiver's available resources for providing adequate care (including limitations on time and energy due to competing role demands). In the stress management approach, caregivers can control the amount of stress they experience by learning effective methods of managing the patient's behavior and by obtaining the necessary assistance with caregiving tasks.

Related to the stress management approach are models that utilize a coping and resources framework to explain the psychological impact of caregiving on the caregivers. In this approach, coping behaviors and other resources (psychological, social, and financial) mediate the stress of the caregiving situation. Pratt et al. (1985) applied this model to an analysis of distress among caregivers of Alzheimer's patients.

Other researchers have used a vulnerability or risk model to explain the psychological consequences of caregiving. For example, Fiore et al. (1983) argue that depression is an expectable outcome from the caregiving relationship, because it contains situational elements associated with depression, such as impaired relations with a significant other (care-recipient) and a chronic global stressor (caretaking duties), that limits one's control over one's life and induces considerable guilt.

All of these models, as applied in studies of caregiving, are subject to similar criticisms. Although the theories these models are drawn from are broad-based and generally well developed, the models that are derived from them to explain the psychological impact of caregiving are overly simplistic.

The models examine a restricted number of factors and focus only on a portion of the total caregiving situation. Complex interrelationships between variables are not considered. More elaborate and better specified models need to be investigated. Two examples of recent attempts to advance the field in this direction are contained in this volume.

Kahana and Young (Chapter 3) point out that most research on caregiving has focused exclusively on the caregivers and the negative consequences for them of carrying out the responsibilities of their role. They assert that more elaborate paradigms should be employed, especially ones that consider the caregiver–care-recipient dyad and the positive as well as negative consequences of that relationship for each party. As they note, the actions of each party have implications for the consequences of the relationship for the other, and recursive models that reflect this need to be investigated.

The research by Chiriboga, Weiler, and Nielsen (Chapter 5) argues for broadening the examination of stressors beyond those related to the caregiving situation. They studied the contribution to caregivers' well-being of general life events and the hassles of everyday living, in addition to the perceived burden of care and the amount of actual care provided. Their findings showed that general types of stressors, not just those restricted to the caregiving role, can impact on caregivers' well-being.

Future Research

Several directions for future research into the psychological consequences of caregiving are suggested by this review of extant studies. First, efforts must be made to develop sampling frames that better represent the diverse kinds and levels of responsibilities and tasks caregivers assume. Relatedly, methods must be adopted to ensure more adequate representation of various subpopulations of caregivers, especially men and nonwhites. A stratified sampling design might be one strategy for achieving this end. In addition, study samples must be large enough to permit subgroup comparisons. While sample size is often constrained by available research funds, it must be recognized that small samples will frequently not provide adequate size to detect significant weak or moderate relationships.

Regarding the identification of caregivers, researchers must fully explicate their selection criteria or procedures so that potential bias may be evaluated. It is probably most fruitful to establish a priori criteria, for example, based on the kinds of tasks performed or level of assistance provided to the care-recipient. If the criteria are not explicit or established before the time of accrual, there is likely to be considerable inconsistency in determining who is eligible to be interviewed as a caregiver. Further, if one relies on the care-recipient to nominate the caregiver, they may be inclined to nominate the person whom they feel would be either most likely to agree to participate in the research or, perhaps worse, least likely to be burdened by the interview because they are providing little assistance to the patient.

Future research should investigate the caregivers of a greater variety of care-recipient populations. We are currently conducting longitudinal investigations of the psychological consequences of providing informal care and social support in two less-commonly-studied patient populations: gay men with AIDS, and adult cancer patients. The value of a noncategorical approach, as suggested by Stein and Jessop (1982), Pless and Perrin (1985), and Hamburg et al. (1982), also deserves further attention. Efforts should be made to identify those generic dimensions of the caregivers' responsibilities or situations that might influence the psychological distress experienced in that role.

Investigations also need to incorporate comparison groups into the design. The question of whether caregivers experience elevated psychological distress associated with their role can be meaningfully answered only by comparing their psychological well-being with a comparable sample without similar responsibilities. When existing population norms must be employed as a cost-efficient compromise, efforts must be made to obtain a population sample matched on several key background characteristics (e.g., sex, age, and/or income).

Given the dynamic nature of caregiving, it is also essential that the agenda for future research should include more longitudinal investigations of caregivers. Issues concerning process and change over time cannot be adequately addressed with cross-sectional studies. Longitudinal studies are, of course, expensive and have their own inherent problems (e.g., attrition and reactive effects associated with repeated interviews). However, by following longitudinally even a randomly selected subsample of a larger sample, one would gain insight into a number of dynamic issues.

The identification and synthesis of the many dimensions of the psychological impact of caregiving investigated in different studies needs to be begun to determine which are distinct and which are overlapping. Once these dimensions are clearly conceptualized and defined, attention should be turned to developing a comprehensive multidimensional measure of the psychological impact of caregiving applicable across a wide range of caregiver populations. Such a measure would provide a unified conceptual and methodological approach to the study of the psychological consequences of caregiving. It would also permit a more meaningful comparison of findings across studies, greatly facilitating the accumulation of knowledge in this field.

Another priority for future research should be the development of a strong theoretical focus. The field has been greatly handicapped by the absence of a theoretical framework to guide the selection of variables for investigation and to permit the formulation of meaningful research hypotheses. Researchers need to work toward integrating the various theoretical frameworks and "less specified" conceptualizations currently being employed into a more unified body of theory so that models which are empirically grounded in the research can be applied and tested in a variety of caregiving situations. As Kahana and Young point out, we must begin to investigate more elaborate paradigms, such as the caregiver–care-recipient relationship and its consequences for each party. These dynamic, or relational, models have the potential to enlarge greatly our understanding of the factors that limit or shape the caregiving situation. Their examination, however, will pose new methodological challenges in this field.

Conclusion

In summation, this review has shown that studies of the psychological consequences of caregiving are subject to a number of methodological shortcomings which limit the generalizability of the research findings, compromise the integrity of the inferences that investigators seek to draw, and impede the development of explanatory models of the psychological impact of performing the caregiver role. Research in the field is characterized by relatively small samples that are predominately female and white, and often drawn from one or two institutional settings. Furthermore, the majority of investigations have focused on caregiving to dementia patients and the frail elderly, with caregivers of other populations much less studied. There is great variability in how the psychological impact of caregiving is conceptualized and measured in the various studies, and this has impeded the comparison of findings across studies. The field is characterized by a lack of a strong theoretical focus, and future research is hampered by a weak integration of the findings from diverse caregiving situations and diseases.

Note

1. A number of research reports of studies of caregivers contained in the literature omit significant information concerning their design and methodology. Most characteristically the reports do not contain clear or complete information about the procedures used in sample selection, and rarely are the participation and refusal rates provided. Frequently, information is lacking on the reliability and validity of the measures employed, especially indicators on psychological burden or impact.

When reports omit basic methodological information, it is difficult to assess the probable validity of the study's findings, the integrity of the inferences drawn from the data, and the degree to which the results can be generalized to other groups or populations. Several studies which examined the psychological consequences of caregiving could not be considered in this review because sufficient information about research design and methodology was not provided.

References

Adams, B.N. (1968). *Kinship in an urban setting.* Chicago: Markham.

Allan, J.L., Townley, R.R.W., & Phelan, P.D. (1974). Family response to cystic fibrosis. *Australian Paediatric Journal, 10,* 136-146.

Anthony, E.J. (1970). The impact of mental and physical illness on family life. *American Journal of Psychiatry, 127,* 138-146.

Beck, A.T. (1967). *Depression: Clinical, experimental and theoretical aspects.* New York: Harper & Row.

Booth, A., & Babchuk, N. (1972). Seeking health care from new resources. *Journal of Health and Social Behavior, 13,* 90-99.

Bradburn, N.M. (1969). *The structure of psychological well-being.* Hawthorne, NY: Aldine.

Brody, E.M. (1977). *Long-term care of older people.* New York: Human Sciences Press.

Brody, E.M. (1981). "Women in the middle" and family help to older people. *The Gerontologist, 21* (5), 471-480.

Brody, E.M. (1985). Parent care as a normative family stress. *The Gerontologist, 25* (1), 19-29.

Brody, S.J., Poulshock, S.W., & Masciocchi, C.F. (1978). The family caring unit: A major consideration in the long-term support system. *The Gerontologist, 18,* 556-561.

Brown, D.J., Craick, C.C., Davies, S.E., Johnson, M.L., Dawborn, J.K., & Heale, W.F. (1978). Physical, emotional and social adjustments to home dialysis. *The Medical Journal of Australia, 1,* 245-247.

Burke, R.J., & Weir, T. (1976). Personality characteristics associated with giving and receiving help. *Psychological Reports, 38,* 343-353.

Bywater, E.M. (1981). Adolescents with cystic fibrosis: Psychosocial adjustment. *Archives of Disease in Childhood, 56,* 538-543.

Cantor, M.H. (1983). Strain among caregivers: A study of experience in the United States. *The Gerontologist, 23* (6), 597-604.

Cassileth, B.R., Lusk, E.J., Strouse, T.B., Miller, D.S., Brown, L.L., & Cross, P.A. (1985). A psychological analysis of cancer patients and their next-of-kin. *Cancer, 55,* 72-76.

Chenoweth, B., & Spencer, B. (1986). Dementia: The experience of family caregivers. *The Gerontologist Society of America, 26,* 267-272.

Croog, S.H., & Fitzgerald,E.F. (1978). Subjective stress and serious illness of a spouse: Wives of heart patients. *Journal of Health and Social Behavior, 19*, 166-178.

Croog, S., Lipson, A., & Levine, S. (1972). Help patterns in severe illnesses: The roles of kin network, non-family resources and institutions. *Journal of Marriage and the Family, 34*, 32-41.

Cummings, S.T. (1976). The impact of the child's deficiency on the father: A study of fathers of mentally retarded and of chronically ill children. *American Journal of Orthopsychiatry, 46* (2), 246-255.

Cummings, S., Bayley, H., & Rie, H. (1966). Effects of the child's deficiency on the mother: A study of mothers of mentally retarded, chronically ill and neurotic children. *American Journal of Orthopsychiatry, 36*, 595-608.

D'Afflitti, J.G., & Swanson, D. (1975). Group sessions for the wives of home-hemodialysis patients. *American Journal of Nursing, 75*,(4), 633-635.

Deimling, G.T., & Bass, D.M. (1986). Symptoms of mental impairment among elderly adults and their effects on family caregivers. *Journal of Gerontology, 41* (6), 778-784.

DiMatteo, M.R., & Hays, R. (1981). Social support and serious illness. In B.H. Gottlieb (Ed.), *Social networks and social support* (pp. 117-148). Beverly Hills, CA: Sage.

Duke Center for the Study of Aging and Human Development. (1978). *Multidimensional functional assessment: The OARS methodology. A manual.* Durham, NC: Duke University.

Featherman, D. (1980). Retrospective longitudinal research: Methodological considerations. *Journal of Economics and Business, 32*, 152-169.

Fengler, A.P., & Goodrich, N. (1979). Wives of elderly disabled men: The hidden patients. *The Gerontologist, 19* (2), 175-183.

Field, D. (1981). Retrospective reports by healthy intelligent elderly people of personal events of their adult lives. *International Journal of Behavioral Development, 4*, 77-97.

Fife, B., Norton, J., & Groom, G. (1987). The family's adaptation to childhood leukemia. *Social Science and Medicine, 24* (2), 159-168.

Fiore, J., Becker, J., & Coppel D.B. (1983). Social network interactions: A buffer or a stress. *American Journal of Community Psychology, 11*(4), 423-439.

Funch, D.P., & Marshall, J.R. (1984) Measuring life stress: Factors affecting fall-off in the reporting of life events. *Journal of Health and Social Behavior, 25*, 453-464.

George, L.K., & Gwyther, L.P. (1986).Caregiver well-being: A multi-dimensional examination of family caregivers of demented adults. *The Gerontologist, 26* (3), 253-259.

Gilhooly, M.L.M. (1984). The impact of caregiving on caregivers: Factors associated with the psychological well-being of people supporting a dementing relative in the community. *British Journal of Medical Psychology, 57*, 35-44.

Gilleard, C.J., Belford, H., Gilleard, E., Whittick, J.E., & Gledhill, K. (1984). Emotional distress amongst the supporters of the elderly mentally infirm. *British Journal of Psychiatry, 145*, 172-177.

Gourash, N. (1978). Help-seeking: A review of the literature. *American Journal of Community Psychology, 6* (5), 413-423.

Grad, J., & Sainsbury, P. (1963). Mental illness and the family. *The Lancet, 9*, 544-547.

Grad, J., & Sainsbury, P. (1968). The effects that patients have on their families in a community care and a central psychiatric service—a two-year follow-up. *British Journal of Psychiatry, 114*, 265-278.

Grandstaff, N.W. (1976). The impact of breast cancer on the family. *Frontiers of Radiation Therapy Oncology, 11*, 146-156.

Gurin, G., Veroff, J., & Feld, S. (1960). *Americans view their mental health.* New York: Basic Books.

Hafstrom, J.L., & Schram, V.R. (1984). Chronic illness in couples: Selected characteristics, including wife's satisfaction with the perception of marital relationships. *Family Relations, 33*, 195-203.

Hamburg, D.A., Elliott, G.R., & Parron, D.L. (1982). *Health and behavior: Frontiers of research in the biobehavioral science.* Washington, DC: National Academy Press.

Hinds, C. (1985). The needs of families who care for patients with cancer at home: Are we meeting them? *Journal of Advanced Nursing, 10*, 575-581.

Hoenig, J., & Hamilton, M.W. (1966a). Elderly psychiatric patients and the burden on the household. *Psychiatric Neurology (Basel), 152*(5), 281-293.

Hoenig, J., & Hamilton, M.W. (1966b).The schizophrenic patient in the community and his effect on the household. *International Journal of Social Psychiatry, 12*, 165-176.

Holroyd, J., & Guthrie, D. (1979). Stress in families of children with neuromuscular disease. *Journal of Clinical Psychology, 35* (4), 734-739.

Holroyd, J., & Guthrie, D. (1986). Family stress with chronic childhood illness: Cystic fibrosis, neuromuscular disease, and renal disease. *Journal of Clinical Psychology, 42* (4), 552-561.

Hooyman, N., Gonyea, J., & Montgomery, R.(1985). The impact of in-home services termination on family caregivers. *The Gerontologist, 25* (2), 141-145.

Horowitz, A. (1985). Sons and daughters as caregivers to older parents: Differences in role performance and consequences. *The Gerontologist, 25*, 612-617.

Horowitz, A., & Shindelman, L.W. (1983). Reciprocity and affection: Past influences on current caregiving. *Journal of Gerontological Social Work, 5* (3), 5-20.

Jenkins, T.S., Parham, I.A., & Jenkins, L.R. (1985). Alzheimer's disease: Caregiver's perceptions of burden. *Journal of Applied Gerontology, 4* (2), 40-57.

Jessop, D.J., & Stein, R.E. (1985). Uncertainty and its relation to the psychological and social correlates of chronic illness in children. *Social Science and Medicine, 20*, 993-999.

Jones, D.A., & Vetter, N.J. (1984). A survey of those who care for the elderly at home: Their problems and their needs. *Social Science and Medicine, 19*(5), 511-514.

Kammeyer, K., & Bolton, C. (1968). Community and family factors related to the use of a family service agency. *Journal of Marriage and the Family, 30*, 488-498.

Kazak, A.E. (1987). Families with disabled children: Stress and social networks in three samples. *Journal of Abnormal Child Psychology, 15* (1), 137-146.

Kutner, B., Fanshel, D., Togo, A.M., & Langner, T.S. (1956). *Five hundred over sixty.* New York: Russell Sage.

Langner, T. (1962). A 22-item screening score of psychiatric symptoms indicating impairment. *Journal of Health and Human Behavior, 3*, 269-276.

Lawler, R.H., Nakielny, W., & Wright, N.A. (1966). Psychological implications of cystic fibrosis. *Canadian Medical Association, 94*, 1043-1046.

Levine, F., & Preston, E. (1970). Community resource orientation among low income groups. *Wisconsin Law Review, 1*, 80-113.

Lewis, F.M. (1986). The impact of cancer on the family: A critical analysis of the research literature. *Patient Education and Counseling, 8*, 269-289.

Lewis, F.M., Ellison, E.S., & Woods, N.F. (1985). The impact of breast cancer on the family. *Seminars in Oncology Nursing, 1* (3), 206-213.

Miller, A.R. (1976). Retrospective data on work status in the 1970 census of population: An attempt at evaluation. *Journal of the American Statistical Association, 71*, 286-292.

Montgomery, R.J.V., Gonyea, J.G., & Hooyman, N.R. (1985). Caregiving and the experience of subjective and objective burden. *Family Relations, 34*, 19-25.

Montgomery, R.J.V., Stull, D., & Borgatta, E.F. (1985). Measurement and the analysis of burden. *Research on Aging, 7*(1), 137-152.

Morrow, G.R., Carpenter, P.J., & Hoagland, A.C. (1984). The role of social support in parental adjustment to pediatric cancer. *Journal of Pediatric Psychology, 9* (3), 317-329.

Morycz, R.K. (1980). An exploration of senile dementia and family burden. *Clinical Social Work Journal, 8,* 16-27.

Morycz, R.K. (1985). Caregiving strain and the desire to institutionalize family members with Alzheimer's disease. *Research on Aging, 7*(3), 329-361.

National Center for Health Statistics. (1968). The influence of interviewer and respondent psychological and behavioral variables on the reporting in household interviews. *Vital and Health Statistics,* (PHS Pub. No. 1000, Series 2, No. 26, Public Health Service), Washington DC: U.S. Government Printing Office.

National Center for Health Statistics. (1977). A summary of studies of interviewing methodology. *Vital and Health Statistics,* (DHEW Pub. No. 77, Series 2, No.69, Health Resources Administration). Washington, DC: U.S. Government Printing Office.

Neighbors, H.W., & Jackson, J.S. (1984). The use of informal and formal help: Four patterns of illness behavior in the black community. *American Journal of Community Psychology, 12* (6), 629-643.

Niederehe, G., & Fruge, E. (1984). Dementia and family dynamics: Clinical research issues. *Journal of Geriatric Psychiatry, 17* (1), 21-56.

Noelker, L., & Wallace, R.W. (1985). The organization of family care for impaired elderly. *Journal of Family Issues, 6,* 23-44.

Pfeiffer, E. (1979). A short psychiatric evaluation schedule: A new 15-item monotonic scale indicative of functional psychiatric disorder. In the Proceedings of the Bayer-Symposium, 7. *Brain function in old age* (pp. 228-236). New York: Springer.

Pless, I.B., & Perrin, J.M. (1985). Issues common to a variety of illnesses. In N. Hobbs & J.M. Perrin (Eds.), *Issues in the Care of Children with Chronic Illness* (pp. 41-60). San Francisco: Jossey-Bass.

Poulshock, W.S., & Deimling, G.T. (1984). Families caring for elders in residence: Issues in the measurement of burden. *Journal of Gerontology, 39* (2), 230-239.

Pratt, C.C., Schmall, V.L., Wright, S., & Cleland, M. (1985). Burden and coping strategies of caregivers to Alzheimer's patients. *Family Relations, 34,* 27-33.

Rabins, P.V., Mace, N.L., & Lucas, M.J. (1982). The impact of dementia on the family. *Journal of the American Medical Association, 248* (3), 333-335.

Rakowski, W., & Clark, N.M. (1985). Future outlook, caregiving, and care-receiving in the family context. *The Gerontologist, 25,* 623-628.

Robinson, B.C. (1983). Validation of a caregiver strain index. *Journal of Gerontology, 38* (3), 344-348.

Robinson, B., & Thurnher, M. (1979). Taking care of aged parents: A family cycle transition. *The Gerontologist, 19,* 586-593.

Rosenblatt, A., & Mayer, J.E. (1972). Helpseeking for family problems: A survey of utilization and satisfaction. *American Journal of Psychiatry, 28,* 126-130.

Sabbeth, B. (1984). Understanding the impact of chronic childhood illness on families. *Pediatric Clinics of North America, 31* (1), 47-57.

Sainsbury, P., & Grad de Alarcon, J. (1969). The psychiatrist and the geriatric patient: The effects of community care on the family of the geriatric patient. *Journal of Geriatric Psychiatry, 4,* 23-41.

Satterwhite, B.B. (1978). Impact of chronic illness on child and family: An overview based on five surveys with implications for management. *International Journal of Rehabilitation Research, 1* (1), 7-17.

Scott, J.P., Roberto, K.A., & Hutton, J.T.(1986). Families of Alzheimer's victims: Family support to the caregivers. *Journal of the American Geriatrics Society, 34*, 348-354.

Shanas, E. (1979). The family as a social support system in old age. *The Gerontologist, 19* (2), 169-174.

Sheehan, N.W., & Nuttall, P. (1988). Conflict, emotion, and personal strain among family caregivers. *Family Relations, 37*, 92-98.

Spanier, G. (1976). Measuring dyadic adjustment: Scales for assessing the quality of marriage and other dyads. *Journal of Marriage and the Family, 38*, 15-28.

Stein, R., & Jessop, D. (1982). A non-categorical approach to chronic childhood illness. *Public Health Reports, 97*, 361-378.

Stetz, K.M. (1987). Caregiving demands during advanced cancer: The spouse's needs. *Cancer Nursing, 10* (5), 260-268.

Stoller, E.P. (1983). Parental caregiving by adult children. *Journal of Marriage and the Family, 45*, 851-858.

Stone, R., Cafferata, G.L., & Sangl, J. (1987). Caregivers of the frail elderly: A national profile. *The Gerontologist, 27*, (5), 616-626.

Test, M.A., & Stein, L.I. (1980). Alternatives to mental hospital treatment: II. Social cost. *Archives of General Psychiatry, 37*, 409-412.

Thompson, D.M., & Haran, D. (1985). Living with an amputation: The helper. *Social Science and Medicine, 20* (4), 319-323.

Thompson, E.H., & Doll, W. (1982). The burden of families coping with the mentally ill: An invisible crisis. *Family Relations, 31*, 379-388.

Vachon, M.L.S., Freedman, K., Formo, A., Rogers, J., Lyall, W.A.L., & Freeman, J.J. (1977). The final illness in cancer: The widow's perspective. *CMA Journal, 117*, 1151-1154.

Venters, M. (1981). Familial coping with chronic and severe childhood illness: The case of Cystic Fibrosis. *Social Science and Medicine, 15A*, 289-297.

Wellisch, D., Landsverk, J., Guidera, K., Pasnau, R.O., & Fawzy, F. (1983). Evaluation of psychosocial problems of the homebound cancer patient: I. Methodology and problem frequencies. *Psychosomatic Medicine, 45*(1), 11-21.

Worcester, M.I., & Quayhagen, M.P. (1983). Correlates of caregiving satisfaction: Prerequisites to elder home care. *Research in Nursing and Health, 6*, 61-67.

Wortman, C. (1984). Social support and the cancer patient. *Cancer, 53*, 2339-2360.

Zarit, S.H., Orr, N.K., & Zarit, J.M. (1985). *The hidden victims of Alzheimer's Disease: Families under stress.* New York: New York University Press.

Zarit, S.H., Reever, K.E., & Bach-Peterson, J. (1980). Relatives of the impaired elderly: Correlates of feelings of burden. *The Gerontologist, 20* (6), 649-655.

Zarit, S.H., Todd, P.A., & Zarit, J.M. (1986). Subjective burden of husbands and wives as caregivers: Longitudinal study. *The Gerontologist, 26*, (3), 260-266.

Zarit, S.H., & Zarit, J.M. (1986). Dementia and the family: A stress management approach. *The Clinical Psychologist, 39*, 103-105.

3

Clarifying the Caregiving Paradigm

Challenges for the Future

EVA KAHANA
ROSALIE YOUNG

Caregiving research, just as research in the field of aging, has started out in search for commonalities which underlie the caregiving process. The concept of burden (Zarit, Orr, & Zarit, 1985) emerged as a unifying notion which was shared by diverse caregivers to diverse groups of elderly. However, as research on caregiving has come of age, it has been confronted with both conceptual limitations and lack of empirical support for a unidimensional view. Accordingly, increased attention is directed at diversity in the processes and outcomes of caregiving based on the different populations of caregivers and care-recipients considered. We are learning that caregiving to a demented elder differs in some significant ways from giving care to an elder recovering from a heart attack or hip fracture. It is also becoming increasingly apparent that caregiving involves complex interactions with potentially positive or negative consequences for both care-recipients and caregivers. The major goal of this chapter is to outline a framework for considering dyadic aspects of the caregiving paradigm which allows for flexibility, diversity, and multidimensionality, and expands on prevalent conceptual

AUTHORS' NOTE

The assistance of Ms. June Novatney and Ms. Reva Taylor in conducting the literature review is greatly appreciated.

orientations to the study of caregiving. Such expanded conceptual frameworks are necessary if future research is to integrate converging developments in gerontology and related disciplines which are salient to understanding caregiving to the elderly.

Caregiving has often been studied as a unidimensional and unidirectional process primarily reflecting the burdens and health and mental health problems experienced by caregivers based on their efforts to provide aid to elders. Yet, closer examination reveals multiple dynamisms in caregiver/care-recipient interactions. In an effort to search for meaningful conceptual frameworks which help to organize caregiver/care-recipient interactions better, the authors have previously focused on the utility of a stress, resources, and recovery paradigm (Young & Kahana, 1989). In this paradigm, caregiving is considered as an adaptive arrangement in the face of serious or chronic illness. Our conceptualization of strain focused on stressors, as well as mediating resources, which may help explain positive outcomes for both elderly who suffered heart attacks and for their caregivers. Our dual focus on caregiver and care-recipient outcomes has sensitized us to the importance of clearly conceptualizing paradigms regarding the caregiver/care-recipient interactions. In the following discussion, we will draw upon the general framework of stress theory (Dohrenwend & Dohrenwend, 1974) in an effort to further clarify alternative models of caregiving research.

While the relationship between two central individuals comprises the focus of most caregiving studies (Johnson, 1983), the alternative conceptual models implicit in such analyses have seldom been explicated. The caregiving arrangement may produce either symmetrical outcomes with ultimate benefits to both caregivers and care-recipients, or asymmetrical outcomes where caregivers may suffer great burden even as care-recipients recover. Alternatively, caregivers may experience few adverse effects in situations where the older patient's needs are not being met. Characteristics of caregivers, their resources, specifics of the caregiving situation, the patient's characteristics, and resources may all intervene in either negative or positive ways to influence outcomes of caregiving.

Dyadic Models of Caregiving

In order to develop a useful conceptual framework for considering different elements and dimensions of caregiving and to develop a useful way of comparing existing research findings, a brief overview of implicit models of caregiving will be given. In this effort, we aim to delineate structural as well

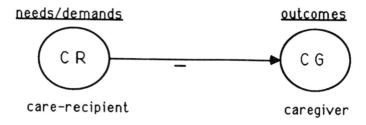

Figure 3.1 Caregiver Centered Asymmetrical Paradigm

as functional properties of the caregiving paradigm. The models are subdivided into: (a) Static caregiving outcome models and (b) Dynamic caregiving outcome models. In an effort to reduce the level of complexity, presentation of these models is restricted to consideration of a dyad consisting of major caregiver and care-recipient. The proposed models are depicted in Figures 3.1 through 3.8.

I. Static Caregiving Outcome Models

1. Asymmetrical Models

a. *Caregiver-centered one-directional model.* Structurally the simplest and most commonly studied unit has been that of the major caregiver/care-recipient dyad (Figure 3.1). Research has extensively focused on the impact of caregiving responsibilities resulting from needs and/or demands of the care-recipient on the well-being of the caregiver (Zarit et al., 1985). It is common to find studies of caregiver burden among caregivers who assume different roles in the family. Comparisons may thus be made between burdens of spouse caregivers versus child caregivers or of daughters versus sons (Brody, 1978, 1981).

In the caregiver-centered model, the care-recipient is generally assumed to serve as the source of stress to the caregiver, demanding commitments of time and energy. As a result of this stress, the caregiver is expected to experience subjective burden and develop adverse psychosocial outcomes. While this model structurally involves a dyad, actual interactions of the members of this dyad are not generally specified. Furthermore, focus is typically only on adverse outcomes or burdens rather than on positive outcomes for the care provider.

b. *Care-recipient-centered one-directional model.* A second emphasis using a structural unit of the dyad centers on the impact of caregiving on the

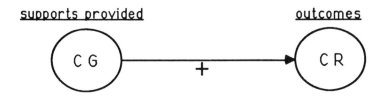

supports provided   outcomes

Figure 3.2 Care-Recipient Centered Asymmetrical Paradigm

care-recipient. In this view, focus is on the impact of various caregiving arrangements on satisfaction and/or physical and emotional welfare of the care-recipient (Figure 3.2).

In terms of stress theory (Kahana & Kahana, 1984), this model defines the caregiver as a resource or support to the care-recipient. Efforts and actions of the caregiver are expected to reduce the adverse impact of frailty or illness on the care-recipient. This emphasis is less often used in the gerontological literature than the caregiver-centered paradigm. When the focus is on the care-recipient, studies have emphasized the positive roles of the caregiver. Caregiver support may be viewed as a buffer or mediator of illness-induced stress for the care-recipient (George, 1989).

   c. Caregiver-centered bidirectional model. Caregiving theory and research have both generally centered on instrumental needs of the frail elder and instrumental assistance provided by the caregiver. In this context it is assumed that the caregiving relationship is one-directional: the caregiver gives and the care-recipient receives assistance. The question arises then: what can keep such a one-way relationship viable? The only personal return the caregiver might expect is burden. Yet, recent research on caregiving (Kinney & Stephens, 1989; Stephens & Christianson, 1986) reveals that there are uplifts as well as strains and burdens associated with caregiving. How could such uplifts come about?

   One basis for expecting such positive consequences of caregiving relates to often overlooked resources of frail elderly. Care-recipients may not always be totally without resources for giving. A person who is physically dependent may still be a great correspondent, a raconteur, or a great listener. Thus, the caregiving relationship need not always be as one-sided as it might appear on the surface.

   A second explanation may relate to needs of the caregiver for nurturance or the opportunity to express altruistic behaviors where the greatest reward may be the witnessing of increased well-being by the care-recipient (Kahana, Midlarsky, & Kahana, 1987; Schulz, Chapter 1 of this book).

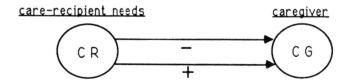

Figure 3.3 Bidirectional Caregiving Paradigm: Caregiver Centered Model

Furthermore, caring for another human being who is dependent may also enhance a sense of competence or of usefulness, and generate a kind of intimacy which is borne of sharing. A strong bonding may occur between caregiver and care-recipient.

A more comprehensive view of the outcomes of a caregiving relationship thus includes consideration of potential positive as well as negative influences of uplifts as well as burdens among caregivers. Figure 3.3 depicts a bidirectional model of caregiver outcomes allowing for this added level of complexity.

Understanding of benefits derived as well as burdens experienced plays a useful role as we try to reinforce strengths in caregivers and enhance outcomes of the caregiving experience.

d. Care-recipient-centered bidirectional model. Consideration of alternative outcomes for care-recipients calls for acknowledgment of potential adverse influences of caregivers on care-recipients. While research evidence supports the view that the role of caregivers is generally a positive one (facilitating functioning, recovery, and well-being of care-recipients), a comprehensive paradigm also calls for recognition of potential negative impact of caregivers on care-recipients. Evidence for such adverse outcomes comes from the clinical literature which notes adverse sequelae of overprotectiveness, neglect, or even potential abuse of care-recipients by caregivers (Silverstone & Hyman, 1982). Elderly care-recipients have been viewed as being at risk for physical abuse, neglect, or other forms of exploitation by resentful caregivers (Kosberg, 1983). Alternatively, recent research has called attention to the potential role of frustrated elderly care-recipients as abusers of elderly caregivers (Pillemer & Wolf, 1986). In addition, in some cases such as mental illness, the possibility exists that caregivers may have had an etiologic influence in the development of conditions which necessitate subsequent caregiving. To the extent that caregivers may exert both positive (supportive) and negative (stressful) influences on care-recipients, we may anticipate that the net benefit derived by care-recipients would be mini-

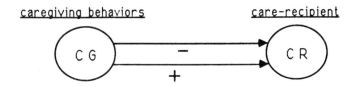

caregiving behaviors   care-recipient

Figure 3.4 Bidirectional Caregiving Paradigm: Care-Recipient Centered Model

mized. Figure 3.4 depicts a care-recipient-centered bidirectional caregiving model. It should be noted that one is still considering a static and asymmetrical model where caregivers or care-recipients are alternatively viewed as influencing outcomes for the other group.

2. Symmetrical Models

Symmetrical caregiving outcome models involve simultaneous consideration of outcomes for caregivers and care-recipients (Figure 3.5). Caregiving arrangements may be usefully evaluated in terms of the combined caregiver/care-recipient outcomes. Such arrangements may result in benefits to both parties, adverse outcomes for both, or they may benefit only caregivers or only care-recipients (Young & Kahana, 1989). Thus, for example, a daughter who moved in with her parents and devotes her life to caring for them may experience great burden while her parents may express a high level of satisfaction with the caregiving arrangements. It should be noted that while this model considers outcomes for both members of the dyad, interaction and feedback between caregivers and care-recipients is not explicitly taken into account.

Consistent with the emphasis of the caregiving literature on caregiver well-being, outcomes have generally been limited to assessments of caregiver burden and to health or mental health problems of caregivers. A more comprehensive or systemic view of caregiving also includes consideration of caregiving outcomes on care-recipient well-being and quality of life. Furthermore, effectiveness of caregiving may also be considered in terms of the therapeutic value of caregiving, including its ability to foster greater autonomy in care-recipients. In instances of caregiving to those recovering from illness and being rehabilitated, caregiver effectiveness may be assessed in terms of diminished future needs for caregiving.

Research on caregiving effectiveness has generally focused on subjective evaluations of effectiveness (Townsend, Noelker, Deimling, & Bass, 1988).

C G

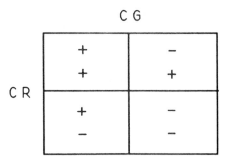

C R

Figure 3.5 Symmetrical Model of Caregiver/Care-Recipient Outcomes

A few researchers have recently distinguished between objective and subjective caregiving burdens in considering outcomes of caregiving (Montgomery, Goneya, & Hooyman, 1985). It is noteworthy that subjective caregiver burden is largely unrelated to the degree of recipient dependency. Greater use of symmetrical caregiving models should contribute to further specification of conditions under which positive outcomes for both caregivers and care-recipients may be maximized.

While symmetrical models permit the simultaneous consideration of caregiver/care-recipient outcomes, they do not necessarily posit a relationship between those two sets of outcomes. An important further direction for understanding the complexities of caregiving involves consideration of the impact of caregiving interactions on both caregivers and care-recipients in the framework of relational or dynamic models. Such models permit explication not only of the impact of caregivers and care-recipients on outcomes for one another but also of the mechanisms by which alternative outcomes are generated.

II. Relational and Dynamic Models of Caregiving

In a relational view of caregiving, the interactions between caregivers and care-recipients are seen as the central factors which impact on outcomes for both groups. In order to specify the nature of these interactions, assumptions about the relationship must be explicated, and the most important dimensions of interactions must be identified. We will attempt to illustrate the value of a dynamic model here by focusing on dependency as the salient dimension to consider in describing caregiver/care-recipient interactions. Dependency represents one critical aspect of caregiving relationships. We feel that a focus on a single dimension permits a closer illustration of alternative caregiving models and presents a framework for the study of other dimensions salient to diverse caregiving situations.

The very existence of a caregiver/care-recipient dyad is predicated on the dependency needs of an elder and the fulfillment of those dependency needs by a caregiver. The concept of dependency is one which is central to the understanding of all caregiving paradigms, yet it has been curiously missing in many discussions of caregiving.

In the following discussion, we will suggest three potentially useful relational or dynamic models of caregiver/care-recipient interactions which center around dependency. The general models outlined are applicable to other dimensions of interaction as well. Research addressing these models involves examples of formal caregiver/care-recipient dyad relationships (agency and institutional based) as well as informal (family based) caregiving arrangements. We will first outline a contingency model of caregiving outcomes, followed by a feedback model, and, finally, present a congruence model of caregiver/care-recipient interactions and outcomes. It should be noted that relational and dynamic models may be considered either as asymmetrical models, focusing only on caregiver or care-recipient outcomes, or as symmetrical models focusing on both. Since there are, as yet, relatively few examples of research using these models, we will present each in its more comprehensive symmetrical format.

   a. Contingency model of caregiver/care-recipient interaction. The focus of this model is on the reinforcement of dependency which may result in learned helplessness in care-recipients and may also increase burdens on caregivers. Some of the most careful empirical work on development and maintenance of dependency in late life has been done by Baltes and her associates (Baltes & Baltes, 1986; Baltes & Reisenzein, 1986) in an operant conditioning framework. This learning based model stresses reciprocity and mutual influences between the older person and his or her social environment. The focus of this work has been on the conditions under which older persons exhibit dependent behaviors and, in particular, in the reinforcing effects of significant social partners. Since this work has been largely conducted in institutional settings, its focus has been on staff influences on patient dependency.

When dyadic interactions have been observed which consider the behavior of frail aged as a consequence of the behavior of the caregiver staff, there appears to be a highly responsive pattern. Dependency-inducing behaviors of staff generally are followed by dependent behaviors of patients while independence-inducing behaviors of staff are generally followed by independent patient behaviors. While the interaction of family caregivers

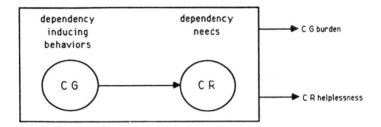

Figure 3.6 Contingency Model of Caregiver/Care-Recipient Interactions and Outcomes

and elderly care-recipients have not been systematically studied in terms of dependency-inducing caregiver behaviors and patient responses, the usefulness of a similar model for the study of caregiver/care-recipient dyads is readily observable. Thus, it would appear that caregivers' behavior may influence care-recipient dependency while care-recipient dependency may contribute to patient helplessness as well as caregiver burden. A contingency model reflecting the impact of interactions related to dependency between caregivers and care-recipients is shown in Figure 3.6.

The model in Figure 3.6 depicts a useful but simplified view of a paradigm which takes into account the interactions between caregivers and care-recipients centered around functional dependency. This contingency model looks at the activation of care-recipient dependency by caregivers. Alternatively, it would be possible to consider a contingency model which focuses on caregiver behavior as a function of care-recipient input. In the contingency model in Figure 3.6, caregiver behavior is seen as the stimulus, while care-recipient behavior is viewed largely as a response, and the impact of care-recipient dependency on caregiver behavior is not considered. Such a one-directional model is particularly appropriate to consideration of relationships between formal caregivers and care-recipients. Caregiver attitudes or behaviors may be seen as having evolved primarily through professional socialization experiences and have not generally been viewed as a direct result of care-recipient characteristics (Kahana & Kiyak, 1984; Wolinsky, 1988). However, consideration of informal caregiver/care-recipient interactions may be more accurately depicted considering a "nonrecursive" feedback model of mutual influences.

b. Feedback model of caregiver/care-recipient interactions and outcomes. Late life caregiving situations typically arise when there is a sudden or gradual onset of health decline in an elderly family member. It is reason-

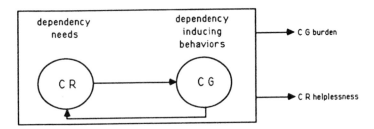

Figure 3.7 Feedback Model of Caregiver/Care-Recipient Interactions and Outcomes

able to argue that dependency-inducing behaviors of informal caregivers are, in fact, a function of care-recipient dependency needs. Care-recipient dependency needs may thus be seen as activating a cycle which involves more dependency-inducing behaviors by caregivers who start to "do for" care-recipients. This, in turn, may reinforce dependent behaviors of the older patient and a cycle of care-recipient helplessness accompanied by caregiver burden may be generated. Figure 3.7 depicts a nonrecursive or feedback model of caregiving and dependency (Blalock, 1971).

As shown in this model, the mutual interactions of caregivers and care-recipients may explain the development of adverse outcomes among both caregivers and care-recipients. The nonrecursive model is a truly dynamic, rather than just a relational, model; and it calls attention to the mechanisms underlying caregiving outcomes. A limitation both of contingency and of feedback models relates to their propensity to account primarily for negative rather than for both positive and negative outcomes. The contingency and feedback models outlined here may also be seen as normative models. A relational model which accounts for individual differences in caregiver/care-recipient interactions may be found in the congruence model of dependency presented below.

c. Congruence model of caregiver behavior and patient dependency. Dependency-inducing behaviors of caregivers have been described above as potentially contributing to reduced functioning or helplessness of care-recipients. The concern about the adverse impact of caregiving relationships relates to a fear that dependency may be encouraged and reinforced by caregivers. Yet, it may be equally problematic if caregivers direct insufficient attention to meeting dependency needs. In cases of severe chronic illness, expectations of autonomy, or even of improved functioning on the part of the frail elderly, may be unrealistic. Self-reliant behaviors may be beyond

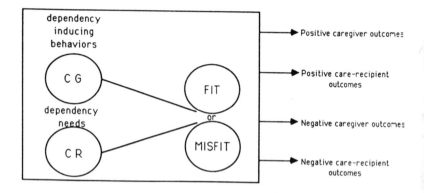

Figure 3.8 Congruence Model of Caregiver/Care-Recipient Interactions and Outcomes

the "adaptation level" of the patient, and unrealistic demands may contribute to patient depression or maladjustment (Lawton & Nahemow, 1973). There is a tendency in the caregiver literature to focus on the excessive or unrealistic demands placed by many elderly on their caregivers and the burden of caregiving. Yet, there is a parallel, but seldom connected, literature on elder abuse (Pillemer & Wolf, 1986) that calls attention to the neglect of the elderly and the failure of some caregivers to attend properly to the legitimate dependency needs of the elders they do or should care for.

These alternative expectations may be resolved if one considers a congruence model of interactions between caregivers and care-recipients (see Figure 3.8).

The congruence model of caregiver/care-recipient interactions is concerned less with the factors which generate or reinforce dependency and more with the match or mismatch between patient dependency needs and caregiver behaviors directed at meeting dependency needs. In this model, positive outcomes (for both caregivers and care-recipients) are seen as resulting from a close fit between the degree of patient dependency needs and caregiver responses to those needs. Negative outcomes are likely when an imbalance exists between patient competence or dependency and caregiver support. Such mismatch or disequilibrium may exist as a permanent state (e.g., the caregiver has insufficient time or resources to meet caregiver needs due to role strains). Mismatch may also arise as the dependency needs of the patient change or the caregivers' ability to meet those needs changes (e.g., because of illness of caregiving spouse or competing role demands on caregiving daughter).

The congruence model is thus well suited for consideration of evolving and changing uplifts and burdens of caregiving, as well as of different levels of satisfaction with care on the part of care-recipients. This model is less well suited to instances where few individual differences exist or where the focus is on normative effects.

Previous Research Involving Dynamic or Relational Models

There have been few studies utilizing relational or dynamic models of caregiver/care-recipient interactions around issues of dependency or other salient dimensions. It is important to note that while our illustrations of relational models centered around issues of dependency, the models are equally applicable to other aspects of caregiver/care-recipient interactions, including those of control, stimulation, or affective support.

The majority of research focusing on relational aspects of caregiving has considered similarities and differences in perceptions of dependency, service needs, or assistance provided by caregivers and care-recipients. Cicirelli (1981) studied congruence in reported service provisions by adult children and aged parents. His study indicates that the elderly reported receiving more services than children reported giving. Elderly parents also felt closer to their children than the children felt toward parents.

Most severe stress effects in caregiving families have been found to be associated with restrictions on the caregiver's personal time and caregiver–elder conflict (Noelker & Wallace, 1985). Resentments which may develop between caregivers and care-recipients were seen as undermining the dyadic relationship and exacerbating caregiving burden experienced by older care-providers. Alternatively, satisfaction with family relationships has also been found to have a profound influence on life satisfaction of the elderly (Scharlach, 1987). Mutual satisfaction of caregiver and care-recipient with their interaction and relationship appears to be a better predictor of psychosocial well-being of elderly care-recipients than is the actual amount of support provided (Baruch & Barnett, 1983).

Directions for Future Research— Clarifying Elements of the Caregiving Paradigm

In order to develop useful and empirically validated relational caregiving models around the outcomes discussed, clarification of several components of the caregiving paradigm is necessary. Of particular importance is clarification of the concept of dependency, specification of motivating factors in caregiving, and recognition of similarities and differences in paradigms relevant to informal family caregivers and formal caregiver/care-recipient dyads. Finally, the temporal dimension in the dyadic caregiving paradigm must be explicated. We will now turn to a discussion of each of these issues.

While dependency in a caregiving context has been generally related to functional status, it is important to recognize that dependency is a multidimensional construct (Kahana, Kahana, & Riley, 1989). As we move from functional to psychological aspects of dependency, dependency is increasingly recognized as a form of coping or an avenue for gaining passive control over one's environment. This view is consistent with Goldfarb's (1969) typology where an older patient may seek control over those around him or her by exhibiting passive and dependent behaviors.

Furthermore, functional dependency must be differentiated from powerlessness in a relationship. It is thus possible that the care-recipient who is highly dependent in functional terms actually holds greater power in the dyadic relationship. An important challenge to research on caregiver/care-recipient dyads is the specification of interdependencies which exist between partners. In addition, research must differentiate functional dependencies from psychological dependency and from interdependence in the dyadic relationship.

Interdependence in Caregiving

It has come to be accepted by gerontologists in recent years that the social ties of older people cannot be characterized as reflecting one-sided dependency. Research exploring social ties of the aged provides compelling evidence for reciprocity, interdependency, and even altruism as defining social interactions (Kahana, Midlarsky, & Kahana, 1987; Quadagno, 1985). Yet, the growing field of caregiving research has focused primarily on dependencies of late life and, as a rule, has not addressed the assumptions made when interdependence versus dependency are the conceptual underpinnings of research.

Attempting to integrate these two orientations may be particularly useful if we are to understand the dynamics of caregiver burdens, on the one hand, and learned helplessness on the other. These two adverse outcomes have frequently been associated with being a caregiver or a care-recipient, respectively. To the extent that caregivers and care-recipients can maintain a measure of interdependence in their relationship, uplifts of caregiving, as well as competence of care-recipients, may be maximized. The caregiving literature suggests that spouse caregivers are less likely to suffer from caregiver burden than are adult child caregivers (Johnson, 1983). Perhaps one explanation for this advantage is the interdependence of elderly spouses who are more likely to assume alternatively caregivers and care-recipient roles than are adult child/elderly parent dyads. Thus, it is not uncommon for elderly spouses to serve as caregivers to one another, as both may suffer from chronic illness. Similarly, research has found that the elderly who receive assistance from peers are more likely to maintain a sense of reciprocity (Payne & Bull, 1985). Thus the psychological interdependence may persist even at a time when there is physical dependency. Equity theory (Thibaut & Kelley, 1959) provides a meaningful conceptual basis for exploring adverse sequelae of interactions which are exclusively dependent by the elderly and exclusively "giving" by those who assist them. Contributing too little or too much in a relationship can each result in experience of strain (Keith & Schafer, 1985).

Consideration of interdependence even in the face of illness and frailty is particularly relevant in caregiving situations where physical illness, rather than mental impairment, creates the need for caregiving. To the extent that caregiving paradigms are developed around caregiving situations involving terminal illness or dementing illness, a strict dependency model may be most applicable. However, normatively there are many caregiving situations involving primarily physical health problems, such as heart attacks or illnesses necessitating surgery, from which a good recovery may be anticipated. In such situations, anticipation of recovery where the patient will once again have the ability to reciprocate and engage in interdependent interactions, allows for psychological expectations of interdependence which may diminish caregiving burden.

Research focusing on caregiving by adult children at the time of a health crisis (Fischer & Hoffman, 1984) also suggests the view that burden may be relatively minimal in temporary caregiving situations. Furthermore, one can also look at interdependence as part of a long-term commitment to repay elders (particularly parents) for care which they had provided earlier in life.

In summary, the interdependence in caregiving relationships may exist because: (a) there is ongoing reciprocity during the caregiving relationship; (b) there is anticipation of future reciprocity; and/or (c) there is acknowledgment of past reciprocity.

Motivating Factors in Caregiving

In attempting to explain sustained informal caregiving arrangements, major motivating factors of attachment and filial obligations have been identified (Cicirelli, 1981). Attachment represents an enduring emotional bond which promotes contact and communication and ultimately leads to protectiveness toward the attached individual. Helping behavior which may be expressed in caregiving may be seen as a logical outgrowth of attachment between kin. The concept of attachment may be seen as particularly well suited for the study of dyadic relationships. While attachment has been viewed as a useful concept in psychological research, there has been relatively little research using this concept in the field of gerontology.

Sociologists and anthropologists have generally focused on related but distinct concepts of filial obligations or family solidarity and cohesiveness in explaining assistance provided to elders (Adams, 1968). While attachment and obligation are likely to explain the high degree of assistance provided by kin toward one another, family conflict is likely to reduce caregiving assistance. These concepts may also provide a useful first step toward explaining the nature of interactions in the course of caregiving. Accordingly, attachment may enhance the quality of interactions while conflict is likely to lead to less satisfactory interactions. Furthermore, motivation to help must be coupled with ability or competence to help in order to sustain a successful caregiving relationship (Adams, 1968).

Family Roles and Caregiving

In discussing diverse models of dyadic caregiver/care-recipient interactions, we have focused on generic models without taking into account the family positions and kin relations of caregivers and care-recipients. Recent work by Cantor (1983) has taken an important step toward specifying the relationship between type of caregiver and strain of caregiving, indicating that where the bond is closer caregiving roles appear more stressful. This research also points to the important influence of family attitudes in impacting outcomes of caregiving.

Overall, research supports the view that caregiving relationships involving adult children and parents are more problematic for both caregivers and recipients than are spouse caregiving relationships. Accordingly, Johnson (1983) found that over 80% of spouses accepted the caregiving role without reservation whereas only 56% of the adult child caregivers did so. Furthermore, older care-recipients were generally more satisfied with care from spouse than from children. Although spouse caregivers appear less burdened than child caregivers, they nevertheless encounter special problems. Older wives find caregiving chores to dependent husbands particularly restrictive of their social relationships (Noelker & Wallace, 1985). Furthermore, frailty of spouses often makes them particularly vulnerable to stress of major caregiving responsibilities.

Middle-aged daughters perceive their parents as having greater needs for help than do middle-aged sons (Cicirelli, 1981). Conflict in family relationships appears to be particularly problematic for married adult children and especially for those with young children of their own. Role overload has been cited as a plausible explanatory variable for these conflicts.

While the work of Cantor (1983), Johnson (1983), and others calls attention to the differential roles of caregivers who hold different positions in the family, more work needs to focus on the specific interrelationships between members of these caregiver/care-recipient dyads and the influence of these dynamic relationships on caregiver/care-recipient outcomes.

The caregiving models outlined above may help elucidate the influence of family roles and the efficacy of caregiving arrangements. Specifically, asymmetrical models may be useful in determining the degree to which caregiving by different family members is likely to result in positive outcomes for caregivers, for care-recipients or for both. Consideration of "feedback" models allows for understanding mutual influences of caregivers and care-recipients as a function of the family connections. Thus, for example, child–parent caregiving dyads may be compared with spouse–spouse caregiving dyads in terms of dependency-inducing behaviors of caregivers, on the one hand, and help-seeking behaviors of care-recipients on the other. It is possible that based on greater tolerance for dependency of spouses than of parents, the same types of help-seeking behaviors expressed by elders will result in differential outcomes of caregiver burden for child caregivers than for spouse caregivers.

Temporal Dimensions in Caregiving

Consideration of dynamic interactions and mutual satisfaction of caregivers and care-recipients is difficult enough when it is considered at one point in time, given definable needs of a frail elder and available resources, as well as motivation of the caregiver. Yet, in reality, caregiving is part of a process of change in time; and dyadic interactions are likely to be effected by the course of the illness and the upward or downward trajectory of the patient as well as the reactions and the changing life circumstances of the caregiver.

Thus, it is very likely that dyadic interactions between patient and caregiver will differ greatly for the Alzheimer's patient and his or her caregiver from that of the elderly victim of a heart attack. In the first case, the patient's trajectory is almost certain, taking an erratic but ultimately predictable course downward. Furthermore, at some point in the course of the illness process, the patient is likely to become unable to reciprocate even on an emotional or cognitive level. In the case of the elderly heart attack patient, there are far more divergent courses taken by the illness, and outcomes may also vary greatly.

In regard to the temporal dimensions of caregiving, limited research has focused on the long-term effects of caregiving on informal providers of care. Research by Townsend et al. (1988) did not support the wear-and-tear hypothesis which suggests increasing ill effects over time. It has been argued that sustaining long-term caregiving may be more difficult for caregivers who are frail or very old themselves (Noelker & Townsend, 1987). It has also been suggested that family supports erode and diminish over time when chronic illness places continuing strain on caregivers (Eggert, Granger, Morris, & Pendleton, 1977). Conversely, relationships can also improve over time in caregiving situations as positive experiences may diminish old conflicts and lead to forgetting of prior sources of bitterness (Silverstone & Hyman, 1982). Maladaptive interactions patterns may also be diminished with improved communication and problem-solving skills (Springer & Brubaker, 1984).

The dynamic models of caregiving outlined above are particularly well suited for consideration of temporal dimensions in caregiving. Thus, care-recipient needs are likely to change in the course of illness and recovery. If caregivers do not respond by changing their caregiving behaviors, incongruence may emerge, destabilizing an otherwise successful and congruent caregiving arrangement, and resulting in adverse caregiving outcomes.

Formal Versus Informal Caregiver Dyads

In order to gain a greater understanding of dyadic influences between family caregivers and the elderly, research on formal caregivers should complement studies of dyadic interactions between family caregivers and care-recipients. There is a large body of literature on patient–physician relationships and connections (Haug, 1981; Pendleton & Hasler, 1983) which could be fruitfully reconsidered in terms of caregiving relationships between elderly patients and their most significant formal caregivers. Interestingly, when the caregiver is an informal one, such as a spouse, child, or other family member, they are generally viewed as meeting a need as responders rather than initiators in the caregiving role. In contrast, formal caregivers, especially nursing staff in health care institutions, have been considered in a more proactive rather that reactive light (Baltes & Baltes, 1986). They are often discussed in terms of dependency- or independence-inducing attitudes which they might manifest. It poses an important question of whether dependency- or independence-inducing behaviors of caregivers may have greater or lesser effects on behaviors of care-recipients in a family context than they do in an institutional setting.

Expanding the Caregiver Paradigm— A Glimpse Beyond Dyadic Perspectives

The foregoing discussion has focused on dyadic relationships involving major formal and informal caregivers and care-recipients. It is important to acknowledge, however, that, in reality, caregiving arrangements are far more complex, generally involving entire family systems, on the one hand, and a network of formal caregivers on the other. It is beyond the scope of this chapter to provide a detailed discussion of caregiving models involving these more complex units of analysis. Nevertheless, we will briefly note significant elements of the broader system. These elements include the family and informal support systems and formal health care providers.

While it is true that most ailing elderly persons have a single major caregiver, a number of different caregivers typically play significant auxiliary roles providing either direct care to the patient or direct assistance to the major caregiver (Noelker & Shaffer, 1986). Caregiver burden has been found to be greatest when alternative caregivers are not available (Couper & Sheehan, 1987; Montgomery et al., 1985). While the availability of additional caregivers and the extensiveness of the caregiver network are generally seen as diminishing caregiver stress, family involvement can also cause greater stress when conflicts are present (Brody, 1981; Springer & Brubaker, 1984).

Brody (1978) has aptly called for extending the focus of caregiving research from the major caregiver/care-recipient dyad to encompass the entire family system. Such expansion of the caregiver paradigm has thus far seldom been implemented in empirical studies although it is generally acknowledged in the clinical literature (Silverstone & Hyman, 1982). Perhaps a major reason for lack of attention to the family system and family dynamics in caregiving research rests in the methodological difficulties of operationalizing dynamic rather than static relationships and including networks of divergent size rather than only the neatly quantifiable caregiver and care-recipient dyad. The alternative caregiving models we outlined for the dyad of caregiver and care-recipient could be further expanded to incorporate multiple members of the family system, as well as friends and family who comprise the broader unit of informal caregivers.

In addition to acknowledging the reciprocal interactions between caregivers and care-recipients, we should also note that the formal health care system and its representatives (physicians, nurses, and other health care providers) play critical roles in bringing about, shaping, and/or limiting the nature of caregiver/care-recipient interactions. Consideration of pivotal individuals from the formal support system as alternative caregivers who define the caregiver/care-recipient dyad may be a useful first step in reevaluating the proposed dyadic models. Beyond consideration of dyadic paradigms which include a key formal caregiver, it is useful to consider such individuals in the framework of a caregiver "triad." The family physician may be usefully viewed as such a third party whose central role, along with the major caregiver, renders him or her a member of a caregiving triad. Future research could thus consider implications of the absence of symmetry in interactions of such a caregiving triad, as well as other considerations which would limit the applicability of the dyadic models presented and/or suggest new ways to explain observed relationships.

Expanding the paradigm even further, one may move from the individual to the systemic levels and explore models which would apply to interrelationships of patients, family, and the formal support network on an organizational rather than individual level. The relationship between informal and formal caregiving systems has been generally conceptualized as complementary (Cantor, 1979; Litwak, 1985). An alternative systems model (Noelker and Townsend, 1987) posits that changes in the care-recipient's needs, in the family's resources, or in the community's resources each precipitate readjustments in the other two units. Presentations of systemic models which describe these relationships pose yet another challenge to conceptual development in caregiving research.

Conclusions

This chapter aimed to outline and make explicit assumptions and orientations involved in alternative caregiving paradigms applicable to gerontological research dealing with the caregiving dyad. In so doing, we focused on the most basic and extensively studied unit, consisting of a major donor and recipient of aid (Johnson, 1983).

Caregiving research in the field of gerontology has been generally propelled by an applied orientation and a desire to develop useful guidelines for ameliorating burdens of caregivers to frail elders. As such, each new study aims to provide a response to a meaningful set of questions relevant to the well-being of caregivers and/or care-recipients. Each research project also comprises a building block in a structure of accumulating knowledge. Nevertheless, there has not been any over-reaching theory or even plan-guiding research in this area. Consequently, a number of areas have received extensive attention while other relevant questions have not been subjected to systematic study. Our aim in the present chapter has been to provide a map for consideration of the full spectrum of caregiving models which have been implicit in research on caregiving to elders. Because of the great many permutations possible in considering even the simplest unit of analysis, only dyadic models have been presented. Our hope is that this chapter will serve as an impetus to further mapping of potential models in caregiving involving the more complex family and formal care delivery systems briefly touched upon in the latter part of the chapter. We also hope that the explication of the models involved in diverse studies will facilitate integration of research and eventually lead to the development of more comprehensive theoretical frameworks which, in turn, may guide future research.

References

Adams, B.N. (1968). *Kinship in an urban setting*. Chicago, IL: Morkham.

Baltes, M.M., & Baltes, P.B. (1986). *The psychology of control and aging*. Hillsdale, NJ: Lawrence Erlbaum.

Baltes, M.M., & Reisenzein, R. (1986). The social world in long-term care institutions: Psychological control toward dependency? In M.M. Baltes & P.B. Baltes (Eds.), *The psychology of control and aging*. Hillsdale, NJ: Lawrence Erlbaum.

Baruch, G., & Barnett, R.C. (1983). Adult daughters' relationship with their mothers. *Journal of Marriage and the Family, 45*, 601-606.

Blalock, H.M. (1971). *Causal models in the social sciences*. Chicago: Aldine-Atherton.

Brody, E.M. (1978). The aging of the family. *The Annuals of the American Academy, 438*, 13-27.

Brody, E.M. (1981). Women in the middle and family help to older people. *The Gerontologist, 21*, 471-480.

Cantor, M. (1979). Neighbors and friends: An overlooked resource in the informal support system. *Research on Aging, 1*, 434-463.

Cantor, M. H. (1983). Strain among caregivers: A study of experience in the United States. *The Gerontologist, 23*(6), 597-604.

Cicirelli, V.G. (1981). *Helping elderly parents: The role of adult children*. Boston, MA: Auburn House Publishing.

Couper, D.P., & Sheehan, N.W. (1987). Family dynamics for caregivers: An educational model. *Family Relations, 36*, 181-186.

Dohrenwend, B., & Dohrenwend, B. (1974). *Stressful life events: Their nature and effects*. New York: John Wiley.

Eggert, C., Granger, V., Morris, R, & Pendleton, S. (1977). Caring for the patient with a long term disability. *Geriatrics, 22*, 102-114.

Fischer, L.R., & Hoffman, C. (1984). Who cares for the elderly: The dilemma of family support. *Research in Social Problems and Public Policy*, *3*, 169-215.

George, L.K. (1990). Vulnerability and social factors. In Z. Harel, P. Erhlich, & R. Hubbard (Eds.), *Understanding and serving vulnerable aged*. New York: Springer.

Goldfarb, A.I. (1969). Predicting mortality in the institutionalized aged. *Archives of General Psychiatry*, *21*, 172-176.

Haug, M. (1981). *Elderly patients and their doctors*. New York: Springer.

Johnson, C.L. (1983). Dyadic family relations and social support. *The Gerontologist*, *23*(4), 377-383.

Kahana, B., & Kahana, E. (1984). Stress reactions. In P. Lewinsohn and L. Teri (Eds.), *Clinical geropsychology*. Elmsford, NY: Pergamon.

Kahana, E., Kahana, B., & Riley, K. (1989). Person-environment transactions relevent to control and helplessness in institutional settings. In P.S. Fry (Ed.), *Psychological perspectives of helplessness and control in the elderly*. New York: Elsevier North-Holland.

Kahana, E., & Kiyak, A. (1984). Attitudes and behavior of staff in facilities for the aged. *Research on Aging*, *6*(3), 395-416.

Kahana, E., Midlarsky, E., & Kahana, B. (1987). Beyond dependency, autonomy, and exchange: Later life adaptation. *Social Justice Review*, *1*, (4), 439-459.

Keith, P.M., & Schafer, R.B. (1985). Housework, disagreement and depression among younger and older couples. Special issue: Developmental tasks in late life. *American Behavioral Scientist*, *29*(4), 405-422.

Kinney, J.M., & Stephens, M.A.P. (1989). Hassles and uplifts of giving care to a family member with dementia. *Psychology and Aging*, *4(4)*.

Kinney, J.M., Stephens, M.P., & Brockman, A.M. (1987). Personal and environmental correlates of territoriality and use of space: An illustration in congregate housing for older adults. *Environment and Behavior*, *19*(6), 722-737.

Kosberg, J.I. (1983). The special vulnerability of elderly parents. In J.L. Kosberg (Ed.), *Abuse and maltreatment of the elderly; Cause and intervention* (pp. 263-275). Boston: John Wright.

Lawton, M.P., & Nahemow, L. (1973). Ecology and the aging process. In C. Eisdorfer & M.P. Lawton (Eds.), *Psychology of adult development and aging*. Washington, DC: American Psychological Association.

Litwak, E. (1985). *Helping the elderly: The complementary roles of informal networks and formal systems*. New York: Guilford Press.

Montgomery, R.J.V., Goneya, J.C., & Hooyman, N.R. (1985). Caregiving and the experience of subjective/objective burden. *Family Relations*, *34*, 19-26.

Noelker, L.S., & Shaffer, G. (1986). Care networks: How they form and change. *Generations*, *10*(4), pp. 62-64.

Noelker, L.S., & Townsend, A.L. (1987). Perceived caregiving effectiveness: The impact of parental impairment, community resources, and caregiving characteristics. In T. H. Brubaker (Ed.), *Aging, Health and Family: Long-Term Care* (pp. 58-79). Newbury Park, CA: Sage.

Noelker, L.S., & Wallace, R.W. (1985). The organization of family care for impaired elderly. *Journal of Family Issues*, *6*(1), 23-44.

Payne, B., & Bull, C. N. (1985). The older volunteer: The case for interdependence. In W.A. Peterson & J. Quadagno (Eds.), *Social bonds in later life: Aging and interdependence* (pp. 251-272). Beverly Hills, CA: Sage.

Pendleton, D., & Hasler, J. (1983). Doctor-patient communication: A review. In D. Pendleton & J. Hasler (Eds.), *Doctor-patient communication* (pp. 5-53). New York: Academic Press.

Pillemer, K.A., & Wolf, R.S. (1986). *Elder abuse: Conflict in the family*. Dover, MA: Auburn.

Quadagno, J. (1985). Introduction. In W.A. Peterson & J. Quadagno (Eds), *Social bonds in later life: Aging and interdependence*. Newbury Park, CA: Sage.

Scharlach, A.E. (1987). Relieving feelings of strain among women with elderly mothers. *Psychology and Aging*, 2(1), 9-13.

Silverstone, B., & Hyman, H.K. (1982). *You and your aging parents*. New York: Pantheon.

Springer, D., & Brubaker, T.H. (1984). *Family caregivers and dependent elderly: Minimizing stress and maximizing independence*. Newbury Park, CA: Sage.

Stephens, S.A., & Christianson, J.B. (1986) *Informal care of the elderly*. Lexington, MA: Lexington Books.

Thibault, J., & Kelley, H. (1959). *The social psychology of groups*. New York: John Wiley.

Townsend, A., Noelker, L., Deimling, G., & Bass, D. (1988). *The longitudinal impact of caregiving on adult-child caregivers' mental health*. Cleveland: The Benjamin Rose Institute.

Wolinsky, F.D. (1988). *The sociology of health: Principles, practitioners and issues*. Belmont, CA: Wadsworth.

Young, R., & Kahana, E. (1989). Age, medical advice about cardiac risk reduction, and patient compliance. *Journal of Aging and Health*, 1(1), 121-134.

Zarit, S.H., Orr, N.K., & Zarit, J.M. (1985). *The hidden victims of Alzheimer's disease: Families under stress*. New York: New York University Press.

4

Theoretical Questions and Ethical Issues in A Family Caregiving Relationship

ROMA S. HANKS
BARBARA H. SETTLES

Introduction

Family caregiving is predicted to increase as publicly funded programs are carefully regulated and restricted to specific populations and as costs of private care escalate; therefore, it is appropriate to examine the relationships of family members who are caregivers and dependents. Differentials in power within the family may produce ethical conflicts within the caregiving relationship. Furthermore, the actors in the caregiving situation bring both history and expectations which influence the character of caregiving decisions within the framework of past relationships. The purpose of this analysis is to present an in-depth case study of family caregiving and euthanasia. This chapter explores spousal interactions as manifestations of role transfer and change. The interactions of the family with community service-providers are investigated as they relate to role perception and enact-

AUTHOR'S NOTE

The authors wish to thank Professors Paul T. Durbin, Department of Philosophy, University of Delaware; Carlfred Broderick, The James A. Peterson Human Relations Center, University of Southern California; and Joan M. Patterson, School of Public Health, University of Minnesota, for their comments on earlier drafts of this paper.

ment. In addition, this chapter extends theoretical perspective by applying appropriate ethical theories to the issues raised in the case.

The issues of relative power between family and organization and among family members involved in the care of infirmed relatives has been dramatically demonstrated in the case of Roswell and Emily Gilbert. This chapter explores ethical issues in a symbolic interaction framework to trace developments in the Gilbert case at three levels of interaction: (a) on the individual level in the perception of self by the caregiver and the dependent; (b) in the marital dyad in role performance before and after the onset of the illness; and (c) on the organizational level in the confrontation of family and society in decision making.

The Gilbert Case

Emily Gilbert suffered for 10 years from Alzheimer's disease and osteoporosis. Neighbors reported that she had pleaded with her husband "Please let me die" (Givens, Agrest, & Prout, 1985). On March 4, 1985, Roswell Gilbert, a retired electronics engineer, gave his wife of 51 years a sedative, then fired a shot from his 9mm Luger into her temple. When he checked her pulse and found that she was still living, he returned to his shop, reloaded the gun and came back to the living room to fire a fatal shot.

On May 9, 1985, a Broward County, Florida, jury found Mr. Gilbert guilty of first-degree murder in Emily's death, and the judge sentenced him to 25 years in prison with no chance for parole. Roswell Gilbert is 76 years old. Friends and family portrayed Gilbert as "a private and selfless person who was completely devoted to his wife—so much so that, in the end, he gave her the gift of euthanasia that she wanted" (Plummer & Marx, 1985). A prosecutor called him a "cold, calculating scientist who killed his ailing wife because she embarrassed and inconvenienced him, not from any feeling of mercy or compassion."

Although the reasons are unclear, evidence suggests that the Gilberts had several options for support, such as permanent nursing home placement and professional respite care, which they did not use in coping with her illness ("Gilbert Issue," 1985). Friends, neighbors, and family members insisted that Mr. Gilbert's determination to care for Emily himself grew out of his concern for her peace of mind and her refusal to cooperate with the professionals who did try to help.

Martha Gilbert Moran, the only daughter of the Gilberts, found her father's willingness to assume total caregiving responsibility for her mother to be characteristic of his treatment of the family in other situations. "Daddy catered to mother's whims all the years they were married. . . . Daddy deprived himself to make mother happy," she recalled in one interview (Plummer & Marx, 1985).

Apparently, Roswell Gilbert's desire to protect the women in his family extended to his daughter. "My father didn't want to upset me with mother's condition," Moran told reporters (Plummer & Marx, 1985). The parents of Ms. Moran's husband had suffered severe medical problems over a 25-year period. Since she and her husband had been closely involved with their care, she felt that her father wanted to shield her from the problems of her mother's illness. In addition, she felt that her father's negative image of nursing homes grew out of her unpleasant experiences with caregiving institutions during the long illness of her in-laws (Moran, 1985).

The fact that Roswell Gilbert committed an illegal act in shooting his wife is not altered by his desire to keep her out of an institutional system he felt was hostile to her needs and temperament or even by his humane intention to end her suffering. Active euthanasia is still illegal in all jurisdictions of the United States. Perpetrators of the crime are typically convicted, but the sentences are reduced or suspended (Triche & Triche, 1975).

Treatment of Gilbert has been called a "gross inequity" by Derek Humphrey, executive director of the Hemlock Society, the Los Angeles-based right-to-die group (Hemlock Society, 1985). Jurors in Gilbert's case stand by their verdict (Jurors defend, 1985). Proposals for conditional release and clemency were rejected (Florida cabinet, 1985; Connor reiterates, 1985). Gilbert maintains that his decision was morally right, and he stands by his defense. Furthermore, he has had strong support from his family in fighting his conviction. Emily Gilbert's sister has written letters to officials pleading for the release of her brother-in-law. Martha Gilbert Moran has carried her father's case to the public through newspaper, magazine, and television interviews. A sympathetic treatment of the case aired as a television movie.

The family's definition of Emily's illness and Roswell's action are important in the analysis, both morally and theoretically. Goode (1956, pp. 205–206) suggested that the relationship between marital roles is "backed by moral sentiment." Kinship groups and the larger society act as "third party" to any particular role set, confirming and censuring role enactment. Expectations for obligations and rights within a role set exist both within the relationship unit (dyad) and between the unit and the third party. In the Gilbert case, family expectations for Roswell's role as caregiver can accommodate euthanasia because the expectations for Emily's role as dependent accommodate total reliance on her husband's judgment.

In the Gilbert family, role expectations grew out of a relationship of dependency/caregiving that Roswell and Emily had built during the 40 years of their marriage preceding her illness. Although the family may have been shocked initially by Roswell's dramatic action, they did not find his motives or his decision-making process to be inconsistent with their expectations. Swensen (1979) concluded that couples make readjustments in later years of marriage using the same set of skills they have used to face problems and to cope with other readjustments in the past.

Accepting the act of euthanasia as an extension of the relationship of Roswell and Emily allows examination of other ethical issues in the case. Perhaps the most basic of these issues is the right of a marital partner to determine the personhood of a spouse. What family dynamics led the Gilberts to a point in their marriage at which he, the caregiver, decided to kill her, the dependent? Did the act indicate a loss of personhood by Emily, the dependent spouse, at least in the perception of Roswell, the caregiving spouse? Was that loss of personhood related more to Emily's illness or to the dynamics of the marriage relationship? Do marital partners have a moral responsibility to maintain autonomy or to state explicitly the conditions under which they agree to relinquish power in decision making to a spouse?

It may be argued that Roswell and Emily established patterns of interaction based on her total dependency on him and compliance with his decisions. Indeed, she may have expected him to act on her expressed wish to die since he had acted to fulfill so many of her wishes during their 51-year marriage. In that case, the shooting could be called voluntary active euthanasia.

A feminist perspective questions the moral justification of Emily's position in the marital dyad. Even before her illness, both Roswell and Emily behaved as if she were less of a person than he and less capable of autonomous decision making. This assumption may have negatively influenced Roswell's evaluation of his wife's state of deteriorating health. Furthermore, this perspective forces the examination of ethical issues in the caregiving/dependency dimension of spousal relations. The question then becomes: Does a marriage partner ever have the right or responsibility to assume such a total caregiving role that the dependent spouse loses perceived personhood?

Theoretical and Ethical Perspectives

Dependency and Autonomy

Reference Group Position

It is possible to gain some insight into the marital relationship of Roswell and Emily Gilbert through published reports of interviews, Mr. Gilbert's testimony at the murder trials, and personal statements of those close to the case. Martha Gilbert Moran described her parents' marriage as traditional and typical of the marriages of the 1940s and 1950s (Moran, 1985). Structural-functional family theorists have emphasized the utility of role designation in family interaction. Roles are maintained by economic and social pressure (Parsons & Bales, 1955). Roswell Gilbert was, over the course of his marriage to Emily, the primary wage-earner. He was an electrical engineer, a corporate vice president, and a business consultant. Rapoport and Rapoport (1968) noted that "work and family modes of interaction tend to be isomorphic; they affect each other in such a way as to induce similar structural patterns in both spheres" (p. 55). Stryker (1959) notes that people are categorized and that behavior toward them is organized by such categories. Gilbert's professional position and Emily's supporting role may have categorized their own expectations for their interactions, as well as expectations of family and friends.

The corporate decision-making process, based on utilitarian analysis of alternatives, was familiar to Roswell Gilbert and may have been incorporated into his family decision-making style. Furthermore, Emily Gilbert was described by her daughter as "a typical 1950s housewife." She played bridge, loved beautiful clothes and jewelry, and seemed content with her role as corporate wife. She may have internalized the role to the extent that she participated in decision making with her husband in a manner similar to that of his corporate staff, that is, gathering and presenting information for him to use in making the final decision.

Lindesmith and Strauss (1966), in reviewing the work of Sherif, Merton and Kitt, Newcomb, Hyman, and Festinger, state that "a person's thought is influenced by his particular position in a social hierarchy and by the positions of the groups with which he identifies himself" (p. 254). Roswell Gilbert's career position in the corporate managerial structure removed him from the information gathering function in decision making. His job was to act on information brought to him by others. In his caregiving role, he assumed a similar position. Doctors informed him of his wife's illness and its prognosis. Emily stated her preference for home care over hospital care. Eventually, she stated her desire to die. Roswell acted on the information presented to him with the decisiveness characteristic of his professional role.

It is important to note that the Gilberts had lived abroad in societies that hold different views of euthanasia and that many of their friends support voluntary active euthanasia. Furthermore, the Gilbert family holds high standards for quality of life that must be taken into account in an analysis of this case (Moran, 1985).

Marital Power

Bahr (1982, pp. 90–91) reported, "A particularly interesting interaction between norms of control and competence occurs in the provider role . . . [with the strongest relationship] when husbands are perceived to be exceptional providers" and when norms are patriarchal. Mr. Gilbert was a successful man. His success as "provider" was a resource which he brought to the family and which increased his power in the relationship. He had the additional resource of societal confirmation of his control in the marriage, particularly after Emily's health began to decline. Emily was mentally ill, physically suffering, and accustomed to the role of dependent wife.

Blood (1972) examined the effects of power structure on the marital relationship. He suggested that the greater the power differential between marriage partners, the more deferential and respectful the wife is to the husband. Roswell Gilbert portrayed Emily as "so dependent on me that I began to think that this was a mistake we had made in our lives . . . she should have been more independent" (Gilbert, 1985). In response to Emily's emotional dependence and her physical and mental deterioration, Roswell increased his instrumental role in the marriage, thereby increasing his power in the relationship.

Symbolic Loss of Personhood

Alzheimer's was both physically and symbolically debilitating for Emily. It threatened her self-definition as well as her health (Barbour, 1985). The diagnosis of Alzheimer's may have so altered Emily's definition of herself as to call into question the existence of that self. Strauss (1985) and his associates refer to diagnosis as the beginning of an illness trajectory that modifies the image of the patient and routinizes care and interaction. Following diagnostic labeling, the patient and those who care for him/her respond to the direction of that trajectory. By Stryker's (1959, p. 115) definition, "One's self is the way one describes to himself his relationship to others in a social process." Severe impairment of physical and mental functioning would change Emily's descriptors of herself from an interactive perspective as well as from a physical perspective. When the dimensions of Emily that described her as a person were gone, Emily was gone. Therefore, it is possible to argue that when Roswell killed Emily, he merely confirmed the reality of her total dependence on him and the preceding process of the death of everything that defined her personhood. The act of killing Emily was a confirmation of reality as both Roswell and Emily perceived it.

Kant allows that persons derive dignity solely from their rationality and the freedom that accompanies that rationality (Bayles & Henley, 1983; Beauchamp, 1982). Thus, he is able to separate the rational self from all other aspects of the self. He is concerned with the integrity of the agent as a rational being. Therefore, the question of Emily's rationality in making choices becomes important. If Emily realized that her disease would cause progressive deterioration of her ability to make decisions, she may have rationally decided to give Roswell increasing decision-making power. Although Kant does not allow moral justification of suicide, he does allow choosing a role for oneself if that choice is made rationally. Emily chose the dependent role while she was still able to act as a rational agent. It may be argued that the choice to give Roswell decision-making power implies her consent to the decisions he made for her. The question of whether she understood the full range of possible outcomes of total dependency, including the possibility that Roswell would decide that death was her best option, is important in understanding the possibility of her victimization.

The question of Emily Gilbert's autonomy is complex. If Emily was an autonomous individual, she should be self-governing and therefore able to decide for herself whether or not she would act on her expressed wish to die. If, however, she had voluntarily surrendered her autonomy, she might expect and even desire that her husband act on that desire for her. Evidence has been cited that Roswell believed that his wife had become very dependent on him. In his perception, she had surrendered her life to him. Neo-Kantian argument, based on autonomy in choice, allows that "it is permissible for a competent person to exercise his autonomy to choose death, it is also permissible for another to kill him if he rationally and voluntarily chooses it" (Bayles & Henley, 1983, pp. 150–151).

Family Perception of Situation

Martha Moran believes that her mother's loss of the ability to maintain her physical appearance would have been sufficient cause for Emily to have desired death. "My mother was a very vain woman," Moran said. "She never opened the door without checking the mirror." (Moran, 1985). She elaborated by noting that her mother had apparently attempted to hide the progress of her physical disability even from Roswell. When Martha cleaned her parents' apartment after her mother's death, she found soiled clothing hidden and food-stained dresses neatly draped in plastic bags and hung in the closet as if nothing were wrong with them. She feels that pride in appearance was an integral part of her mother's definition of herself (Moran, 1985). The dual affliction of Alzheimer's disease and osteoporosis offered little hope that Emily would be able to hide the progress of both diseases.

The suggestion that Emily's physical condition was seen by Emily and other family members as stigmatizing is perhaps distasteful, but it is important in light of the research of Zimmerman (1971) and Goffman (1963) on shared definitions of stigma. The nature of Emily's physical and mental deterioration presented to the Gilbert family a situation much like that faced by parents of developmentally disabled or chronically ill children (Farber, 1959; Farber, Jenne, & Toigo, 1960; Settles, 1987; Waisbren, 1980). Their lack of access to support services made the family's definition of Emily's illness even more critical.

Evidence was presented at Roswell's trial that Emily's condition was not bad enough to warrant his extreme action. Objective examination of the facts may raise serious questions about the accuracy of the perceptions of Emily's condition by the family. But the basis for Roswell's and Emily's evaluation of her illness was the definition of quality of life shared by their family. Lindesmith and Strauss (1966) point out that "socially transmitted traditions of thought determine, among other things, which problems are important, which unimportant; which questions are crucial, which trivial; which solutions are to be rejected out of hand and which ones judged acceptable, and so on" (p. 233).

The actions that were taken by Roswell were indeed based on his perception of his wife's condition within the context of a shared family definition of quality of life. The accuracy of that perception becomes important in the justification of his actions as both caregiver and killer. Bayles and Henley (1983) discuss the issue of perception as it relates to moral justification in Kantian ethics: "Most immoral conduct results not from ignorance of what is right but from selfishness, confusion and self-deception" (pp. 58-59). Roswell Gilbert did not perceive his actions as immoral because they were based on the definition he had of the situation in which he found himself and his family. To a large extent that definition was supported by his historical and current reference groups. The question of morality may lie in the inaccuracy of that definition and Mr. Gilbert's failure to broaden his awareness of viable options and other perspectives on the illness. Although Roswell chose rationally to be Emily's sole caregiver, he may have based that choice on inaccurate perceptions of the institutional care that could have relieved his burden. His choice was based on his perception of institutional caregiving and of his wife's needs. His conviction that Emily's primary need was to be with him was so strong that he found it easier to kill her than to place her in institutional care.

Society agrees with Roswell Gilbert on some dimensions of his assessment of his situation (Harris, 1985). The dimension of Roswell's definition that is more difficult to measure is that of quality of life. The Gilberts' tolerance for the debilitation brought on by Emily's illness may be the significant break between their definition of the situation and the definition shared by the larger society from which was drawn the jury that convicted Roswell. To the Gilberts, Emily's quality of life had deteriorated to the intolerable, but her condition did not fit the social definition of a potential candidate for euthanasia.

Duty and Autonomy

Gilbert's adoption of the caregiving role was based not only on his love and concern for his wife, but also on his determination to perform his duty in the role of husband. An excerpt from Roswell's testimony reveals this attitude (Gilbert, 1985, p. 398):

Q. But you rejected all offers of assistance. Why did you do this?
A. Well, I rejected them. By "help" you mean watch over her. No, I didn't want any help, no. That was my job I thought.
Q. You say it was your job?
A. To help her, yes.

In the Kantian view of morally correct action, it was precisely Gilbert's recognition of his duty that made his adoption of the caregiving role praiseworthy. If he had acted as caregiver just because he could not find suitable aid from family or community sources, his action would have been morally correct but would have lacked moral worth. The same would be true if Gilbert had chosen the role just because he loved his wife. For Kant, either external circumstances or internal passions can impede autonomy. Roswell Gilbert consciously chose to follow the moral principles by which he lived. He chose to do his duty as he defined it. His choice was autonomous because it was independent of necessity or emotion. The choice was based on Gilbert's perception of duty and the moral good.

It is appropriate to examine Roswell's decisions and good behavior from a Kantian perspective because his background suggests a rigoristic approach to decision making. The Gilbert family is not religious in a formal sense, but both Roswell and Emily attended colleges with conservative Protestant histories. The family apparently adheres to a rather strict moral code which stresses the performances of duty and acceptance of responsibility in decision making (Moran, 1985). It is possible for the rigorist religious influence to be translated into a rule-deontological moral perspective as religious orientation is secularized into an ethical system based on reason. Evidence of Roswell's preference for rule-dominated social institutions is seen in his choice of a career, electrical engineering, which requires formal disciplinary training, and in the formality of role structure in his family relationships.

Justice and Family Value Systems:
Nozick's Entitlement Theory Applied

Although Kantian ethics best fit Roswell's definition of duty and family structure, an argument for his actions can also be made from the libertarian perspective. Throughout his trial and subsequent appeal, Roswell has had the support of his family. The Gilberts' daughter and Mrs. Gilbert's sister have been especially vocal. Perhaps their support grows out of the family's definition of the events of the case. Ms. Moran revealed in a personal, but nonconfidential, interview that her father's actions were consistent with previous family decisions. On at least two other occasions, family members have decided not to use extraordinary means to prolong the lives of suffering relatives (Moran, 1985). If the family belief system involves some shared definition of the quality of life and its relationship to the desire to live, it may be argued that the family has a right to act in a way consistent with that belief system and to make life and death decisions based on it without interference.

Based on his interpretation of individual rights and their relation to justice in transfer, Nozick (1974, 1981) developed a defense of minimal government intervention in the lives of citizens—and then only in protection of right and entitlement. To extend this argument to include family groups as well as individuals, it is necessary to return to Lockean tradition. Locke allows that the formation of a community, in this case a family, implies the formation of one body, empowered to act as one body, presumably with the consent of the majority. Although Locke would disallow suicide or voluntary euthanasia on the grounds that people cannot possess or transfer the power to destroy life, he would allow the power of decision making to remain in the family. Nozick would not only allow, but would insist, that the decision-making power remains outside the political realm.

Nozick's entitlement theory, developed from an economics base, is historical in perspective. It requires that a holding that is initially acquired in accordance with a mutually held principle of justice may be transferred in accordance with the principle of justice to anyone chosen by the holder. If it is applied to justice in the distribution of family roles, the principle of justice in acquisition of the role becomes relevant to assessment of justice in transfer. In the Gilbert case, the issue of how Roswell got his power over Emily is relevant. Entitlement theory requires only that a person entitled to a holding transfers it by some principle of justice to another person. There is no pattern in the distribution of holdings under entitlement theory. Equality of resources can no more be assumed than inequality. Individuals transfer resources, in this case power, by their own choice to people they choose. Therefore, choice becomes the critical test of justice.

Within the marital dyad, it is certainly possible to establish choice. Weitzman (1984) has researched marital contracting as a means of formalizing agreements between marital partners. Since couples routinely interact face-to-face, they have the opportunity to renegotiate contractual agreements periodically. It is possible, of course, that the relationship that develops through successive interactions may nullify the objectivity needed to assure that those renegotiations are based on any originally agreed upon principle of justice.

Retrospective analysis of the development of shared belief systems in families is plagued by uncertainty because of the private nature of family interaction. Interpersonal relationships in American society are rarely formalized to the extent that any written definition of mutually held tenets is recorded either at the onset or over the developmental course of the relationship.

To return to the Gilbert case as an example, it is doubtful that Emily would have agreed early in marriage to transfer to Roswell the almost total control over her body and her decisions that he held at the end of her life. Therefore, if the marriage is considered within the historical context of a mutually held principle of distributive justice, it is also doubtful that Roswell did indeed obtain power in the marriage according to such a principle of justice in transfer. The injustice lies in the restriction of Emily's choice which resulted from the interactions in the marriage relationship. If, however, justice in transfer could be assured by agreement on principle of distribution, Nozick's theory would allow family members to bestow power as well as goods on each other without interference from social organizations outside the family unit.

Indeed, Nozick (1981) has already argued that the application of political morality, with its emphasis on rights, to political and nonpolitical groups is a result of the decline of institutions which were once held morally significant (among them presumably are church and family):

> In no way does political philosophy or the realm of the state exhaust the realm of morally desirable or moral oughts. It is a mark of the politicization of our times, and of the decline of other institutions that used to support the fabric of how we ought to act, that so many people nowadays see the state as the basis of all human decency and decent society, if not as coextensive with it. (p. 503)

Would the state involve itself in issues of elder care and euthanasia if the family had not lost many of its former functions to larger social institutions? Libertarian arguments for Roswell Gilbert's action would give the family power to decide when a relative can no longer maintain the quality of life required to make the person autonomous. It would defend the family, rather than the state, as possessor of institutional power. However, Nozick's theory would uphold the right of the state to interfere in family interaction on behalf of an individual whose rights and entitlements were being violated. Once again, the key concept is the just acquisition and transfer of a holding (in this application, a belief system).

Paternalism and Autonomy

Arguments against Roswell Gilbert's action may be presented from a feminist perspective. Feminist theory would assert Emily Gilbert's right to decide for herself whether the quality of her life had so deteriorated that she wished to die, and it would even extend that right to allow her to seek her husband's assistance in acting on her wish to die. Although the act Roswell committed can be justified under feminist theory, the chivalrous and paternalistic relationship which fostered his development as family decision maker cannot, since it constituted the base of potential victimization of Emily. The problem in the Gilbert case, from the feminist perspective, is not with the decision that was made but with the mechanism that was employed in making the decision. Bernard (1971) refers to coercion as the true basis of woman's inferior status. The importance of the woman's ability to retain control of her own body is a major contention of feminist ideology (Grossman et al., 1980).

The structure of the relationship of Roswell and Emily lent itself to the development of paternalism as she became less functional and he became more powerful. The caregiving relationship began with love and concern. Childress (1982) notes that paternalism develops from love when the focus turns to "needs" rather than "rights." As Emily was seen as less autonomous, her needs became the focus of the relationship. Since she had demonstrated compliance with Roswell's decisions in the past, it was easy for him to assume that he could make decisions for her as long as he saw them to be in her best interest.

The problem with paternalism is that it almost always involves coercion and deception (Childress, 1982). Testimony in the Gilbert case revealed that although Emily had expressed a desire to die, she and her husband had not discussed the possibility of his killing her. The act was a paternalistic decision made for her by Roswell because he decided that it was her best alternative (Gilbert, 1985, p. 389).

Q. And now you told the detective that you had never discussed with Emily about shooting her; isn't that a fair statement?
A. Oh, never, no.
Q. You never discussed at all with her?
A. Never, no.
Q. In fact, that's why you basically came up from behind her; isn't that a correct statement?
A. Well, naturally I don't want her looking down the muzzle of a gun when I do it, no. I came up along-side her, yes.

Chivalry and Autonomy

Perhaps it is most accurate to describe the Gilberts' relationship as chivalrous. The following excerpt from Roswell's testimony reflects the basis for this conclusion (Gilbert, 1985, p. 363):

Q. During all this time, can you tell this Court and Jury whether you were either angered or disenchanted with Emily because of the so-called burdens you'd been receiving?
A. No, never. I loved her very much and we were two rather different people. You know. I was a professional scientist. She was a fine lady. But kind of like two adjacent pieces of the jigsaw puzzle. They don't look alike but they sure fit together, and this is a mutual thing, and after all those years the cement hardens and you don't break apart lightly.

The concept of a chivalrous relationship as a symbolic interaction follows from the contention that symbols organize behavior with reference to that which is symbolized (Stryker, 1959). Roswell's reference to himself as "a professional scientist" and Emily as "a fine lady" suggests a set of interactions organized under those labels. Martha Gilbert Moran describes her father's treatment of her mother as chivalrous. She remembers that he did not complain when her mother spent money on clothing or jewelry (Moran, 1985). She often felt like an outsider since her parents had a close relationship and an active social life. Emily loved beautiful things and exciting parties. Many family photographs show the couple dining and dancing in fashionable clubs.

Family therapists, philosophers, and feminists alike have addressed the issue of chivalry in marital relationships. Blood (1972) noted that chivalry does not imply that the female's position has been elevated above the male's. Rather, chivalry is a "gift" which still-superior men bestow on women. Blood found that chivalrous marriages have great power differentials between the marriage partners and a patriarchal power structure. Chivalry does not empower women but grants them a special status in which they are treated to special favors, which they may or may not desire, based on men's perceptions of their needs.

Lipman-Blumen (1984) examines gender roles in middle and upper class families. The major sources of power for women in such families are social influence and vicarious achievement. In a broader discussion of the mechanisms of male domination, she points to two myths that perpetuate male control and keep women from renegotiating the power relationship. The first myth assures women that men are best in control because they have more knowledge and are more capable; the second is that men have the best interests of women at heart. The traditional structure in the Gilbert's marriage helped to perpetuate these myths by denying both partners the flexibility to experiment with the boundaries of control.

As Emily's illness progressed and her chivalrous "knight" became her caregiver, the assumption grew stronger in both Roswell and Emily that she needed someone to determine what was in her best interest. In the end, when her caregiver became her executioner, she was assumed to have so yielded herself to another person's care and judgment that she needed his strength even to make the final decision that it was time for her to die. The problem from the feminist perspective is not simply that Roswell shot Emily, but that both probably expected him to take charge and do something about an apparently hopeless situation—even if that something was a violent act.

An additional problem is that it is not at all clear that Emily understood that euthanasia might result from her dependence on Roswell to care for her as her illness progressed. The danger of submission lies in its preponderance toward irreversibility. By the time the power differential in the Gilbert marriage became evident, Emily was too physically ill and emotionally dependent to have the resources for a strong negotiating position.

Consent and Personhood

O'Neill (1985), in an extensive discussion of consent, relates the notion of treating others as persons to intimate personal relationships between adults. She concludes that difficulties in determining whether consent has been given in situations where formal procedures are lacking exists in at least three areas: (a) boundaries of explicit consent are unclear; (b) consent given may not match the activities it supposedly legitimates; and (c) abilities to consent and dissent may be impaired. Although O'Neill's discussion develops from the question on consent in sexual behavior, implications for the Gilbert case are evident.

Morally significant consent requires that the consenting person not be seriously misled about the consequences of the action for which consent is being given. Emily Gilbert consented to being cared for by her husband. The boundaries of her consent are unclear, and there are serious questions as to whether her consent to be dependent on Roswell can be extended as far as it was taken without serious threat to her autonomy. Based on Rawl's priority of justice, Bandman and Bandman (1983) insist that, "Just and beneficent euthanasia entails full disclosure and freely given consent. Otherwise, it is neither just nor beneficent, but killing of another kind. Kindness alone will not do" (p. 170). Emily Gilbert's right to consent or dissent was impaired not only by her illness, but also by Roswell's failure to discuss with her the option of death at his hands.

In intimate personal relationships, goals are often shared to the extent that a couple is seen to act as one. Roswell felt that his purpose and Emily's purpose were the same—namely, the termination of her suffering. Their daughter affirms the singleness of purpose which she saw in her parent's marriage by her decision to keep her mother's ashes until the death of her father so that she can scatter them both together over the waters off the Florida coast. "They have always been together and I know they would want to remain so," (Moran, 1985).

Consent is an issue not only from Emily's perspective, but also from Roswell's. The role in which he found himself had exceeded the boundaries by which it was defined when he originally gave his consent to fulfill it. He agreed to be Emily's caregiver. He did not foresee the evolution of the role of mercy killer from that commitment. If Emily truly wanted to die, why did she not commit suicide? Was Roswell being used when she repeatedly asked him to "let me die?" Could that request imply some expectation that he do something? Caregivers often feel that the demands of their role far exceed their original expectations (Steinmetz, 1988).

Some caregivers turn the gun on themselves in suicide. Bill was in his mid-sixties, and Louise was near 70 when she suffered a series of strokes that severely limited her mobility and mental functioning and left her dependent on Bill for daily physical care. Theirs had been a stormy marriage with periodic talk of divorce "when the kids leave home," but in their later years, they seemed to have reached a peaceful understanding and mutual enjoyment of their quiet rural life. Their daughter and her children made frequent visits and assisted Bill in Louise's care.

Retired as a master carpenter, Bill managed to continue part-time work while caring for Louise. The family secured the services of a housekeeper by allowing her to live in a house they had formerly used as rental property. Suddenly the demands on the caregiving arrangements changed dramatically. Bill's son-in-law was injured in an accident, requiring the daughter to spend more time caring for him and less time caring for her mother. Bill suffered a mild stroke, confining him to his home and increasing the caregiving requirements on the housekeeper.

Although Bill's physical recovery progressed rapidly, he began to show depressive symptoms. He found it difficult to sleep; he feared being in crowds; and he often cried when he spoke about his family's problems. One morning, about six months after his stroke, Bill stood in his garden beside his favorite rose bush and shot himself.

There will be no trial in Bill's case—no jury to establish guilt, no television talk show invitations for his daughter, no movie treatment of his story, and no special interest groups rallying to his cause. Is Bill's story so different because the gun was pointed in a different direction?

The case of Bill and Louise raises the argument that the caregiver's personhood can be sacrificed just as surely as the dependent's in the performance of a role for which consent has been given without full knowledge of the boundaries of commitment or of the activities to which consent may lead.

Conclusions

Roswell Gilbert's act was a dramatic clarification of some important issues in home health care that families face in a technologically advanced society. His solution was atypical and calls forth emotional and esthetic feelings about "the good death" and the position of members in family interactions. While ordinary families may not choose to conclude caregiving with violent means, they are, in increasing numbers, asked to make life-and-death decisions. The same ethical dilemma may be clothed in terms that suggest kindness rather than violence as family members are asked: "Shall we give more pain medication?"; "Would you like to take your mother home now?"; or "Do you want us to give the child more oxygen?" Medical professionals have developed skill in offering termination in language that they and the family members can accept.

As health care moves out of professional settings, family members will have chances to apply their own perceptions to the options that are available and to participate not only in decisions about treatment but also in the ethical decisions about life and death. The return of health care to the home is a function both of technological development and of the current political and economic climate. While families are being involved in the work and decision making that was formerly assigned to professionals whose behavior was guided by professional codes of ethics, little attention has been given to equipping families with skills that facilitate solutions of the moral dilemmas they may face in caregiving.

Philosophers have worked with professionals (Mitcham, 1985) in medicine, engineering, and human resources to illuminate technical decision making with ethical analysis techniques and theories. Similar work with families awaits development. Maddock (1986), in a plenary address to the Groves Conference on Marriage and the Family, urged researchers and policy makers to consider the tools of ethical analysis in formulating intervention strategies.

Family life researchers and therapists can help to identify potentially dysfunctional caregiving relationships and to develop educational and therapeutic strategies for specific patient/caregiver dyads. Research from the family perspective can enrich inquiry into ethical issues by identifying processes of ethical decision making in intergenerational and marital relationships. The family as a small group offers an interesting focus for the study of applied ethical analysis. The family is a private group, sharing and transmitting values within and across generational lines; the family exists over time, building a history of interaction; and the family is part of the larger social system, interpreting and relating cultural norms to ethical dilemmas in the family relationships (Hanks, 1988; Larzelere & Klein, 1987).

The Gilbert case illuminates the need for family professionals and applied ethicists to work together to: (a) frame ethical questions about family caregiving in terms of family theory so there is a common language for discourse from both applied ethical and family perspectives; (b) clarify ethical issues surrounding chronic illness and long-term family caregiving; and (c) develop educational strategies to help families and primary service-providers recognize potential ethical dilemmas in family caregiving relationships.

Significant work has begun on clarification of issues surrounding chronic illness and the long-term family caregiving so often associated with it (Jennings, Callahan, & Caplan, 1988). The Hastings Center identified a multidisciplinary team for a three-year project funded by the Henry Luce Foundation. Attention was primarily on the patient/professional relationship, but the team also addressed issues of family obligation to provide and pay for the care of chronically-ill family members. Conclusions about the family appeared in the project report:

Family life, and especially the moral obligations that family members have toward one another, is challenged by severe chronic illness in two ways: first by the burdens imposed on families by chronic care; and second by virtue of the fact that severe chronic illness in a family can pose a crisis for our traditional moral expectations concerning family life. Should we, in the name of individual autonomy, both for the chronically ill and for family members, move toward replacing family-based care with such innovations as group homes, programs to encourage independent living, professionalized home care services, and greater access to long-term care institutions for those needing only unskilled nursing and "custodial" care? It remains to be seen whether our society will be able to move toward a system that responds to the complex needs of both families and individuals. (pp. 12-13)

Any analysis of the costs and benefits of family caregiving that takes into account the various needs and resources of individual family members, the family as a group, and the larger social system supporting the care, quickly leads to a realization that the level of analysis makes a difference in the variables to be considered. The affectional ties and dependencies among family members may carry greater weight than physical resources in a family's resolution of caregiving needs. The family may never consider access to community support if they are, as the Gilberts were, unfamiliar with using a larger social system for support.

The Gilbert case suggests issues beyond the availability of services to the chronically ill and their family caregivers. Even with services available, there are an inestimable number of families whose shared values keep in place expectations that the family will take care of its own dependent members. These expectations form family-centered barriers to access to services. Programs that focus on increasing the number or distribution of available facilities will have little impact on these families. Policy makers and program designers must recognize the potential in families for dysfunctional family autonomy that inhibits help-seeking before it becomes an issue of access or availability, cost, or quality.

Chronic illness forces a rethinking of the individual autonomy that is the basis for patient/professional relationships and current medical treatment models. Long-term family caregiving suggests a complementary rethinking of individual autonomy within family relationships and of family autonomy within service-providing and santion-imposing communities. Who draws the lines between family privacy, self-determination, and dysfunctional autonomy? In some communities, familial and cultural values and traditions undermine efforts to provide effective support for caregiving families.

This chapter is based on a single case study and requires further investigations, but it does begin to identify some of the salient ethical issues in family caregiving and allows formulation of preliminary conceptualizations. The family has the option of supporting interactions that are not supported by general social norms if those interactions fit shared expectations for performance of intrafamilial roles. Role performance is perceived by the family as morally correct or incorrect depending on the family's definition of the event which precipitates interaction. Families will make life-and-death decisions based on shared expectations for quality of life; those expectations may or may not be objective or consistent with social norms codified in the legal system.

The issues and decisions surrounding family caregiving can be either individual or collective (shared by family members and generations). Therefore, it is necessary to define the moral unit to which policy and intervention is addressed and ethical accountability is assigned. Symbolic interaction as applied to family theory provides an objective amoral framework for understanding relationships, interactions, and consequences. It does not provide the basis for developing ethical codes which protect either decision makers or potential victims in life-and-death family care situations. The symbolic interaction perspective as a bridge between family and ethical theory is useful in the Gilbert case.

The authors have proposed that the effect of Alzheimer's disease and osteoporosis caused Emily to lose the descriptors of herself that defined her personhood. When Emily asked to die and when Roswell killed her, both were acting on the perception that "Emily" was gone. Symbolic interaction theory allows the conceptualization of the separation of perception from objective physical evaluation. Kantian ethics allow the separations of the rational self from other aspects of self and the explanation of how the loss of rationality alters personhood. At the time of her death, both Roswell and Emily were acting on their perceptions of her condition. It is at this point that feminist theory questions the historical development of those perceptions in the context of the marital relationship. This case questions the ability of actors to be morally correct in acting on perceptions that grow out of power differentials that obscure objectivity. It also raises the issue of support for family caregiving in a pluralistic society in which conceptualizations of moral issues vary widely.

This chapter uses symbolic interaction as a theoretical tool for exploring a caregiving relationship. Alzheimer's disease, as it is associated with loss of personhood, is particularly suited to a symbolic interaction perspective. The ethical dilemmas in other chronic illnesses and other family caregiving situations could be developed from other theoretical perspectives on the family. For example, an ethical analysis of the allocation of health care resources could draw upon the institutional frame of reference that focuses on the family as one of a number of interacting institutions in society or on the economic framework that views the family as a unit of consumership. The case study approach is useful in developing interdisciplinary discussions of ethical issues in family caregiving among researchers familiar with family analysis, philosophers familiar with applied ethical analysis, and professional service providers and policy makers familiar with the needs and resources of their clients and constituents.

References

Bahr, S. J. (1982). Exchange and control in married life. In F. I. Nye (Ed.), *Family Relationships: Rewards and costs* (pp. 81-95). Beverly Hills, CA: Sage.

Bandman, B., & Bandman, E. (1983). Rights, justice, and euthanasia. In M.D. Bayles & K. Henley (Eds.), *Right conduct: Theories and applications* (pp. 164-172). New York: Random House.

Barbour, J. (1985, November 17). Alzheimer's: A loss of self. *Sunday News Journal*, Wilmington, DE, p. G1.

Bayles, M.D., & Henley, K. (Eds.). (1983). *Right conduct: Theories and applications.* New York: Random House.

Beauchamp, T.L. (1982). *Philosophical ethics.* New York: McGraw Hill.

Bernard, J. (1971). *Women and the public interest.* Chicago: Aldine-Atherton.

Blood, R.O. (1972). *The family.* New York: Free Press.

Childress, J.F. (1982). *Who should decide? Paternalism in health care.* New York: Oxford University Press.

Connor reiterates opposition to Gilbert clemency. (1985, September 11). *United Press International*, Tallahassee, FL.

Farber, B. (1959). Effects of a severely mentally retarded child on family integration. *Monograph of Social Research and Child Development, 24* (2, Serial No. 17).

Farber, B., Jenne, W.C., & Toigo, R. (1960). *Family crisis and the decision to institutionalize the retarded child.* Reston, VA: Council for Exceptional Children.

Florida cabinet denies freedom to mercy killer. (1985, August 27). *The Washington Post,* p. A4.

Gilbert, R. (1985, May). Roswell Gilbert v. State of Florida.

Gilbert Issue. (1985, August 24). *Miami Herald,* p. 22a.

Givens, R., Agrest, S., & Prout, L. (1985, September 9). Mercy or murder? *Newsweek,* p. 25.

Goffman, E. (1963). *Stigma: Notes on the management of spoiled identity.* Englewood Cliffs, NJ: Prentice-Hall.

Goode, W.J. (1956). *After divorce.* New York: Free Press.

Grossman, F.K., Eichler, L.S., Winickoff, S.A., Anzalone, M.K., Gofseyeff, M.H., & Sargent, S.P. (1980). *Pregnancy, birth, and parenthood.* San Francisco: Jossey-Bass.

Hanks, R.S. (1988, November). A conceptual framework for ethical analysis in family research

118118   Theoretical Questions and Ethical Issues

and treatment. Paper presented in B.H. Settles & R.S. Hanks, *Issues in developing an ethical code for an emerging family science discipline.* Ethics and Issues in Family Science. Annual conference of the National Council on Family Relations, Philadelphia, PA.

Harris, L. (1985, March 4). Support increases for euthanasia. *The Harris Survey, #18.* Orlando, FL: Tribune Media Services.

Hemlock Society asks clemency for mercy killer. (1985, August 27). PR Newswire, Los Angeles.

Jennings, B., Callahan, D., & Caplan, A.L. (1988, February/ March). Ethical challenges of chronic illness. Special supplement to *The Hastings Center Report, 18* (1), 1-16.

Jurors defend verdict in mercy killing trial, hope court reduces Gilbert sentence. (1985, May 12). United Press International, Fort Lauderdale, FL.

Larzelere, R.E., & Klein, D. (1987). Methodology. In M. B. Sussman & S. K. Steinmetz (Eds.), *Handbook on Marriage and the Family* (pp. 125-155). New York: Plenum.

Lindesmith, A.R., & Strauss, A.L. (1966). *Social psychology.* New York: Holt, Rinehart and Winston.

Lipman-Blumen, J. (1984). *Gender roles and power.* Englewood Cliffs, NJ: Prentice-Hall.

Maddock, J. (1986, July 16-20). Plenary address, Groves Conference on Marriage and the Family, London.

Mitcham, C. (1985). Industrial and engineering ethics: Introductory notes and annotated bibliography. In P.T. Durbin (Ed.), *Research in philosophy and technology, Vol. 8* (pp. 251-265). Greenwich, CT: JAI Press.

Moran, M. G. (1985, October 30). Personal interview.

Nozick, R. (1974). *Anarchy, state, and utopia.* New York: Basic Books.

Nozick, R. (1981). *Philosophical explanations.* Cambridge, MA: Harvard University Press.

O'Neill, O. (1985). Between consenting adults. *Philosophy and Public Affairs, 14* (93), 252-277.

Parsons, T., & Bales, R.F. (1955). *Family, socialization and interaction process.* New York: Free Press.

Plummer, W. , & Marx, L. (1985, May 27). An act of love or selfishness? *People*, p.100.

Rapoport, R., & Rapoport, R. (1968). Work and family in contemporary society. In M.B. Sussman (Ed.), *Sourcebook in marriage and the family* (pp. 53-65). Boston: Houghton Mifflin.

Settles, B.H. (1987). A perspective on tomorrow's families. In M.B. Sussman & S.K. Steinmetz (Eds.), *Handbook on marriage and the family* (pp. 157-180). New York: Plenum.

Steinmetz, S.K. (Ed.). (1988). *Duty bound: Elder abuse and family care.* Newbury Park, CA: Sage.

Strauss, A.L. (1985). *The social organization of medical work.* Chicago: University of Chicago Press.

Stryker, S. (1959). Symbolic interaction as an approach to family research. *Marriage and Family Living, 21* (2), 111-119.

Swenson, C. (1979). *Marriage relationship and problems of retired married couples.* (Unpublished manuscript, Purdue University, 1978), reported in *Families*, National Institute for Mental Health Monograph, Vol. 1 (pp. 249-286).

Triche, III, C. W., & Triche, D.S. (1975). *The euthanasia controversy (1812-1974): A bibliography with select annotations.* Troy, NY: Whitson.

Waisbren, S.E. (1980). Parent's reactions after the birth of a developmentally disabled child. *American Journal of Mental Deficiency, 84* (4), 345-351.

Weitzman, L. J. (1984). *The marriage contract.* New York: Macmillan.

Zimmerman, C.C. (1971). *The future of the family in America.* Burgess Award Address, National Council on Family Relations, Estes Park, CO.

PART II

Research—Cognitive and Physical Impairment

5

The Stress of Caregivers

DAVID A. CHIRIBOGA
PHILIP G. WEILER
KAREN NIELSEN

In this chapter we examine the multiple domains of stressors that potentially affect the lives of caregivers. The first sections deal with stress as a general topic and examine why it is applicable to the caregiving context. The later sections then turn to findings from a specific research project. The target population in this project consisted of adult children who provide care to a parent afflicted with Alzheimer's disease. The general argument to be presented is that a more comprehensive understanding of the stress of caregivers will be obtained when the researcher or practitioner considers not only those stressors specific to the role of caregiving but those that represent other areas of the caregiver's life. This latter perspective has been absent from most caregiving research.

Stress as an Integrating Model

Although the burdens of caregiving are well recognized (e.g., Brody, 1985; Ory et al., 1985; Zarit, Orr, & Zarit, 1985), the scope of conditions that affect caregivers has, to date, received only minimal attention. This lack

AUTHORS' NOTE

This research was supported by National Institute on Aging grant #R01 AG005150-04.

of attention may stem in part from the fact that the source of distress, for example the caregiving situation, is viewed as self-evident. There is substantial justification for studying caregiver experiences within the larger framework of stress research in general.

One reason is to cast caregiving within a life span context. There is a growing interest among theoreticians in the developmental implications of stress experiences. A number of researchers (e.g., Baltes & Baltes, 1980; Elder, 1981; Gergen, 1977) have provided convincing arguments for an interaction not only of place along the life course, but also the historical moment, in understanding how an individual will react to a particular kind of stress exposure. Their findings suggest that the importance of a stress condition, such as caregiving, may depend heavily on when it is studied. Currently, for example, a distinguishing characteristic of Alzheimer's disease is the absence of any curative agents or effective means of symptomatic relief. The potential impact on caregivers of effective techniques of secondary or tertiary prevention for Alzheimer's disease would be enormous, if only because it would provide a modicum of hope.

Perhaps a more compelling reason for the inclusion of stress paradigms is the demonstrated importance of stress exposure for physical and mental well-being. Over the past three decades, stress exposures have been linked to a host of physical and psychological problems, many of which are particularly relevant to adult child caregivers. For example, stress exposure has been implicated in the etiology of hypertension, a condition that places many middle-aged men and women at increased risk of mortality and morbidity (e.g., Kaplan, 1985). Stress, especially the loss of significant others, has been associated with an increased incidence of coronary heart disease (e.g., Lynch, 1977), clinical depression (e.g., Brown & Andrews, 1986; Brown & Harris, 1978), and many other physical and mental health problems of concern to middle-aged populations. There is even evidence that stress depresses the function of the immune system, including the production of interferon, which may lead to an increased risk of multiple health problems, including cancer (Stein & Schleifer, 1985).

The experience of any kind of loss, social or otherwise, in sum has been associated with physical and emotional illness. In the case of family caregivers, we are of course dealing not with a single loss but with a potentially infinite range of losses, some directly linked to the caregiver role, some indirectly linked, and some that might normally be expected at the caregiver's stage of life. Middle-aged caregivers, for example, may be facing loss of social status, loss of leisure time, economic loss resulting from caregiving expenses, loss of friends who are made uncomfortable by the presence of the dementing parent, and the loss of the parent's selfhood and companionship. They may also be facing the departure of children, death of friends due to heart attacks, loss of physical vigor and youthful attractiveness, and all the other "exit events" that begin to accrue in the second half of life and that should be considered as portends of increased risk (Brown & Andrews, 1986; Chiriboga, 1989a; Paykel, 1982).

Definitional Issues

From both a theoretical and an applied perspective, the concept of stress may provide a useful vehicle to further our understanding of caregiving. As we delve into specific issues and ideas about loss and the family caregiver, it is helpful to examine how differently people use the term "stress," as well as its basic components and potential contributions.

The term stress is a very confusing one, in part because it encompasses so many different concepts and is used in so many different ways. The concept of stress has a host of meanings. For some health professionals, stress is the physical and psychological response of a person to some noxious condition. This interpretation actually is the oldest. Selye (1956), for example, defined stress as the nonspecific response made by the organism to trauma or insult. More recent research has broadened the definition of stress considerably. For example, according to the research team headed by Richard Lazarus, perhaps the modern guru of stress research, the term stress:

> refers to any event in which environmental demands, internal demands or both tax or exceed the adaptive resources of an individual, social system or tissue system (Monat & Lazarus, 1985, p.3)

The typical stress paradigm will usually consider three basic components: stressors, mediators, and responses. Implicit to this paradigm is the idea that the stress process is not a mechanical and preordained relationship but one that works through a variety of mediators, such as social supports, self-esteem, and coping strategies. The stressors are impinging agents, including life events as well as the more durable or chronic situations that may last for years. Stressors include both positive and negative agents since both may provoke change (Chiriboga, 1989b; George, 1987). Responses are reactions to the stressors. Most investigators consider the negative consequences: either some physical health response, such as stroke or hypertension or the common cold; or psychological responses, such as anxiety or depression. A few investigators also study positive responses, such as morale, since in the long run, even a negative stressor may lead to psychological growth and development (Chiriboga & Cutler, 1980). The mediators orchestrate the relationship of stressor to response, with the most commonly studied mediators being social supports and coping strategies.

Stressors: What Are They?

As the focus of this chapter really is on stressors, we need to spend a little more time thinking about these elements of the stress paradigm. Stressors come in many sizes and shapes. As a means of categorizing and evaluating these differences, some researchers draw a distinction between those stressors that are acute in nature and those that are more durable, in that they may persist for lasting periods of time. Acute stressors have probably received more attention than the more durable or chronic stressors. The well-known "life event" research (e.g., Holmes & Rahe, 1967) falls into this acute stress category. Life events have been found to predict all sorts of physical, mental, and social dysfunction. Everything, in fact, from coronary heart disease (e.g., Lynch, 1977) to general psychiatric symptomatology (e.g., Chiriboga, 1984; Dohrenwend, 1986) to depression (e.g., Brown & Harris, 1978; Paykel, 1982; Pearlin, 1982).

While acute events or stressors have received the bulk of attention, some of the more interesting and exciting research at the level of chronic stress has focused on what are called day-to-day hassles. Lazarus and Folkman (1984) have examined the importance of day-to-day hassles for the physical and emotional well-being of middle-aged men and women. They conclude that hassles exert a stronger influence on our mental health and well-being than does exposure to the more well-known life events. Similarly, Pearlin (1985) reports a better showing of what he calls "durable" events over those that reflect acute or time-limited conditions.

Caregiver Stress: An Empirical Study

In the remainder of this chapter, the focus will shift to an empirical consideration of how stress exposure may affect the lives of one particular subgroup of caregivers: adult children who provide care to a parent afflicted with Alzheimer's disease. Adult children are not only a major source of help for demented parents, but often are the preferred caregiver (Biegel, Shore, & Gordon, 1984; Brody, 1985; Wan, 1982). One review concludes that "family members provide an extraordinary amount of assistance to their older family members" (Springer & Brubaker, 1984, p. 16). This is especially true in the case of Alzheimer's disease, where the caregiver is faced with a major burden and can only expect the situation to get worse. Hence, caregiving in the context of Alzheimer's disease provides a good illustration of the stress context of caregiving.

In studying the stress exposure of adult caregivers, one basic decision that had to be reached concerned how broad a range of stressors should be included. We have already seen that stressors are sometimes operationalized as life events, sometimes as more chronic problems, such as continuing friction with colleagues at work, or the need to provide care to a dependent parent. They may be major events, such as the birth of a child or the death of a spouse, and they may be day-to-day events, such as getting tied up in traffic or running out of cereal in the morning. They may even be positive experiences if these experiences create major change and disequilibrium in the person's life.

Clearly, there are a host of stressors that can affect the well-being of caregivers, and these stressors are not necessarily related directly to caregiving. Because of their potential, the analyses to be described included not only stressors specific to caregiving but those of a more general nature, such as work and financial stressors. In order to explore the potential role of these stressors, their associations with three of the more frequently studied measures of psychological well-being were considered.

The Sample

Subjects were part of a larger study, conducted in the Central Valley area of Northern California, of adult child caregivers and their parents. The 255 adult children included in the present analyses all had parents with probable diagnoses of Alzheimer's disease who were: (a) geriatric clients who had sought services in two hospitals, two clinics, three community health centers, and six home health care agencies; (b) residents of board and care facilities; (c) residents of skilled and intermediate care facilities; or (d) clients whose child belonged to either of two Alzheimers Disease and Related Disorders Association (ADRDA) groups serving the catchment area. The patient diagnosis was reviewed by a physician on the basis of medical history, assessments by either a geriatric nurse practitioner or a third-year medical student, and structured instruments and tests.

The sample ranged in age from 27 to 67, with 50 representing the average age. Reflecting the fact that caregiving is most often performed by women, 30% were men and 70% were women. This was not an elite sample: over

50% had not completed their college education. However, reflecting the affluence of the agricultural area from which the sample was drawn, only 21% had family incomes of less than $20,000, and 27% reported incomes of $45,000 and over. Nine percent felt they did not have enough money to make ends meet, and one-third had just enough to get by.

The overwhelming majority, approximately 90%, represented whites of European descent. The remainder included blacks (4%), Hispanics (3%), and Asians (1%). Seventeen percent had no children, while 29% had already launched their children. The mean age of their children was 25. Most of the subjects were either Catholic (20%) or Protestant (53%), but two-thirds either never attended services or did so only on religious holidays.

Measures. Measures were based on responses to interviews and to a questionnaire that was also given to all of the adult children.

Basic demographic information. These four measures included information on age and sex of the adult child; financial status of the caregiver; and gender of the afflicted parent.

Parent characteristics. These measures, based on interviews with the adult child, included three descriptors of parent with Alzheimer's disease: how long it had been since the first symptoms were noticed by the caregiver; the present severity of impairment; and frequency of contact with parent.

Social supports. These nine measures assessed whether the caregiver had friends who also had a demented parent; number of friends living nearby; number of close kin living nearby; involvement in self-help groups; frequency of contact with the nondemented parent (if available); number of siblings; marital status; whether subject was primary caregiver; and whether or not the subject had children.

Stressors. Since a major goal of this investigation was to assess not only stressors that were directly related to caregiving, but the stressors of everyday life, a variety of stress indices were included. These tapped general life events, hassles, perceived burden of care, and amount of actual care reported.

1. *Life Event Inventory.* This 37-item inventory is based on a larger inventory (Chiriboga, 1977, 1984) that is applicable to persons at all stages of life. The shorter version is more focused on the kinds of life events faced by persons in middle and later life. Although the instrument includes data on perceptions of events, the measures used in this paper consider the frequency of exposure to events in the following dimensions: work, marital, family, nonfamily, social life, financial, and miscellaneous.

2. *Hassles Inventory.* A 13-item Hassles Inventory (Chiriboga & Cutler, 1980; see also Chiriboga, 1984) that assesses hassles in the six areas of work, mari-

tal, family, nonfamily, financial, and caregiving. Ratings were made on a 5-point scale (1 = "all the time"; 5 = "never") for items such as "Hassled by my helping responsibilities." Subscales based on factor analyses and item content were developed in each of the six areas.

3. *The Caregiver Burden Scale.* A 22-item instrument assessing both emotional and behavioral-relational strain imposed upon caregivers (Zarit et al., 1985). The items are similar to those in other instruments (e.g., Montgomery, Gonyea, & Hooyman, 1985) but have better content validity. Internal reliability for the total score has been reported at .79 (Zarit et al., 1985). Although usually treated as a single unitary score, the burden data were subjected to factor analyses in order to explore the dimensionality of subjective burden.

Alpha factoring and an oblique rotation (SPSS-X, 1988) yielded five interpretable factors that together accounted for 61% of the original variance. The scales were as follows:

   a. General Burden (α = .90). An 11-item factor in which higher scores indicate caregivers feel they have lost control of their lives, overall feel burdened, feel their social life has suffered, feel caught between competing responsibilities, feel they don't have enough time for themselves, feel their health has suffered, feel caregiving has affected their social relationships adversely, and so forth.

   b. Burden of Guilt and Uncertainty (α = .65). A 4-item scale in which higher scores indicate caregivers feel they should be doing more for the parent, that they could be doing a better job of caring, feel uncertain about what to do, and fear the future.

   c. Burden of Social Embarrassment (α = .69). A 3-item scale in which lower scores indicate caregivers feel uncomfortable about having friends over, embarrassed over their parent's behavior, and angry when around parent.

   d. Burden of Parental Demand (α = .72). A 3-item scale in which higher scores indicate caregivers feel the parent definitely expects them to provide care, asks for more help than needed, and is dependent upon them.

   e. Financial Burden. A single-item scale in which higher scores indicate caregivers feel they lack the financial resources necessary to take care of the parent.

4. *Instrumental Demands of Daily Life (IDDL).* This instrument represents a modification of the IADL instrument included in the OARS Multidimensional Functional Assessment Questionnaire (Duke University, 1978). Designed to assess the level of impairment in functioning of the patient, the original IDDL was modified for this study to ask how often caregivers assisted their parent with each of 14 behaviors. For example, how often did they make phone calls for the parent, take them to the doctor, help in the preparation of meals, and so forth. In each case, an 8-point rating scale was used, where "1" = never and "8" = more than once a day. The IDDL was designed to provide a more objective indicator of caregiver burden than the Zarit Burden Scale described above.

In a factor analysis with oblique factor rotation, two factors were obtained that together accounted for 67% of the original variance:

a. Basic IDDLs ($\alpha = .95$). Ten items that assess the frequency with which caregivers help their parent with basic activities, such as dressing, toileting, and grooming.

b. Instrumental IDDLs ($\alpha = .65$). Four items that deal with more complex activities: taking the parent someplace for social reasons, taking the parent someplace for medical or therapeutic reasons, assisting in financial matters, and making phone calls for the parent.

Stress Response. While the response component of the stress paradigm is inherently multidimensional, it is often assessed by means of a single measure, such as depression (Elliott & Eisdorfer, 1982). Since the association of stressors with caregiver distress was a major concern, three established indicators of psychological functioning were included in this study. One indicator, Affect Balance, was oriented to what might be called the "normal range" of functioning, and covers positive and negative emotions that anyone might experience. The remaining two were designed to detect problems in emotional functioning. Depression is not only the most commonly employed indicator of stress response (Elliott & Eisdorfer, 1982) but one with demonstrated sensitivity to stress conditions involving the loss of a relationship (e.g., Brown, Bifulco, Harris, & Bridge, 1986). Anxiety is also employed frequently as an index of stress response, with a history going back to Freudian concepts of "signal anxiety" as a stress-alert mechanism. In the present study, all three measures were significantly ($p = .001$) associated with each other. Affect Balance correlated at $-.48$ with Anxiety and $-.62$ with Depression, while the latter two correlated at the .73 level.

1. *Affect Balance.* This (Bradburn, 1969; Bradburn & Caplovitz, 1965) assessed the ratio of positive to negative affect. The positive affect score summarized responses to four questions (how often did the respondent [R] feel on top of the world, particularly excited about something, pleased, and proud); the negative score also summarized responses to four questions (how often did the R feel very lonely, couldn't get going, depressed, and bored).

2. *Anxiety.* Drawn from the Hopkins Symptoms Checklist-90 (Derogatis & Cleary, 1977), this was the 10-item Anxiety subscale. A single summated score was used in which higher scores indicated greater anxiety.

3. *Depression.* Also drawn from the HCL-90, this consisted of the 13-item depression subscale. The measure of depression represented a summation of scores for all 13 items; higher scores indicated greater depression.

Results

Before turning to the central question of whether the stressors experienced by caregivers affected their well-being, several characteristics of the sample will be reviewed that provide a background for interpreting results. One important characteristic is that these adult children, by and large, were not isolated from other family members; for example, most saw siblings more than once a month. About 60% felt they were the primary caregiver, with 33% saying it was a sibling. Perhaps because the majority lived less than one hour's drive away from their parent, contact was frequent: 33% saw their afflicted parent daily, and another 38% saw their parent on a weekly basis.

In addition to family contact, 21% of the adult children belonged to a self-help group for families with a member afflicted with Alzheimer's disease, and 86% reported that they had turned to someone for help and advice about the problems associated with their parent. The resource most commonly accessed was a medical doctor: over 64% sought advice from a doctor. The second most frequently accessed resource was a sibling (35%), while friends came in third (29%). Despite the use of social resources, 39% currently felt themselves to be "very much" to "extremely" troubled by the situation they found themselves in. At the other extreme, 24% were either "only a little" or "not at all" troubled.

The Prediction of Affect Balance

In order to examine the relationship of the several different types of stress indicators to psychological functioning, hierarchical set regression analyses were computed with each of the three criterion. In each regression, the sets of variables were entered in the following order: (a) basic demographics; (b) parent characteristics; (c) social supports; (d) subjective and objective burden; and (e) events and hassles. Two regression analyses were run for each criterion, with the first including four or five measures in each set, and the second analysis including only those measures that exhibited significant or near significant relationships with criterion.

In the analyses focused on Affect Balance, entry of the basic demographic set indicated that adequacy of finances played a minor but beneficial role in the morale of caregivers (Table 5.1). This is certainly not a new, or surprising, finding. In fact, Bradburn and Caplovitz (1965) found much the same results when they first reported findings on Affect Balance based on national surveys.

Table 5.1   Hierarchical Regression Predicting Affect Balance

Set #	Zero Correlation	Beta	R^2 Change	Total R^2	MR
1. *Basic demographics*					
Finances ok/end month					
(+ = good)	.16	.16	.03*	.03	.16*
2. *Parent characteristics*					
Contact with AD parent	−.21	−.21			
How long AD obvious	.18	.14	.06***	.09	.30***
3. *Social supports*					
Contact with other parent	.13	.15			
Have friends with AD parent	−.14	−.13			
Self not primary caregiver	−.04	−.15	.06**	.14	.38***
4. *Objective/subjective burden*					
Burden of guilt, uncertainty	−.22	−.20			
Burden of parental demands	−.19	−.04	.04	.18	.43***
5. *Events and hassles*					
Work events	−.19	−.16			
Hassles in social relations[1]	.26	.28			
Work hassles[1]	.34	.30	.17***	.35	.59***

[1] Low score indicates more hassles.   *$p = .10$;   **$p = .05$;   ***$p = .01$.

With the entry of the next set, that dealing with parent characteristics, the importance of caregiver context began to emerge. Greater contact with the parent was associated with lower morale; but the longer the parent had been recognized to have the disease, the higher the morale. Following parent characteristics was a set of variables having to do with social supports available to the caregiver. Comparatively speaking, social supports played a somewhat less important role. One significant contributor was contact with the nondemented parent. In contrast to contact with the afflicted parent, where greater contact was associated with lower morale, greater contact with the nondemented parent was associated with higher morale. Also associated with higher morale was friendship with other people who, like the caregiver in our study, had a parent with Alzheimer's disease. Being the primary caregiver, surprisingly, emerged as associated with higher morale in the regression analysis but not in the zero-order correlation.

The objective and subjective indices of burden did not contribute to morale, either individually or as a set. However, the measures of life events and hassles, entered as the fifth and final set, did make a contribution. In fact, for the regression equation predicting Affect Balance, the largest contribution came from the general noncaregiver events and hassles and not from the indices focused specifically on caregiver stress and strain. More specifically, fewer work events, fewer work hassles, and fewer hassles in social relationships together accounted for a substantial 17% of the variance in Affect Balance.

What these last findings imply is that for researchers interested in the morale of caregivers, a focus on predictive indices, such as objective or subjective burden, may represent too narrow a view. In fact, researchers and clinicians may be better off examining the overall array of stressors confronting the caregiver, who has other worries and concerns, in addition to that entailed by the presence of a dependent parent or sibling. At the same time, it should also be kept in mind that the more focused measures also contributed significantly to the prediction of caregiver morale, and certainly are worthy of consideration.

The Prediction of Anxiety

In the first regression analyses, the criterion was Affect Balance, a measure often used to study psychological well-being in community populations. With Anxiety as the criterion, however, a measure was introduced that assessed indications of psychopathology. The basic demographic characteristics of caregiver and patient, and the characteristics associated with the parent's illness, did not predict anxiety (Table 5.2). Social supports provided only one measure contributing to the regression equation, a measure assessing friendship with someone whose parent also had Alzheimer's disease. As was the case with Affect Balance, this type of friendship also seems to carry weight with feelings of anxiety: those with friends who are also caregivers felt significantly less anxious.

Unlike the prediction of Affect Balance, however, the measures of objective and subjective burden made a significant contribution. As a set, these measures accounted for 9% of the variance in anxiety. Most important were two indicators of subjective burden. Persons who felt more guilt over the care of their parent, and who also felt uncertain about what to do, were higher in anxiety. Similarly, caregivers who felt embarrassed by their parent's behavior in public were likely to feel anxiety.

Once again, however, it was the non-Alzheimer's disease related events and hassles that made the greatest contribution. As was true in the prediction of morale, work events, work hassles, and hassles with social relationships

Table 5.2 Hierarchical Regression Predicting Anxiety

Set #	Zero Correlation	Beta	R^2 Change	Total R^2	MR
1. *Basic demographics*					
Finances ok at end of month	−.12	−.12			
Gender of caregiver	.11	.11	.03	.03	.16
2. *Parent characteristics*					
None relevant					
3. *Social supports*					
Have friends with AD parents	−.14	−.14	.02*	.05	.22***
4. *Objective/subjective burden*					
Burden of parental demands	.05	.04			
Burden of guilt, uncertainty	.28	.27			
Burden of social embarrassment[1]	.21	.17	.09***	.14	.37***
5. *Events and hassles*					
Work events	.23	.24			
Hassles in social relations[2]	−.33	−.30			
Work hassles[2]	−.36	−.27	.20***	.34	.58***

[1] Reverse scored for this table.
[2] Low score indicates more hassles.   *$p = .10$;   **$p = .05$;   ***$p = .01$.

were associated with greater anxiety. Together they accounted for approximately 20% of the variance in anxiety of caregivers. The contribution of these variables is made especially interesting because it was these same stressors that accounted for the greatest proportion of variance in Affect Balance.

The Prediction of Depression

As was the case for Affect Balance and Anxiety, the regression of depression on stressors and mediators produced a highly significant predictive equation. In this case, the equation accounted for a respectable 49% of the variance in caregiver depression.

To begin by examining the contribution of basic demographic characteristics, this set of variables was significantly associated with depression (Table 5.3). The variables making a significant contribution included income and gender of the caregiver: those in poorer financial circumstances, and women, were more likely to report depressive symptoms. Such findings are

Table 5.3 Hierarchical Regression Predicting Depression

Set #	Zero Correlation	Beta	R^2 Change	Total R^2	MR
1. *Basic demographics*					
Finances ok at end of month	−.17	−.17			
Gender of caregiver	.18	.18	.06***	.06	.25***
2. *Parent characteristics*					
Contact with AD parent	.14	.12	.02	.08	.28***
3. *Social supports*					
N: close kin living nearby	−.19	−.19	.04**	.11	.34***
4. *Objective/subjective burden*					
Burden of guilt, uncertainty	.37	.36			
Burden of social embarrassment[1]	.24	.15			
Burden of parental demands	.06	−.11	.15***	.27	.52***
5. *Events and hassles*					
Work events	.20	.21			
Hassles with spouse/partner[2]	−.37	−.32			
Hassles in social relations[2]	−.33	−.26			
Work hassles[2]	−.38	−.20	.23***	.49	.70***

[1] Reverse scored for this table.
[2] Low score indicates more hassles.   *p = .10; **p = .05; ***p = .01.

hardly surprising, and are in accord with the general literature on both depression and psychological symptomatology in general (e.g., Chiriboga, 1984; Derogatis & Clearly, 1977; Pearlin, 1982), and for caregivers (e.g., Pruchno & Resch, 1989).

Characteristics of the parent's illness were not significantly related to depression; and when the investigation turned to social supports, the only association with depression was that caregivers with more kin living nearby were significantly less depressed. However, the burden scales did make an important contribution, accounting for 15% of the variance in caregiver depression. The two measures that seemed most important indicated that when the caregiver feels burdened by a combination of guilt and uncertainty, or when he or she feels embarrassed in public by the parent's behavior, depression is more likely.

A third measure of subjective burden, that of unreasonable parental demands, was also involved in the predictive equation. Although involved only to a minor extent, it is worth noting because in the zero-order correlation there was no relationship. However, in the context of the other variables, a suppressed relationship emerged: caregivers who felt their parent made unreasonable demands were less depressed. One explanation may be that perceiving the parent to be unreasonably demanding makes it easier for caregivers to distance themselves from the situation.

Despite the contribution of both demographic and caregiver-related measures, the greatest amount of variance continued to be accounted for by general indices of stress. And, once again, caregivers with greater numbers of work events, more work hassles, and more hassles with social relationships came out as more depressed. One new contributor was spousal hassles: those reporting hassles with their spouse were significantly more depressed.

Some Final Comments

We began this chapter by presenting a theoretical rationale for studying the stressors of caregiving from a broadened perspective, and then proceeded to examine empirical support for this perspective. Analyses with all three criteria of stress response strongly suggested that stressors play an important role in the well-being of caregivers, and that these stressors are not restricted to those that pertain directly to the caregiving role. The results demonstrated that general kinds of stressors, especially those of the hassles type and those dealing with work and social relationships, were most strongly associated with indices of well-being. Such findings bring to mind Freud's apocryphal but enlightening statement (e.g., Hale, 1980) that issues dealing with love and work may be the keys to understanding human nature. The findings also suggest that chronic problems arising from the caregiver role may provide the context for stress overload. In other words, under conditions of chronic strain in one area of life, the individual may begin to fall apart in other areas which, in turn, may exacerbate the basic problem.

To expand on this last point, there seems to be at least two ways in which stress build-up may lead to crisis (Chiriboga, 1989a). In one, we experience a piling up of stressor events that leads to a feeling of overload or crisis. Another, perhaps more insidious, way may involve the individual experiencing stressors that begin to cross over from a particular role, such as caregiving, to work, family, hobbies, and so forth. At a certain point, the individual may be experiencing just about as much stress as he or she can tolerate in all sectors. At that point, any additional stressor may lead to a condition we might refer to as the "Camel's Back Syndrome." Little stressors have built up, and their cumulative load may not even be recognized at the conscious level. The last stressor, perhaps one that seems actually to be relatively minor, such as the care recipient refusing to eat, then acts to trigger all the pent up emotion. It is, in fact, the proverbial "straw that broke the camel's back."

The stressors of caregiving, of course, do not necessarily lead to crisis conditions. In our research, we have encountered individuals heavily stressed in the caregiver part of life but with normal loads in all others. Such people seem to be doing extremely well from a phenomenological point of view. Whether by accident, fate, or skill, they have managed to "contain" the crisis of caregiving. We also encounter, on occasion, individuals who react to the conditions imposed by a dependent parent with a sense of challenge and who, in fact, seem to thrive in the situation. The fact that being the primary caregiver was associated with higher morale in the regression analyses, but was completely unrelated to morale when simple correlations were considered, illustrates the complexity of considering caregiving. These last results suggest that having the primary responsibility for the parent can, under certain conditions, be an advantage, although in the general case the more important considerations are levels of stress experienced by the caregiver, length of time the parent has been ill, and so forth.

Whether the reaction is one of crisis or challenge, the literature and our own results suggest the importance of a careful and comprehensive assessment of the stress context faced by caregivers. Given the relevance of both general and caregiver-specific stressors in predicting the three examples of stress responses included in the study, one conclusion that may be drawn is that health professionals concerned and involved with adult child caregivers might wish to consider the use of a multiple instrument approach to assessing stress in their subjects and clients. While, to date, most instruments designed to assess the stress loads of caregivers have focused almost exclusively on caregiving itself, a number of well constructed and psychometrically sound measures of hassles and other minor events (e.g., Chiriboga & Cutler, 1980; Lazarus & Folkman, 1984; Zautra, Guarnaccia, Reich, & Dohrenwend, 1988), life events (e.g. Lewinsohn, Mermelstein, Alexander, & MacPhillamy, 1985; Murrell, Norris, & Grote, 1988), and chronic strains (e.g., Pearlin, 1982) are readily available (see also Chiriboga, 1989b).

Knowing only the individual's level of stress exposure, however, will not by itself reveal the whole story of how well the caregiver is faring. For example, consistent with the general literature on their role as a stress mediator (e.g., Pearlin, 1982), social supports were directly associated with well-being on all three indicators of stress response. In other words, the more supports available, the better off the caregiver was.

The findings also suggest the importance of time and context. For example, in the prediction of Affect Balance, one contributing variable assessed how long the parent had presented obvious signs and symptoms of Alzheimer's disease. The fact that longer durations of illness were related to higher morale or Affect Balance might appear almost contraintuitive. That is, it would seem obvious that the longer the illness had been manifest, the lower should be the morale of the caregiver. A frequent comment by adult children who attend a geriatric clinic directed by Weiler, for example, concerns how terrible it is to see valued and loved parents gradually lose their individuality and vitality. In fact, however, longer durations of illness were found in this study to associate with higher morale.

Of the many possible reasons for the illness–morale association, one that was brought up by subjects themselves, in their anecdotal comments and in response to questions about the stresses of caregiving, is that in the later stages of the disease the parent makes fewer demands on the caregiver, either because the patient was already institutionalized or because the patient was essentially bedfast and therefore relatively more easy to manage. This interpretation parallels a conclusion of Haley and Pardo (1987), who reported evidence that the stresses imposed upon caregivers may peak during the intermediate phases of Alzheimer's disease, when the patient is still active and possibly more agitated or belligerent.

The role of illness duration highlights once again the fact that caregiving is not a single event but a long and complex process in which many problems, both temporary and lasting, may arise at any given moment, not that many caregivers will present as incapacitated, or as being in crisis. Overall, our findings emphasize the utility of employing more generalized models of stress in studying or attempting to understand the situations in which caregivers find themselves. In particular, the hypothesis was supported that to best understand the conditions affecting the well-being of caregivers, a broad predictive net must be cast. Stressors involved in social relations generally, and in the work context, demonstrated particular salience for levels of psychological well-being. But perhaps the overall conclusion that can be reached on the basis of the data presented is that caregivers are individuals in their own right, not simply caregivers, and that the factors that govern their lives are multiple. Some are unique to the caregiver context, others transcend that context.

References

Baltes, P. B., & Baltes, M. (1980). Plasticity and variability in psychological aging: Methodological and theoretical issues. In C. Guerski (Ed.), *Aging and the CNS*. Berlin: Schering.

Biegel, D.E., Shore, B.K., & Gordon, E. (1984). *Building support networks for the elderly: Theory and applications*. Beverly Hills, CA: Sage.

Bradburn, N.M. (1969). *The structure of psychological well-being*. Hawthorne, NY: Aldine.

Bradburn, N.M., & Caplovitz, D. (1965). *Reports on happiness*. Hawthorne, NY: Aldine.

Brody, E.M. (1985). Parent care as a normative family stress. *The Gerontologist*, 25(1), 19-29.

Brown, G. W., & Andrews, B. (1986). Social support and depression. In M. H. Appley & R. Turmbull (Eds.), *Dynamics of stress: Physiological, psychological and social perspectives*. New York: Plenum.

Brown, G.W., Bifulco, A., Harris, T., & Bridge, L. (1986). Life stress, chronic subclinical symptoms and vulnerability to clinical depression. *Journal of Affective Disorders*, *11*(1), 1-119.

Brown, G. W., & Harris, T. (1978). *Social origins of depression: A study of psychiatric disorder in women*. London: Tavistock.

Chiriboga, D.A. (1977). Life event weighting systems: A comparative analysis. *Journal of Psychosomatic Research, 21*, 422-425.

Chiriboga, D. A.(1984). Social stressors as antecedents of change. *Journal of Gerontology, 39*(4), 468-477.

Chiriboga, D.A. (1989a). Stress and loss in middle-age. In R.A. Kalish (Ed.), *Midlife loss: Coping strategies* (pp. 42-88). Newbury Park, CA: Sage.

Chiriboga, D. A. (1989b). The measurement of stress exposure in later life. In K. Markides (Ed.), *Aging, stress, social supports and health*. New York: John Wiley.

Chiriboga, D.A., & Cutler, L. (1980). Stress and adaptation: Life span perspectives. In L. Poon (Ed.), *Aging in the 1980s: Psychological issues*. Washington, DC: American Psychological Association.

Derogatis, L.R., & Cleary, P.A. (1977). Confirmation of the dimensional structure of the Symptoms Checklist-90: A study in construct validation. *Journal of Clinical Psychology, 33* (4), 981-989.

Dohrenwend, P. B. (1986). Note on a program of research on alternative social psychological models of relationships between life stress and psychopathology. In M. H. Appley & R. Turmbull (Eds.), *Dynamics of stress: Physiological, psychological and social perspectives*. New York: Plenum.

Duke University Center for the Study of Aging and Human Development. (1978). *Multidimensional functional assessment: The OARS Methodology*. Durham, NC: Duke University.

Elder, G. H., Jr. (1981). Historical experience in the later years. In T. K. Hareven (Ed.), *Patterns of aging*. New York: Guilford.

Elliott, G.R., & Eisdorfer, C. (Eds.). (1982). *Stress and human health: Analysis and implications of research*. New York: Springer.

George, L. (1987). Life events. In G. L. Maddox (Ed.), *The encyclopedia of aging*. New York: Springer.

Gergen, K. J. (1977). Stability, change, and change in human development. In N. Datan & L. H. Ginsberg (Eds.), *Life span development psychology*. New York: Academic Press.

Hale, N. (1980). Freud's reflections on work and love. In N.J. Smelser, and E.H. Erikson (Eds.), *Themes of work and love in adulthood*. Cambridge, MA: Harvard University Press.

Haley, W.E., & Pardo, K.M. (1987). *Relationship of stage of dementia to caregiver stress and coping*. Paper presented at 95th annual convention of the American Psychological Association, New York.

Holmes, T., & Rahe, R. (1967). The Social Readjustment Rating Scale. *Journal of Psychosomatic Research, 11*, 213-218.

Kaplan, N. M. (1985). *Clinical psychology*. Baltimore: Williams & Wilkins.

Lazarus, R.S., & Folkman, S. (1984). *Stress, appraisal and coping*. New York: Springer.

Lewinsohn, P. M., Mermelstein, R. M., Alexander, C., & MacPhillamy, D. J. (1985). The Unpleasant Events Scale: A scale for the measurement of aversive events. *Journal of Clinical Psychology, 41*(4), 483-498.

Lynch, J.J. (1977). *The broken heart: The medical consequences of loneliness*. New York: Basic Books.

Monat, A., & Lazarus, R. S. (1985). Psychoanalytic perspectives on normality. In D. Offer & M. Sabshin (Eds.), *Normality and the life cycle: A critical integration*. New York: Basic Books.

Montgomery, R. J. V., Gonyea, J. G., & Hooyman, N. R. (1985). Caregiving and the experience of subjective and objective burden. *Family Relations, 34* (1), 19-26.

Murrell, S.A., Norris, F.H., & Grote, C. (1988). Life events in older adults. In L.H. Cohen (Ed.), *Life events and psychological functioning: Theoretical and methodological issues* (pp. 96-122). Newbury Park, CA: Sage.

Ory, M.G., Williams, T.F., Emer, M., Lebowitz, B., Rabins, P., Salloway, J., Sluss-Radbaugh, T., Wolff, E., & Zarit, S. (1985). Families, informal supports, and Alzheimer's disease: Current research and future agendas. *Research on Aging, 7* (4), 623-644.

Paykel, E. S. (1982). Life events and early environment. In E. S. Paykel (Ed.), *Handbook of affective disorders*. New York: Guilford.

Pearlin, L.I. (1982). The social contexts of stress. In L. Goldberger & S. Breznitz (Eds.), *Handbook of stress: Theoretical and clinical aspects*. New York: Free Press.

Pearlin, L. I. (1985). Life strains and psychological distress among adults. In A. Monat & R. S. Lazarus (Eds.), *Stress and coping: An anthology (2nd ed.)*. New York: Columbia University Press.

Pruchno, R.A., & Resch, N.L. (1989). Husbands and wives as caregivers: Antecedents of depression and burden. *The Gerontologist, 29* (2), 159-165.

SPSS-X user's guide (3rd ed). (1988). Chicago: SPSS.

Selye, H. (1956). *The stress of life*. New York: McGraw-Hill.

Springer, D., & Brubaker, T.H. (1984). *Family caregivers and dependent elderly: Minimizing stress and maximizing independence*. Beverly Hills, CA: Sage.

Stein, M., & Schleifer, S. J. (1985). Frontiers of stress research: Stress and immunity. In M.R. Zales (Ed.), *Stress in health and disease*. New York: Brunner/Mazel.

Wan, T.H. (1982). *Stressful life events, social support networks and gerontological health*. Lexington, MA: D.C. Heath.

Zarit, S.H., Orr, N.K., & Zarit, J.M. (1985). *The hidden victims of Alzheimer's disease: Families under stress*. New York: New York University Press.

Zautra, A. J., Guarnaccia, C.A., Reich, J.W., & Dohrenwend, B.P. (1988). The contribution of small events to stress and distress. In L.H. Cohen (Ed.), *Life events and psychological functioning: Theoretical and methodological issues* (pp. 123-148). Newbury Park, CA: Sage.

6

Service Use and
The Caregiving Experience

Does Alzheimer's Disease Make a Difference?

RHONDA J. V. MONTGOMERY
KARL KOSLOSKI
EDGAR BORGATTA

The past decade has seen a rapid increase in the number of publications and studies focusing on the family role in long-term care. This interest has stemmed from growing numbers of elders with chronic illnesses and a growing awareness of the important role that family members have in providing care for these elders. While the early research focused on families providing care to elders suffering from a wide range of disabilities, more recent work has shown an increasing emphasis on families caring for elders suffering from Alzheimer's disease (e.g., George & Gwyther, 1986; Safford, 1980; Zarit, Reever, & Bach-Peterson, 1980; Zarit & Zarit, 1982; see also Morycz, 1985, for a review).

The intensive focus on caregivers of Alzheimer's victims has undoubtedly stemmed from three forces. First, the drastic consequences of this debilitating disease are so alarming that they have prompted clinicians and those responsible for policy development to sympathize with family members who are caring for Alzheimer's patients. Second, Alzheimer's victims have been brought into clinical settings in numbers that provide a sufficient data base for study. And third, numerous government and grassroots movements have brought the plight of such families to the attention of policy makers. This increasing attention is evidenced by state and federal legislation mandating the development of service demonstration programs and the corresponding requests for proposals. For example, in the Omnibus Budget Reconciliation Act of 1986, Congress allocated $40 million for the Medicare Alzheimer's Disease Demonstration to fund up to 10 projects (Section 9342 of Public Law 99-509 [OBRA-86]). As a consequence, there has been an emergence of programs designated specifically for families dealing with Alzheimer's disease and related disorders. Implicit in these programs is the assumption that those families caring for members having Alzheimer's disease are in especially difficult situations that require targeted services.

There is no definitive empirical evidence that caring for family members with Alzheimer's disease or other cognitive impairments is more difficult or stressful than caring for family members with other types of impairment. Several patterns, however, have been reported that would suggest such a difference, at least for persons in later stages of dementia. The most widely documented effects of caregiving on caregivers have been emotional stress, or subjective burden, and restrictions on time or activities, which are sometimes referred to as objective burden (Horowitz, 1985; Montgomery, 1989). Because elders in early stages of cognitive impairment may require less physical care than elders with other impairments, the caregiving burden initially may be less. But as their dementia progresses, their ability to perform even routine self-care tasks diminishes, making the caregiving task as difficult as that for other types of impairment. Additionally, progressive cognitive impairment is also likely to be accompanied by impaired social functioning and disruptive behavior (Miller, 1977). As a consequence, caregivers of family members with cognitive impairments are likely to experience greater stress (Deimling & Bass, 1986), and a spiraling process ensues in which the caregiver feels a need for increased vigilance resulting in, perhaps, even greater stress. Thus, the expectation that caregivers of cognitively impaired family members experience greater difficulties in caregiving is intuitively plausible.

The purpose of this study was to determine whether the caregiving experience of family members who care for elders with Alzheimer's disease or other mental impairments differs from that of caregivers assisting elders with noncognitive impairments. In particular, analyses were conducted to determine if the type of impairment of an elder is related to the type and extent of caregiving tasks, the caregiver's subjective experiences, and the use of formal services.

Method

Study Participants

Data were collected as part of a larger study on family caregiving and intervention programs conducted in King County (Greater Seattle), Washington (Montgomery & Borgatta, 1989). A total of 541 family units volunteered for participation. For purposes of the study, family units were dyads composed of an elder and a family member who served as the primary caregiver for the elder. When possible, interviews were conducted individually with members of each dyad on two separate occasions 12 months apart. Approximately half of the elders were unable to be interviewed due to mental impairment. Data for these persons were obtained from the caregivers.

Diagnostic Groups

For the analyses reported here, caregivers were placed into three categories corresponding to the type of impairment they reported for elders. At Time 1, 97 of the caregivers reported that the elder for whom they cared had been diagnosed as having Alzheimer's disease. Another 23 reported that, currently, there was a strong suspicion that the elder had Alzheimer's disease, but formal medical diagnosis had not yet been made. The 120 individuals in these two groups were combined to form the "Alzheimer's Probable" group.[1]

The second category of the independent variable was composed of 131 individuals who suffered some cognitive impairment, but for whom Alzheimer's was not a presumed cause. Specifically, respondents were asked whether or not there was any problem with the elder's memory. Responses were coded on a 6-point scale ranging from "no impairment" to "serious problem, severly limiting." Elders who were not identified as Alzheimer's victims, but who were reported to have moderate to severe limitation due to memory dysfunction (scores of 4–6 on a 6-point scale) comprised the second category.

The third and final category in the independent variable was composed of 194 individuals for whom no cognitive impairment was indicated, and Alzheimer's disease was not diagnosed or suspected. In all, 96 of the 541 elders were of uncertain status due to incomplete information. These individuals were omitted from the present analyses since classification in any of the three groups would have been extremely tenuous.

It should be underscored that because the contact with the respondents was a normal research contact and not a medical contact, the information available for classification into the categories of the independent variable was restricted to that directly available from the respondents. While there is a possibility of having medical diagnostic categories clinically defined which are current and acceptable to the medical community, these were not available to the researchers. This limitation need not be viewed as problematic. Rather, it is necessary to emphasize the observation of W. I. Thomas that reality is entirely defined by the perceptions of persons involved. Thus, presumably, those who identify their impaired elder as having been diagnosed with Alzheimer's disease will treat them accordingly. Similarly, those caregivers who suspect Alzheimer's disease will respond in accord with their beliefs, as will persons reporting their elder to be mentally impaired. Of course, caregivers who have not raised Alzheimer's disease as a viable diagnosis will certainly operate under their own *definition of the situation.* In short, it is argued that it is not the diagnosis per se that is important, but the perception of the presence of the diagnosis that is likely to affect caregivers' behaviors. This is particularly true when we are interested in studying utilization of services created for populations with specific diseases. It does not really matter whether an individual has received an accurate diagnosis when they begin to seek services; it is only important to know what diagnosis it is that they assume to be true, and which guides their caregiving behavior.

Dependent Variables and Covariates

Background information was collected on elders' age, sex, marital status, living arrangement, and income. Information was also collected concerning the extent of elders' informal social contacts, activities of daily living (ADL), self-reported health, including how dependent the elder is on others for help, and their relationship to their caregiver.

Activities of daily living were measured using 12 items on a 3-point scale. Two indices of ADL were constructed based on a principal components factor analysis. Personal Care ADLs comprised items such as bathing, using the toilet, moving in and out of bed or chairs, and eating. Household Task ADLs comprised items such as shopping for groceries or clothes, using transportation to places out of walking distance, preparing meals, and doing housework.

Informal caregiving activities were assessed with a 27-item inventory of caregiving tasks that asks about the amount of time a caregiver spends performing each task per week. A principal components factor analysis was conducted for these items resulting in four factors, from which corresponding indices were constructed. Meal Tasks included three household chores performed for the elder: shopping, preparing meals, and cleaning up after meals. Banking Tasks consisted of assistance with filling out forms, banking, and taking care of legal matters. Transportation Tasks consisted of five items concerned with transporting the elder to appointments, to visit friends, and accompanying the elder while shopping, doing errands, or going to appointments. Personal Care Tasks included changing bed linens and assisting the elder in dressing, bathing, toilet, and hair care.

Caregiver burden was assessed by two indices. Objective burden was represented by changes in the caregiver's life-style in four general areas: time spent for recreation and vacation, time for their own work, time spent with friends and relatives, and time to themselves for solitary activities. Subjective burden was a summary score constructed from five items including stress in the relationship, feeling manipulated by the elder, nervousness/depression, and excessive demands made by the elder.

Caregiver morale was assessed using a 31-item index that asked respondents how often they have felt lonely, anxious, optimistic about life, in good spirits, depressed, and so on. Principal components factor analysis identified 25 items as sharing a common underlying structure, and these were combined to form a single score ($\alpha = .94$).

The *quality of the relationship* between elder and caregiver was assessed using two separate indices constructed from the factor groupings of pooled items. The first measure consisted of items tapping the caregiver's sense of closeness, love, affection, liking, devotion, and attachment to the care-recipient. The second measure reflected the caregiver's sense of duty or obligation toward the elder and included such indicators as social expectations, moral obligations, duty, and perceptions of responsibility. Both measures were found to have reasonably high coefficients of reliability ($\alpha = .89$ and .81, respectively).

The final set of dependent variables was constructed by assessing the number of days that elders had used 15 different types of formal services in the past month: general or psychiatric hospital use, group meals, senior center, physical or inhalation therapy, home health care, transportation services, chore services, mental health services, physician services, speech therapy, adult day care, congregate care, and nursing home care.

Data collection was part of a larger, ongoing, longitudinal study of caregiving in which caregivers had been providing care for varying lengths of time. Using two interviews 12 months apart, it is possible to obtain a temporally extended look at the caregiving career of caregivers with elders suffering from differing types of disabilities. Since the three diagnostic groupings in the study have different trajectories in terms of prognosis and behavioral limitations, service needs are likely to change differentially for families of each type. In this sense, the second measurement time serves as a replication that reflects these changes in the sample.

Results

During the course of the 12-month study, 190 elders (43% of the sample) either died or were placed in nursing homes. This attrition was nonrandom across groups, making the samples of participants substantially different at the two measurement times. Results are therefore reported separately for each measurement time. Comparisons among the three groups of impaired elders are made in terms of (a) background and demographic characteristics; (b) experiences of the caregivers, including the types of tasks they perform and perceptions of burden; and (c) formal service use.

Time 1

Background Characteristics

A comparison of background characteristics serves not only a descriptive function, but may suggest competing explanations for differential service use in addition to that of the diagnostic groupings. That is, if differences in service utilization do exist between groups, the differences may be due to this initial nonequivalence on dimensions related to service use rather than to cognitive impairment per se.

Significant differences on background characteristics among the three diagnostic groups are shown in Table 6.1. The groups were found to differ on age, marital status, relationship of elder to the caregiver (i.e., spouse vs. child), living arrangement, and self-ratings of health and dependence on others.

Members of the cognitively impaired non-Alzheimer's group were approximately three years older on the average than members of the other two groups. The health of the elders in the two non-Alzheimer's groups was reported to be poorer than for those suffering from Alzheimer's. However, this difference was statistically significant only for the cognitively impaired non-Alzheimer's group. Also, these differences were not reflected in the two ADL measures. Given these findings, it seems somewhat incongruous that the two cognitively impaired groups were also seen as being less dependent upon others than the noncognitively impaired group. One possible explanation is that "dependence" is being defined primarily in terms of overt physi-

Table 6.1   Differences in Elder Characteristics by Type of Impairment (Time 1)

Characteristic	Alzheimer's Probable		Other Cognitive Impairment (Non-Alzheimer's)		No Cognitive Impairment	
	N	% of Group	N	% of Group	N	% of Group
Age*						
< 60	0	0	2	1.5	1	0.5
60–69	15	12.5	4	3.1	19	9.8
70–79	48	40.0	32	24.4	67	34.5
80–89	44	36.7	65	49.6	74	38.1
90–99	13	10.8	24	18.3	31	16.0
100+	0	0	4	3.1	2	1.1
Total	120	100.0	131	100.0	194	100.0
Mean/SD:	79.6/7.5		83.4/8.7		80.5/8.5	
Marital Status*						
Single	3	2.5	2	1.5	3	1.6
Married	60	50.0	56	42.7	61	31.4
Divorced	9	7.5	3	3.3	7	3.6
Separated	1	0.8	0	0	2	1.0
Widowed	47	39.2	70	53.5	121	62.4
Total	120	100.0	131	100.0	194	100.0
Generation of Caregiver*						
Spouse	54	48%	38	32%	50	27%
Child	58	52%	79	68%	133	73%
Total	112	100%	117	100%	183	100%
Caregiver Lives with Elder*						
Yes	97	81%	102	78%	133	69%
No	23	19%	29	22%	61	31%
Total	120	100%	131	100%	194	100%
Elder's Health Rating*						
1. Perfect	3	2.5	0	0	6	3.1
2. Very good	31	25.8	18	13.7	27	13.9
3. Good	30	25.0	31	23.7	56	28.9
4. Fair	24	20.0	38	29.0	57	29.4
5. Not good at all	32	26.7	44	33.6	48	24.7
Total	120	100.0	131	100.0	194	100.0
Mean/SD:	3.4/1.2		3.8/1.1		3.6/1.1	
How Dependent Is Elder on Others*						
1. Very dependent	15	12.6	8	6.1	27	13.9
2. Somewhat	11	9.2	11	8.4	26	13.5
3. Not very	19	16.0	31	23.7	54	27.8
4. Not dependent	74	62.2	81	61.8	87	44.8
Total	119	100.0	131	100.0	194	100.0
Mean/SD:	3.3/1.1		3.4/0.9		3.0/1.1	

*Differences between groups are statistically significant ($p < .05$).

cal health and hospital use. As will be seen in a subsequent section on formal service use, the individuals rated "most dependent" also had higher rates of past hospital use.

The three diagnostic groups also differed significantly on marital status at the outset of the study with a higher proportion of Alzheimer's victims married and a lower proportion widowed relative to the other two groups. An important implication of these differences in marital status is that a significantly higher proportion of caregivers for Alzheimer's victims are spouses of the individual they are caring for than are the caregivers of other group members. Indeed, a dummy variable contrasting married versus widowed elders with caregiver status had a correlation exceeding 0.8. Also, a significantly higher proportion of caregivers live with Alzheimer's and other cognitively impaired elders than with the noncognitively impaired elders (roughly 80% for the two cognitively impaired groups vs. 69% for the noncognitively impaired).

No statistically significant differences between the three impairment types were found for gender, income, the number of informal social contacts they have each week, their personal care ADLs, or household task ADLs at Time 1.

The Caregiving Experience

Table 6.2 shows the estimates made by informal caregivers of the time they spend providing specific services. Two major differences in the types of services provided to elders were observed among the impairment groups at Time 1. The first difference is in the amount of time spent shopping, cooking, and cleaning up after meals (Meals). On the average, caregivers were spending approximately 16.5 hours per week on these tasks for the two cognitively impaired groups, but only 12 hours per week for the noncognitively impaired group. One likely explanation for these differences between groups on the Meals index can be traced to preexisting differences between groups in marital status and caregiver status (i.e., spouse vs. child). Specifically, a higher proportion of the cognitively impaired individuals in the present study were married at Time 1 than the noncognitively impaired; and as a consequence, the proportion of spouses acting as caregivers was higher for these individuals as well. Spouses living in the household generally have greater opportunity for meal preparation and related tasks than caregivers who do not live in the household. An analysis of covariance using hierarchical multiple regression (Kerlinger & Pedhazur, 1973) was conducted to evaluate this possibility. When scores on the Meals variable are initially adjusted for preexisting background differences in age, generation of caregiver, living arrangement, and elder's health and dependence upon others, dummy vari-

Table 6.2 Caregiver Experiences/Activities by Type of (Elder) Impairment

Characteristic	N	Alzheimer's Probable Mean/SD	N	Other Cognitive Impairment (Non-Alzheimer's) Mean/SD	N	No Cognitive Impairment Mean/SD
Type of Service Provided						
Meals = hrs. (shopping + preparing meals + cleaning up after meals)						
(Time 1)*	119	16.4/12.2	131	16.5/11.8	193	12.2/11.1
(Time 2 including nursing home)	92	10.3/13.3	86	11.2/13.0	137	9.8/12.0
(Time 2 excluding nursing home)	53	16.2/14.4	62	14.1/13.4	118	11.2/12.3
Banking = hrs. (legal matters + writing checks + banking + filling forms)						
(Time 1)	118	3.2/2.7	131	3.2/3.7	192	2.9/4.1
(Time 2 including nursing home)	92	3.8/5.6	86	2.9/3.2	137	2.7/3.2
(Time 2 excluding nursing home)	53	3.8/5.0	62	2.9/3.5	118	2.8/3.4
Transportation = hrs. (taking elder to appts. + visit friends + accompany on errands + shopping + waiting for appts.)						
(Time 1)	118	7.4/5.9	131	6.6/5.3	193	6.1/4.8
(Time 2 including nursing home)	92	4.7/5.1	86	5.0/4.3	137	4.4/3.7
(Time 2 excluding nursing home)	53	6.4/5.5	62	6.0/4.3	118	4.8/3.8
Personal Care = hrs. (bathing + hair care + dressing + bed linens + toilet)						
(Time 1)	118	9.3/13.2	131	9.0/11.6	193	7.1/12.7
(Time 2 including nursing home)	92	6.8/11.5	86	6.0/8.7	138	4.4/3.7
(Time 2 excluding nursing home)	53	10.3/13.8	62	7.4/9.4	119	6.0/10.0
Number of Months (Combined) Caregiver Has Been Providing the Tasks						
(Time 1)						
Meals	116	203/202	131	178/186	193	163/172
Banking	119	257/251	131	223/228	192	194/221
Transportation	118	226/214	131	211/213	192	223/218
Personal Care	120	67/104	131	75/120	193	79/140
(Time 2)						
Meals	51	209/212	63	175/186	118	141/162
Banking*	54	269/245	63	208/228	118	174/214
Transportation	53	264/233	63	236/230	118	212/230
Personal Care	54	78/136	63	72/118	118	68/128

Table 6.2 continued

	N	Mean/SD	N	Mean/SD	N	Mean/SD
Type of Service Provided						
Subjective Burden						
(Time 1)	120	11.2/2.5	131	10.9/2.8	193	10.6/3.0
(Time 2 including nursing home)	92	7.6/3.1	86	8.6/3.1	138	8.5/3.7
(Time 2 excluding nursing home)	53	9.2/3.9	62	9.1/2.8	119	8.9/3.5
Objective Burden						
(Time 1)	120	15.9/3.6	131	15.5/3.8	193	15.0/3.7
(Time 2 including nursing home)	113	8.0/6.8	126	8.6/5.4	184	8.5/5.6
(Time 2 excluding nursing home)	53	12.8/6.1	62	12.1/4.4	119	11.1/4.8
Morale						
(Time 1)	119	50.1/12.8	130	52.1/10.4	190	51.8/12.4
(Time 2 including nursing home)	112	53.2/12.6	124	55.6/11.2	183	55.8/10.9
(Time 2 excluding nursing home)	52	53.3/12.2	61	55.0/10.8	118	54.5/11.0
Duty/Obligation						
(Time 1)*	120	5.3/1.2	129	4.9/1.7	193	4.6/1.7
(Time 2 including nursing home)	92	4.9/1.4	86	4.7/1.8	128	4.4/1.8
(Time 2 excluding nursing home)	53	4.9/1.5	62	4.8/1.9	119	4.4/1.7
Love/Affection						
(Time 1)	117	14.4/4.0	130	14.3/4.5	193	14.5/3.7
(Time 2 including nursing home)	90	13.7/4.4	86	13.3/5.3	135	14.5/4.4
(Time 2 excluding nursing home)	52	13.2/4.8	62	13.0/5.4	117	14.4/3.7

*Differences between groups are statistically significant ($p < .05$).

ables representing the diagnostic categories failed to produce a significant increment in explained variance. There were no interactions between diagnostic groups and the covariates in this or any of the subsequent analyses, suggesting that the use of a common regression coefficient to adjust for pre-existing differences was appropriate. Also, it should be noted that the marital status dummy variable contrasting married versus widowed elders was not entered as a covariate due to its substantial relationship with generation of the caregiver (r > .8) and attendant problems of multicollinearity. Adding it would have added little to the analysis and logic would suggest that it operates through the caregiver status variable. The analyses of covariance are not reported here due to space considerations and because only the incremental effect for the diagnostic groupings is generally of interest. But of the covariates, the variable representing the generation of the caregiver (spouse vs. child) exerted the largest unique effect on the Meals variable, followed closely by whether or not the caregiver lived with the elder.

The only other difference in caregiver characteristics between impairment groups at Time 1 (Table 6.2) was in the amount of duty/obligation reported by the caregivers, with caregivers in the Alzheimer's group expressing a greater sense of duty/obligation, than caregivers in the other groups. Again, however, when the significant background differences from Table 6.1 are introduced as covariates, the incremental R^2 for diagnostic groups is once again nonsignificant. The apparent difference among diagnostic groups again appears to be a consequence of initial group differences on marital status and the accompanying difference in the relationship of the caregiver to the elder, with spouses indicating a higher sense of duty/obligation than children. It is noteworthy that no differences were found among the caregivers of the three groups in the levels of subjective or objective burden. This finding has important implications for programming and policy issues that will be discussed below.

Formal Service Use

There were only two differences in formal service use among the three diagnostic groups at Time 1: the use of general hospital services, and the use of home health care (see Table 6.3). The differential use of hospital services was characterized by high service use for elders in the noncognitively impaired group compared to the two cognitively impaired groups. These differences persist even controlling for the preexisting differences in background characteristics at Time 1, and thus attribution of these differences to diagnostic groupings remains plausible.

Home health care service shows a slightly different pattern of utilization with impaired non-Alzheimer's and nonmentally impaired elders using such services significantly more than Alzheimer's victims. These differences persist even after adjusting for preexisting differences between groups. Thus, for both home health care and hospital use, diagnostic groupings remain as tenable explanations for differences in rate of use.

Table 6.3 Differences Among Impairment Groups by Use of Specific Services

Characteristic	Alzheimer's Probable		Other Cognitive Impairment (Non-Alzheimer's)		No Cognitive Impairment	
	N	Mean/SD	N	Mean/SD	N	Mean/SD
General Hospital						
(Time 1)*	120	.34/2.10	131	.78/2.64	194	1.71/5.26
(Time 2)	94	.49/1.92	87	.56/3.08	138	.87/3.59
(Time 2 excluding						
nursing home)	54	.59/2.23	63	.42/2.36	119	.71/2.91
Group Meals						
(Time 1)	120	1.40/5.18	131	.86/3.15	194	1.13/4.79
(Time 2)	94	1.22/3.51	87	1.22/3.51	137	.72/3.62
(Time 2 excluding						
nursing home)*	54	2.59/5.70	63	1.68/4.03	118	.83/3.89
Home Health Care						
(Time 1)*	120	.59/1.85	130	1.89/4.84	194	1.57/3.71
(Time 2)	94	.43/1.67	87	.84/3.81	137	.56/2.84
(Time 2 excluding						
nursing home)	54	.74/2.16	63	1.13/4.44	118	.65/3.05
Transportation Service						
(Time 1)	120	.73/3.39	131	.57/2.11	194	.66/2.94
(Time 2)*	94	1.59/4.63	87	.56/2.08	137	.38/1.45
(Time 2 excluding						
nursing home)*	54	2.54/5.83	63	.57/1.94	118	.40/1.55
Adult Day Care						
(Time 1)	120	.58/1.91	131	.41/2.10	194	.27/1.96
(Time 2)*	94	1.73/4.80	87	.59/2.33	138	.12/0.82
(Time 2 excluding						
nursing home)*	54	2.85/6.01	63	.81/2.71	119	.13/0.88
Nursing Home						
(Time 1)	120	.23/1.80	131	.49/3.36	194	.34/2.45
(Time 2)*	94	11.51/14.34	87	7.37/12.82	138	4.09/10.27

Differences between groups are statistically significant ($p < .05$).

One link between hospital use and home health care use may be found in present Medicare eligibility rules. Specifically, in order for home health care to be subsidized by Medicare, the home care must occur no more than three months after discharge. In the present study, the two non-Alzheimer's groups had higher rates of both hospital use and home health care. Thus, hospital use may explain home health use. However, the reason for differences in the rate of hospital use between diagnostic groups is not readily apparent and may simply be due to the self-selection characteristics of the participants.

Time 2

By Time 2, one year later, the pattern of living arrangements of elders had changed substantially. Not surprisingly, the lowest proportion of elders living alone were Alzheimer's victims (3%) compared to the cognitively impaired non-Alzheimer's group (9%) and the noncognitively impaired (15%). In addition, the Alzheimer's group had the highest proportion in nursing homes (34%) relative to the cognitively impaired non-Alzheimer's group (18%) and the noncognitively impaired (10%). It is also noteworthy that the pattern of deaths at Time 2 among the three groups paralleled the self-ratings of health taken at Time 1, with the cognitively impaired non-Alzheimer's group having the highest proportion of deceased (32%) compared to roughly 26% for the noncognitively impaired and 19% for the Alzheimer's victims.

Background Characteristics at Time 2

Given the nonrandom pattern of attrition at Time 2, the three groups were again compared on background and demographic characteristics. As before, the diagnostic groups differed dramatically on marital status, with roughly 40% of the mentally impaired participants being married compared to 23% of the nonmentally impaired elders. As at Time 1, this distribution on the marital status variable is evidenced in differences between groups with respect to the "generation" of the caregiver (i.e., spouse vs. child).

In contrast, self-ratings of dependence on others show a much different pattern at Time 2, with nonmentally impaired elders indicating the least dependence upon others. At Time 1, these elders viewed themselves as being the most dependent. The shift is likely due to selective attrition with a greater proportion of the cognitively impaired being institutionalized between Time 1 and Time 2. The overall level of dependence at Time 2 is also much higher for all three groups, and likely reflects a steady process of deterioration and increasing frailty. As expected, elders remaining in the community at Time 2 were rated as significantly healthier at Time 1 than those who either died or were institutionalized. The fourth and final difference occurred with respect to household task ADLs. At Time 1 there was no difference on this variable. At Time 2, however, both of the non-Alzheimer groups have improved ADL scores; again, this is likely due to selective attrition given the higher proportions of deaths among the more frail elders in these two groups. Unlike Time 1, the remaining participants did not differ in age or self-reported health status.

Characteristics of Caregivers and Informal Service Use at Time 2

It should be noted that the Time 2 analyses of Tables 6.2 and 6.3 are shown with both nursing home placements included and excluded from the sample. This is done because both informal caregiving and formal service use can (and often do) continue even after institutionalization. (One exception to this is the use of nursing home services which could only be conducted using the full sample.)

The only difference in caregiver characteristics among groups at Time 2 is in the length of time that the caregivers have been providing assistance with legal/banking matters (see Banking, Table 6.2). Post hoc comparisons among group means indicated a single significant difference between Alzheimer's victims and the nonmentally impaired elders on this variable. However, when background differences in marital status, generation of caregiver, household task ADLs, and self-reported dependence upon others (i.e., the significant background differences among groups at Time 2) are adjusted for, differences among diagnostic groups in the length of time they have been receiving assistance in Banking matters disappear. Interestingly, there were again no detectable differences among caregivers in subjective or objective burden, morale, or sense of duty/obligation.

Formal Service

Four differences were observed between groups in formal service use at Time 2. Specifically, groups differed in the use of group meals, transportation services, adult day care, and nursing home placement. In each case, Alzheimer's victims used these formal services significantly more than members of the other two groups. These effects for diagnostic grouping persist even after adjusting for background differences at Time 2. Also, these effects were observed for both the full sample and when excluding those in nursing homes. However, the unique effects of diagnostic groups on the various types of service use are weak—never exceeding an 8% increment in explained variance in service use and, in most cases, accounting for only 2 or 3%. Not surprisingly, use of transportation services is not independent of adult day care use; however, the correlation is modest (ϕ = .36) with roughly twice as many elders using transportation as adult day care services.

It is noteworthy that all four of the differences in formal service use occurring at Time 2 were not detected at Time 1. Since Alzheimer's is a chronic progressive disorder, it makes sense that individuals with the disorder will suffer progressive deterioration resulting in the need for increased supervision (e.g., adult day care and transportation). On the other hand, these developmental effects are completely confounded with sample attrition due to death or institutionalization occurring over the course of the study. To gain further insight into the reasons for these changes in utilization over time, we replicated the comparisons from Time 1 using only the subset of elders who were still living in the community at Time 2. If the same differences were observed at Time 1 as Time 2 for these individuals, explaining differences at Time 2 as the result of a developmental process associated with Alzheimer's would be less plausible. However, there were no differences in the use of group meals, transportation services, or adult day care services between groups at Time 1 for this selected subsample. Thus, the possibility of a progressive deterioration of Alzheimer's victims remains a tenable interpretation of the differences observed at Time 2. On the other hand, given the nonexperimental nature of this study, the three diagnostic groups vary not only in mental status, but on myriad other undefined dimensions as well. These other unknown, and perhaps unknowable, differences remain as competing explanations for the differences in service use observed at Time 2.

Discussion

The most pervasive and perhaps most important finding reported in this study is the absence of differences in the majority of the caregiving experiences and use of services among the three comparison groups. These findings call into question any assumptions that might be made about unique service needs of families caring for elders with Alzheimer's disease. For the most part, the data suggest that caregivers have many common experiences regardless of the type of impairment of the elder. Other variables that may be conceived of as contextual variables may be more important factors that define the special needs of a caregiving family than is the type of impairment. In particular, the relationship of the caregiver to the elder (i.e., spouse vs. adult child) and the living arrangement of the caregiver (i.e., same vs. separate household) may be more useful and efficient in identifying caregivers with special needs. For when these variables were entered as covariates at Time 2, only four differences persisted between the diagnostic groups out of a total of 15 comparisons in formal service use and 13 comparisons on dimensions describing the caregiving experience. This is not to say that there are no important differences among the caregiving situations of the three comparison groups, but rather that these differences do not appear to be associated with Alzheimer's disease per se, but with the caregiving context.

These results are consistent with those of a recent study by Birkel (1987). Birkel found no differences among caregivers of demented versus physically impaired elders in morale, in the average amount of time spent caregiving, or in the amount of time spent in various caregiving activities. He did, however, find substantial initial differences between the two groups in household size, composition (i.e., number of children), and disease states and physical health ratings of the elders. These outcomes parallel those of the present study. In addition, Birkel found evidence of differences in the caregiving experience between diagnostic groups. Specifically, he found living arrangement (i.e., household size and composition) to be significantly related to the amount of caregiver strain, with the presence of other residents in the household associated with greater strain for caregivers of physically impaired elders. For caregivers of demented elders, the opposite was true. However, in Birkel's study, there were significant initial background differences between the physically and mentally impaired groups that were uncontrolled, making inferences as to the causes for observed differences between impairment types tenuous.

The implication of such findings for policy is noteworthy. Despite recent trends among policy makers and providers to target support services to caregivers of Alzheimer's patients, it may be more effective, efficient, and equitable to target services using the caregiving context as a criterion rather than a given diagnosis. Certainly it is easier and less costly to assess a caregiver's context than to arrive at a diagnosis of Alzheimer's disease. It would also seem more equitable to provide services to caregivers of similar objective needs despite the direct cause of that need. Because these findings can have such serious implications for policy, it is important to explore two plausible explanations for the findings. The first explanation focuses on the similarities of the three groups of caregivers while the second explanation suggests important differences.

One obvious explanation for the findings of the present study is simply that "caregiving is caregiving," and caregivers tend to use similar types of support services regardless of the specific diagnosis of the elder. This is essentially a restatement of the null hypothesis in the present study. It is the most parsimonious explanation for the present findings in that it requires the fewest assumptions. Thus, while it is clear that there are certain stable relationships between type of impairment (e.g., physical vs. mental impairment) and the experience of caregiving (e.g., caregiver strain or burden), they exist at the bivariate (i.e., zero-order) level. Such relationships serve to foster the belief among observers that caregivers of Alzheimer's victims have special needs. When background differences between Alzheimer's and non-Alzheimer's victims are taken into account, however, many differences in the experience of caregiving disappear. For the most part, these background differences precede any medical diagnosis and, therefore, should be considered causally prior as well.

One might suggest, however, that the differences in background are not random or inexplicable but are, in fact, tied to the diagnoses. That is, they may be due to self-selection of the caregivers into and out of their particular caregiving situations. One possibility is that the effect of Alzheimer's disease on service use is primarily indirect. In such a model, the presence or absence of Alzheimer's disease would affect the caregiving context (e.g., whether the caregiver is a spouse or adult child) which would then influence the use of support services. Data from the present study suggest that there is a pattern associated with the assumption of the caregiving role for Alzheimer's families, and it is this pattern that is reflected in the small number of differences observed. Alzheimer's victims have a much greater proportion of spouses providing care, and it may be the effects of the disease that lead to this selectivity. Nonetheless, even though testing of more elaborate causal models would lead to enhanced understanding of service use patterns, it seems likely that the most efficient targeting of services would still focus on the caregiving context rather than the disease state.

An alternative explanation for the minimal differences in service use among the three groups of caregivers may rest in the temporal pattern of caregiving associated with elders who have differing types of impairments. That is, while the situation of caregivers for elders with the different types of impairment may appear similar in a cross-sectional study, there may be a different trajectory of decline and different pattern of service use if the caregivers are followed over time.

Changes in the composition of the sample from Time 1 to Time 2 support the notion of different developmental trajectories for the three diagnostic groups. The two differences at Time 1 in the use of formal services (i.e., hospital and home health services) suggest less use of services among Alzheimer's victims. This may well reflect the absence of acute conditions of

Alzheimer's victims as compared to the physical impairments of other older persons. By Time 2, however, the initial sample of elders had changed substantially due to death or placement of the most impaired elders in nursing homes. Proportionally, Alzheimer's victims were almost twice as likely to go into nursing homes as the cognitively impaired non-Alzheimer's group, and over three times as likely as those with no cognitive impairments. In contrast, Alzheimer's victims were least likely to be lost to death by Time 2. These outcomes were consistent with ratings of physical health at Time 1. In addition, Alzheimer's victims were described as being the most dependent upon others at Time 2; this is consistent with greater service use (Johnson & Catalano, 1983). Thus, the greater use at Time 2 of group meals, transportation services, adult day care, and nursing home placement among the Alzheimer's group may be seen as an indicator of greater need of Alzheimer's patients associated with their particular trajectory of decline. Furthermore, although the types of tasks caregivers engage in, their sense of burden, and their level of obligation do not tend to be related to the type of impairment, these measures may not tap the difference that caregivers experience in the need for constant supervision or vigilance for elders with differing types of impairments. The fact that these differences do not exist at Time 1 may indicate that this need for vigilance may increase with the progressive deterioration associated with Alzheimer's disease. Ultimately, the need for constant supervision may hasten the institutionalization of the elder.

This possibility that the caregiving experience is substantially different for caregivers of Alzheimer's victims raises an important issue that has serious implications for future research and public policy. Specifically, is there a limit in terms of the amount or types of caregiving that family members can or will provide after which institutionalization becomes almost inevitable? From a research perspective, this question suggests a need to investigate the correlates of institutional placement. Interestingly, preliminary studies in this area suggest that the correlates of institutionalization may be different for demented versus nondemented elders. Such an interaction between "characteristics of the caregiving situation" and "diagnosis of the elder" would support the view that the caregiving careers for caregivers of demented versus nondemented elders is different prior to nursing home placement. For example, Colerick and George (1986) found that the physical health of the elder is not an important predictor of institutionalization for Alzheimer's victims. Only the type of the elder–caregiver relationship (i.e., spouse vs. child) and the caregiver's subjective well-being emerged as significant correlates of institutionalization. In contrast, health and the socioeconomic status of the elder have consistently emerged as predictors from the general population (see Kosloski, Montgomery, & Borgatta, 1988, for a review). Birkel (1987) found that caregivers of demented elders expressed significantly greater negative feelings toward their elders. It also seems likely that demented individuals cannot show appreciation for the help they are given, induce less guilt in the caregiver, and are generally less aware. In any case, identifying variables that may serve to truncate the caregiving career of caregivers (especially caregivers of Alzheimer's victims) and that result in earlier institutionalization should be high on the research agenda. If factors leading to institutionalization are modifiable, knowledge of them may suggest specific types of intervention that can truly assist caregivers of Alzheimer's victims. At this point in time, however, there is little support from previous research or from this study to suggest that support services will prevent institutionalization.

If the caregiving experience as experienced over time is dramatically different between caregivers of Alzheimer's victims and other types of caregivers, the current practice of targeting support services to caregivers of Alzheimer's victims may be seen as practical and appropriate. It might be argued that special services need to be provided to caregivers of Alzheimer's victims to help them delay the decision to institutionalize the elder. This perspective reflects the expectation often held by service-oriented policy makers that more services or new services would make a difference. However, until there is evidence that institutionalization can be so delayed, there remains little support for the expectation that caregivers of Alzheimer's victims will benefit more from services than will caregivers of elders with other types of impairments.

Conclusion

Overall, the data reported here should prompt clinicians, practitioners, and policy makers to be cautious in advocating programs that are restricted to or targeted at caregivers of Alzheimer's victims. The overwhelming evidence is that the caregiving experience is not terribly different for caregivers of Alzheimer's victims who remain in the community than it is for caregivers of elders with other impairments. Even though a few differences in the use of formal services were detected, the unique effect of the diagnostic groupings on the use of the services was very weak. From the perspective of efficient and equitable public policy, this absence of major differences between caregivers of Alzheimer's patients and the caregivers of other impaired elders should raise serious questions about initiatives that employ diagnostic groups as criteria for eligibility. In situations of finite resources where large amounts of public funds are being targeted to a designated group, these funds come at a cost to other groups. In the absence of clear evidence of greater need by caregivers of Alzheimer's patients, there is reason to question this unequal distribution of resources.

On the other hand, more research is clearly needed to guide the development of future policy on ways to assist informal caregivers. This research must move from a simple description of caregiving situations to a deeper understanding of why some individuals are willing to assume the role of caregiver where others will not. In addition, a better understanding must be gained of the conditions that promote an abdication of the caregiving role. One rarely mentioned possibility in the caregiving literature is that it may be impossible to provide enough formal support services to keep elders in the community indefinitely. The results of the present study suggest that this is a possibility that now must be seriously entertained and investigated.

For the time being, the present findings suggest that the needs and experiences of caregivers of Alzheimer's patients who remain in the community are not sufficiently different to defend targeting on the basis of self-perceived need. Instead, the findings point to the context of the caregiving situation as a variable that may be a more fruitful means of explaining differences in the caregiving experience and for designing and targeting programs in the future.

Note

1. It is important to note that initially the 23 suspected cases of Alzheimer's were omitted from the analyses. However, the findings from those analyses parallel those reported, and the two groups were pooled to increase sensitivity of the analyses.

References

Birkel, R. C. (1987). Toward a social ecology of the home-care household. *Psychology and Aging*, *2*, 294-301.

Colerick, E., & George, L. (1986). Predictors of institutionalization among caregivers of patients with Alzheimer's disease. *Journal of the American Geriatrics Society*, *34*, 493-498.

Deimling, G. T., & Bass, D. M. (1986). Symptoms of mental impairment among elderly adults and their effects on family caregivers. *Journal of Gerontology*, *41*, 778-784.

Fillenbaum, G. C. (1975). Reliability and validity of the OARS Multidimensional Functional Assessment Questionnaire. *Multidimensional Functional Assessment: The OARS methodology* (1st ed.). Durham, NC: Duke University, Center for the Study of Aging and Human Development.

George, L. K., & Gwyther, L.P. (1986). Caregiver well-being: A multidimensional examination of family caregivers of demented adults. *The Gerontologist, 26*, 253-259.

Horowitz, A. H. (1985). Family caregiving to the frail elderly. In M. P. Lawton & G. L. Maddox (Eds.), *Annual Review of Gerontology and Geriatrics* (pp.194-246). New York: Springer.

Johnson, C. L., & Catalano, D. J. (1983). A longitudinal study of family supports to impaired elderly. *The Gerontologist, 23*, 612-618.

Katz, S., Ford, A. B., Moskowitz, R. W., Jackson, B. A., & Jaffe, M. W. (1963). Studies of illness in the aged. The index of ADL: A standardized measure of biological and psychosocial function. *Journal of the American Medical Association, 185*, 914-919.

Kerlinger, F. N., & Pedhazur, E. J. (1973). *Multiple regression in behavioral research.* New York: Holt, Rinehart & Winston.

Kosloski, K., Montgomery, R., & Borgatta, E. (1988, November 19-23). *Factors influencing the nursing home placement of the elderly.* Paper presented at the 41st annual meetings of the Gerontological Society of America, San Francisco.

Miller, E. (1977). *Abnormal aging.* London: John Wiley & Sons.

Montgomery, R.J.V. (1989). Investigating caregiver burden. In K.S. Markides & C.L. Cooper (Eds.), *Aging, stress and health.* New York: John Wiley.

Montgomery, R.J.V., and Borgatta, E. (1989). The effects of alternative support strategies on family caregiving. *The Gerontologist, 29*, 457-464.

Morycz, R. K. (1985). Caregiving strain and the desire to institutionalize family members with Alzheimer's disease. *Research on Aging, 7*, 329-361.

Preston, G. A. (1986). Dementia in elderly adults: Prevalence and institutionalization. *Journal of Gerontology, 41*, 261-267.

Safford, F. (1980). A program for families of the mentally impaired elderly. *The Gerontologist, 20*, 656-660.

Zarit, S. H., Reever, K. E., & Bach-Peterson, J. (1980). Relatives of the impaired elderly: Correlates of feelings of burden. *The Gerontologist, 20* (6), 649-655.

Zarit, S. H., & Zarit, J. M. (1982). Families under stress: Interventions for caregivers of senile dementia patients. *Psychotherapy, 19*, 461-471.

7

Absenteeism and Stress Among
Employed Caregivers of the Elderly,
Disabled Adults, and Children

MARGARET B. NEAL
NANCY J. CHAPMAN
BERIT INGERSOLL-DAYTON
ARTHUR C. EMLEN
LINDA BOISE

Only recently have researchers begun exploring the relationships between individuals' work and home responsibilities. Three streams of research have emerged in the literature. One stream of research concerns caregivers of the elderly and their feelings of burden and stress (Horowitz, 1985). Initially, little or no attention was paid to caregivers' employment status. Recent research on these caregivers, however, has begun examining this variable (Brody, Kleban, Johnsen, Hoffman, & Schoonover, 1987). A second stream of research has concentrated on the impact of fulfilling the dual roles of employment and parenting (Crouter, 1984). A third stream of research, appearing in the business and management literature, has examined rates and

AUTHORS' NOTE

The authors are indebted to the following people: Wendy Lebow, for her assistance in data analysis; Darey Shell, for preparing the figures; Maria Talbott and Donna Wagner, for their comments on the manuscript; Paul Koren, for his contributions to the development of the survey instrument; and Patricia Ebert, for her assistance in project management. The data for this manuscript were collected as a part of the Work and Elder Care Project, Regional Research Institute for Human Services and the Institute on Aging, Portland State University, Portland, Oregon, which was funded by the Fred Meyer Charitable Trust.

causes of absenteeism, with family responsibilities (usually whether or not employees have children) as one potential cause (Steers & Rhodes, 1978). This chapter draws upon each of these three areas of research by focusing on the impact of different kinds of caregiving responsibilities on employed caregivers. To date, no studies have compared employees with responsibilities for dependents of distinct types (i.e., children, disabled adults, or elderly persons) with employees not having such responsibilities. Nor have researchers examined the differential impact of various types of dependent care responsibilities on employees. With the increasing recognition of what Crouter (1984) calls the "spillover" from family to work, however, knowledge of the effects of employees' dependent care responsibilities on their work is crucial. Public and corporate policy makers, human resource managers, and social service providers alike will need this information as they attempt to design policies and programs that will ease the conflict between family and work roles.

In an attempt to better inform both policy and practice regarding employed family caregivers, this chapter addresses three questions. First, how do employees with no dependent care responsibilities differ from those with caregiving responsibilities with respect to their levels of absenteeism (i.e., time lost from work) and various types of stress? Second, how do employees with different types of caregiving responsibilities compare with respect to their levels of absenteeism and stress? Third, how do various socioeconomic and job-related characteristics differentially affect employees' levels of absenteeism and stress? Answers to these questions will help to determine whether employees with informal caregiving responsibilities need assistance in their efforts to balance job and family responsibilities and, if so, how these employees might best be helped.

Of interest are four groups of employees: (a) those caring for elderly (age 60 or older) family members or friends; (b) those caring for disabled adults (aged 18 through 59); (c) those having children under the age of 18 in their household; and (d) those having none of the above types of dependent care responsibilities. The following section reviews past research related to each of the three research questions.

Literature Review

Impact of Caregiving Responsibilities

According to Steers and Rhodes (1978), family responsibilities are a major determinant of absenteeism. In addition, time constraints and emotional demands have been found to be substantial for those who both work in paid employment and care for children (Rapaport & Rapaport, 1976), disabled adults (Enright & Friss, 1987), or the elderly (Brody et al., 1987). These separate streams of research suggest that those with dependent care responsibilities carry an extra burden when they fulfill the dual roles of employee and caregiver and led to our first hypothesis: employees with no dependent care responsibilities will experience less absenteeism from work and less stress than those with caregiving responsibilities, whether those responsibilities are for children, disabled adults, or the elderly.

Differences Among Caregiver Types

Because, to date, there has been no systematic attempt to compare employees who are caring informally for children, disabled adults, or elderly, it is necessary to consider research conducted separately on each group. Research on absenteeism suggests that the three groups are likely to experience similar levels of absenteeism. For example, employees who have children in the household (Emlen & Koren, 1984) or large families (Allen, 1980) have a higher incidence of absenteeism. Recent evidence from studies of caregivers for the elderly (Gibeau, Anastas, & Larson, 1986) and disabled adults (Enright & Friss, 1987) also suggests increased absenteeism for these groups due to caregiving, although these studies do not compare caregivers' rates with those of noncaregivers. Researchers studying the effects of caring for children, disabled adults, or the elderly have identified similar stresses for the three caregiver groups. Employees who are parents of minor children, for example, experience financial stress (Oppenheimer, 1982), strains in marital relationships (Whitbourne & Weinstock, 1986), and are more tired and have increased physical ailments, especially those who are employed parents of very young children (Karasek, Gordell, & Lindell, 1987). Similarly, caregivers of the elderly experience health and financial stress (George & Gwyther, 1986) and strains in relationships with other family members (Lebowitz, 1978). For those caring for disabled adults, increased financial burdens (Patterson & McCubbin, 1983) and strained family relationships (Enright & Friss, 1987; Patterson & McCubbin, 1983) have been identified.

These examples suggest that those who are involved in caregiving, whether for children, disabled adults, or the elderly, face similar strains. Due to the lack of systematic research on the differences between employed and nonemployed caregivers, it is unknown whether employment status has a differential effect on the three kinds of caregivers. In the absence of evidence to the contrary, we hypothesized no differences among the employed caregiver groups with respect to absenteeism and stress.

Impact of Personal, Socioeconomic and Job-Related Characteristics

A number of socioeconomic and job-related characteristics have been found to influence employees' levels of absenteeism and stress. Among these characteristics are the employee's gender, partner status, household income, job status, occupation, and flexibility of work schedule.

Women, in general, tend to have higher rates of absenteeism than men (Klein, 1986) and to report more difficulty in combining employment and caregiving (Crouter, 1984). Women's greater responsibility for caregiving, whether for children (Pleck, 1985; Walker & Woods, 1976), adults (Enright & Friss, 1987), or the elderly (Stone, Cafferata, & Sangl, 1987), may account for a significant portion of increased absenteeism and stress.

The presence of a spouse or other partner in the household may represent a resource to an employed caregiver, either as a source of help with caregiving or as someone who can share household responsibilities. Partners who are employed bring additional income as a resource. Individuals who are single parents, for example, must manage childrearing and employment without help and often with limited incomes (Schorr & Moen, 1979); and they have higher absenteeism than their married counterparts (Emlen, 1987). Individuals in dual-earner households, too, experience a number of stresses (Rapaport & Rapaport, 1976; Skinner, 1984). Similarly, fulfilling the demands of caring for elderly relatives or disabled adults, presumably, is stressful for couples where both partners are attempting to provide care as well as maintain employment.

Income is another resource that may make it easier to cope with caregiving responsibility, as it may allow the employee to purchase help with care. Low household income, for example, is highly associated with depression for mothers with young children (Pleck, 1985) and with financial stress for parents (Emlen & Koren, 1984).

With respect to the effects of job characteristics, full-time employees have greater difficulty combining their nonemployment and employment-related responsibilities than part-time employees (Jackofsky & Peters, 1987). Flexible work hours generally have been found to reduce absenteeism (Winett & Neale, 1980) and are often recommended as a way to help employees manage both their job and family responsibilities on a day-to-day basis (Hewlett, Ilchman, & Sweeney, 1986). Finally, employees in managerial or professional jobs may have more flexibility in their work schedules than employees in clerical and other types of jobs, thereby making it easier for them to combine employment and family responsibilities.

The available evidence on socioeconomic and job-related characteristics suggests that these variables influence employees' absenteeism and stress. The third hypothesis tested in this study, then, was: varying socioeconomic and job characteristics will differentially affect absenteeism and stress for the four groups of employees.

Methods

Sample

Data were drawn from a survey of employees conducted in 1987 as a part of the Work and Elder Care Project of the Regional Research Institute for Human Services and the Institute on Aging at Portland State University. The sample for the survey was established by contacting several private and public corporations in the Portland, Oregon metropolitan area to obtain representation according to: (a) type of industry (using the seven major categories of the Standard Industrial Classification) and (b) size (i.e., number of employees: 0–100; 101–500; over 500). A total of 33 corporations agreed to allow their employees to participate in the survey.

Surveys were distributed to 27,832 employees and returned by 9,573 employees of these 33 corporations, for an overall return rate of 34%. This rate is comparable to the response rates of other studies that used similar kinds of distribution methods and involved multiple employers (e.g., American Association of Retired Persons, 1987; Emlen & Koren, 1984; Wagner, Neal, Gibeau, Scharlach, & Anastas, 1989). This rate varied dramatically by company, from a low of 10% to a high of 78%, and even by department within companies.

Because of the fairly low return rate, it is important to note some general characteristics of the sample. Of all the employees who responded to the survey, 59% were women and 93% were white. The mean age was 39.7. Almost 46% classified their occupations as being professional or technical, 18% as management or administrative, and 20% as clerical. Thus, this sample comprises primarily whites, full-time employees, a somewhat greater number of women than men, and a high proportion of individuals in professional and managerial positions.

Employees were asked if they had "responsibilities for helping out adult relatives or friends who are elderly or disabled." They were classified as members of the "elder care" group if they were helping someone age 60 or older and as members of the "adult care" group if they were helping someone age 18 through 59. Employees were classified as members of the "child care" group if they had children under the age of 18 living in their household. It is important to note that employees designated as having "child care" responsibilities simply indicated that there was a child under the age of 18 living in the household, whereas employees designated as "adult care" or "elder care" providers actually identified themselves as providing help to an adult or elder. A total of 23% of the respondents had "elder care" responsibilities, 3% had "adult care" responsibilities, 43% had "child care" responsibilities, and 41% had no dependent care responsibilities. These percentages sum to greater than 100% because some employees had multiple caregiving responsibilities.

To highlight the differences among the employee groups, only individuals who had a single type of caregiving responsibility were considered in the analyses described here; individuals with overlapping caregiving responsibilities were excluded. The resulting sample was composed of individuals with responsibilities for: elder care ($N = 1,192$); adult care ($N = 133$); child care ($N = 2,994$); or no dependent care ($N = 3,482$). Table 7.1 describes the four employee groups with regard to their socioeconomic and job characteristics and, where relevant, the characteristics of the dependents (children, disabled adults, or elderly) for whom they were providing care.

Measures

Data with respect to nine dependent measures were examined in this study. These measures were of two general types: those relating to absenteeism and those relating to stress (Emlen & Koren, 1984). In addition, the study included six variables measuring employees' socioeconomic and job-related characteristics.

Absenteeism

"Absenteeism" was defined to include any time lost from work, including portions of days missed as well as whole days. Specifically, four measures of self-reported absenteeism were used. Respondents indicated how many times in the past four weeks they had: (a) been interrupted at work (including telephone calls) to deal with family-related matters; (b) missed a day of work; (c) been late to work; and (d) left work early or during the day. Only the first measure (times interrupted) specified that this "absence" was due to family-related matters.

Stress

Four types of stress were examined using a 4-point scale (ranging from no stress at all to a lot of stress). Specifically, respondents were asked to indi-

Table 7.1 Description of Employee Groups

	No Dependent Care	Elder Care	Adult Care	Child Care
Age (median)	38	47	39	37
Income (mean)[1]	3.37	3.56	3.09	3.66
	%	%	%	%
Gender (percent female)	62	70	62	55
Partner status				
no partner	41	34	40	17
employed partner	48	52	42	66
nonemployed partner	11	15	18	17
Full-time employment	94	96	93	92
Occupation				
professional, managerial	62	63	61	65
all others	38	37	39	35
Amount of job flexibility				
no flexibility	5	6	10	4
hardly any flexibility	12	17	17	14
some flexibility	54	54	52	53
a lot of flexibility	29	24	21	29
Relationship of care-recipient				
spouse	–	2	10	–
child	–	–	27	100
parent (inc. step; in-law)	–	73	28	–
other relative	–	18	20	–
friend	–	6	11	–
Residence of care-recipient				
in employee's home	–	9	26	100
in own home	–	73	54	–
nursing home	–	16	12	–
other	–	2	8	–
Level of caregiving responsibility				
"only" caregiver	–	12	12	–
"main" caregiver	–	34	32	–
shared equally	–	29	24	–
other is main caregiver	–	25	32	–

[1]Scale is 1 = <$20,000, 2 = $20,000–$29,999, 3 = $30,000–$39,999, 4 = $40,000–$49,999, 5 = $50,000–$59,999, 6 = $60,000 and over.

cate, again in the past four weeks, to what extent several areas of life had been a source of stress to them, including: (a) their own personal health; (b) personal or family finances; (c) family relationships, including extended family; and (d) their job. In addition, a 6-point item (ranging from very easy to very difficult) measured how easy or difficult respondents found it to combine working with family responsibilities.

Personal, Socioeconomic and Job-Related Characteristics

Six different variables measuring employees' personal and job characteristics and socioeconomic status were examined, including the employee's: (a) gender; (b) partner status (no partner, employed partner, nonemployed partner); (c) household income; (d) full- or part-time job status; (e) occupational level; and (f) perceived flexibility in work schedule to handle family responsibilities.

Findings

In response to the first two research questions, that is, the extent to which employees with no caregiving responsibilities differed from those having such responsibilities and the extent to which the caregiving groups differed from each other on the absenteeism and stress measures, a series of one-way analyses of variance were conducted. Scheffé post hoc tests then were conducted on those variables for which there were significant differences to determine precisely which groups were different from the others. The findings from these analyses are presented in Tables 7.2 and 7.3 and are summarized below. Unless otherwise indicated, only significant differences ($p < .05$) are reported. On only two dependent variables—number of days of work missed and job stress—did the one-way analyses of variance reveal no significant differences among the groups. These two variables are not discussed further.

**Question 1: How Do Employees with No Caregiving
Responsibilities Differ from the Three Caregiving Groups
with Respect to Absenteeism and Stress?**

As shown on Table 7.2, absenteeism, (i.e., time lost from work) among employees with no caregiving responsibilities was not clearly less than absenteeism among the caregiving groups. A comparison of the means among the four employee groups on the four measures of absenteeism indicated that only on a single variable (i.e., work interruptions) did the group with no

Table 7.2   One-Way Analyses of Variance and Post Hoc Tests For Absenteeism by the Four Groups of Employees

Work Absenteeism	Means				Post Hoc Tests					
	No Care	Elder Care	Adult Care	Child Care	No Care vs. Elder Care	No Care vs. Adult Care	No Care vs. Child Care	Elder Care vs. Adult Care	Elder Care vs. Child Care	Adult Care vs Child Care
Interruptions[1] $F = 79.27$ signif. $= .00$ $df = 3, 7649$ $N = 7653$	1.16	2.04	2.61	2.97	*	*	*		*	
Days missed[2] $F = 0.82$ signif. $= .48$ $df = 3, 7684$ $N = 7688$	.58	.62	.42	.62						
Arrive late[3] $F = 21.10$ signif. $= .00$ $df = 3, 7665$ $N = 7669$	.41	.30	.41	.71				*		*
Leave early[4] $F = 14.50$ signif. $= .00$ $df = 3, 7665$ $N = 7669$	.64	.57	.63	.86				*		*

[1]Number of interruptions at work due to family-related matters in preceding four weeks.
[2]Number of days missed at work in preceding four weeks.
[3]Number of times late to work in preceding four weeks.
[4]Number of times left work early or during the day in preceding four weeks.
*$p<.05$ (Scheffé post hoc test).

caregiving responsibilities have the lowest mean. Results from the post hoc tests showed that those with no caregiving responsibilities were interrupted at work to deal with family-related matters significantly less often than were all of the caregiving groups. In addition, members of the group without caregiving responsibilities were less likely to arrive late or leave early than the child care group.

In contrast, a comparison of the means on the stress measures revealed that the group with no caregiving responsibilities consistently experienced less stress, with the exception of job stress, than any of the caregiving groups (see Table 7.3). The post hoc tests indicated that those without caregiving responsibilities reported less stress than each of the caregiving groups in their family relationships and in combining work and family responsibilities. Also, they reported less personal health stress than the elder care and the adult care groups and less financial stress than the adult care and child care groups.

Question 2: How Do the Three Caregiving Groups Differ from Each Other in Their Levels of Absenteeism and Stress?

A comparison of the mean rates of absenteeism among the three groups indicated that employees with child care responsibilities had the most absenteeism on all four measures (see Table 7.2). The major differences among groups, as revealed by the post hoc tests, were between the elder care and the child care groups. Specifically, the child care group, as compared to the elder care group, was more likely to be interrupted, to arrive at work late, and to leave work early.

Although the pattern of findings from the post hoc tests was less consistent for the measures of stress (see Table 7.3), the child care and adult care groups reported more stress on a greater number of variables than the elder care group. Both the adult care and the child care groups indicated greater financial stress than the elder care group. The child care group reported more difficulty with combining work and family responsibilities than the elder care group. The elder care and adult care groups, however, reported more personal health stress than the child care group. There were no significant differences among the three caregiving groups in terms of stress with family relationships; all groups indicated some stress on this variable.

Question 3: How Do Socioeconomic and Job-related Characteristics Differentially Affect Employees' Absenteeism and Stress?

In response to the third research question, separate two-way analyses of variance were conducted to relate each socioeconomic characteristic (i.e., gender, household income, and partner status) and job characteristic (i.e., part- vs. full-time, occupation, and perceived job flexibility) to absenteeism and stress by employee group. The results are reported for only two dependent variables: work interruptions (as a representative of the absenteeism measures) and difficulty combining work and family (as a representative of the stress measures). These two dependent variables were chosen because

Table 7.3   One-Way Analyses of Variance and Post Hoc Tests For Stress by the Four Groups of Employees

Kinds of Stress[1]	Means				Post Hoc Tests					
	No Care	Elder Care	Adult Care	Child Care	No Care vs. Elder Care	No Care vs. Adult Care	No Care vs. Child Care	Elder Care vs. Adult Care	Elder Care vs. Child Care	Adult Care vs Child Care
Employee's personal health $F = 9.53$ signif. $= .00$ $df = 3, 7740$ $N = 7744$	2.16	2.30	2.44	2.18	*	*			*	*
Financial $F = 84.46$ signif. $= .00$ $df = 3, 7573$ $N = 7577$	2.31	2.30	2.57	2.66		*	*	*	*	
Family relationships $F = 94.91$ signif. $= .00$ $df = 3, 7685$ $N = 7689$	2.24	2.61	2.64	2.57	*	*	*			
Job $F = 2.51$ signif. $= .06$ $df = 3, 7718$ $N = 7722$	2.88	2.95	2.97	2.90						
Combining work and family $F = 212.26$ signif. $= .00$ $df = 3, 7547$ $N = 7551$	2.25	2.62	2.73	2.98	*	*	*		*	

[1]For health, financial, family relationships and job stress, scale is 1 (no stress) to 4 (a lot of stress). For combining work and family stress, scale is 1 (very easy) to 6 (very difficult).
*$p<.05$ (Scheffé post hoc test).

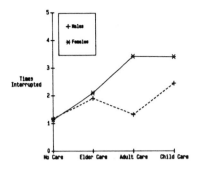
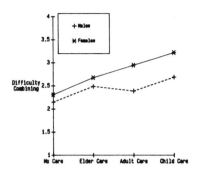

Figure 7.1 Times Interrupted by Group by Gender

Figure 7.2 Difficulty Combining Work and Family by Group by Gender

all three caregiver groups differed significantly from the group with no caregiving responsibilities on each (see Tables 7.2 and 7.3).

Gender

Women reported both significantly more work interruptions, $F(1,7630) = 12.28$, $p<.001$, and more difficulty combining work and family, $F(1,7530) = 41.48$, $p<.001$. In both of these analyses (see Figures 7.1 and 7.2), the interaction term was significant. Women providing adult care or child care were more likely to be interrupted at work than men providing such care; there were minimal gender differences in work interruptions among those with elder care and no dependent care responsibilities, $F(3,7630) = 7.38$, $p<.001$. Similarly, women providing either adult care or child care were more likely to report difficulty combining work and family responsibilities than men providing such care, $F(3,7530) = 14.64, p<.001$.

Partner Status

There were no significant main effects of the partner status variable. The significant interaction terms seemed to derive from the relatively greater importance of partner status for employees with child care responsibilities than for the other three employee groups (see Figures 7.3 and 7.4). Among the employees with children, those without partners showed the highest levels of stress and absenteeism, and those with nonworking partners the lowest both for difficulty combining work and family, $F(6,7430) = 7.12, p<.001$, and work interruptions, $F(6,7535) = 3.41, p<.01$.

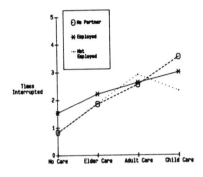

Figure 7.3 Times Interrupted by Group by Partner Status

Figure 7.4 Difficulty Combining Work and Family by Group by Partner Status

Household Income

There was one significant main effect of income: those with higher incomes had fewer problems combining family and work, $F(5,7336) = 4.01$, $p<.01$. The only significant interaction term was also for difficulty combining work and family (see Figure 7.5) and seemed to derive from the importance of income for employees with adult care responsibilities. In general, for employees providing adult care, the lower their income, the more difficulty they reported combining these two roles, $F(15,7336) = 2.46, p<.01$.

Job Status

There were no significant main effects of full-time versus part-time job status. The only significant interaction term (see Figure 7.6) showed that full-time workers who provided either adult care or elder care were more likely than part-time workers to report difficulty combining work and family, $F(3,7527) = 2.81, p<.05$. However, even when working full-time, both of these groups of employees reported somewhat lower mean levels of difficulty than either full- or part-time caregivers to children.

Occupational Status

The professional and managerial employees reported significantly fewer work interruptions than other employees, $F(1,6095) = 8.60, p<.01$. The only significant interaction term (see Figure 7.7) indicated that nonprofes-

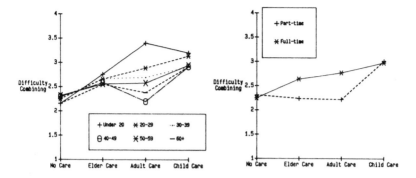

Figure 7.5 Difficulty Combining Work
and Family by Group by
Household Income

Figure 7.6 Difficulty Combining Work
and Family by Group by
Job Status

sional employees providing either adult care or elder care were more likely than professional employees to report work interruptions, $F(3,6095) = 2.86$, $p<.05$. Employees providing child care reported many interruptions regardless of occupation.

Job Flexibility

Those employees who reported the least flexibility in their jobs reported the most difficulty combining family responsibilities and work, $F(3,7438) = 80.01$, $p<.001$. Those with the most flexibility in their jobs, however, reported the most interruptions at work, $F(3,7548) = 3.06$, $p<.05$. The only significant interaction term was for job interruptions (see Figure 7.8). Those providing adult care were the exception to the positive relationship between work interruptions and flexibility. Among the adult care group, those with less flexibility reported more interruptions, $F(9,7548) = 2.29$, $p<.05$.

Discussion

This study examined whether informal caregiving responsibility, in general, is related to perceived stress and absenteeism among employees. It also examined whether different kinds of caregiving responsibility (for a child, a disabled adult, or an older person) are associated with different levels of stress and absenteeism. Also analyzed were the interactions between care-

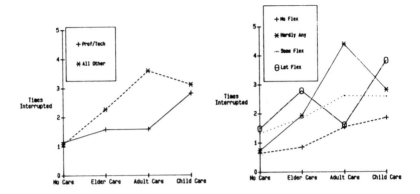

Figure 7.7 Times Interrupted by Group by Occupation

Figure 7.8 Times Interrupted by Group by Job Flexibility

giving responsibility and: (a) socioeconomic characteristics (gender, partner status, household income); and (b) job characteristics (occupational status, part- or full-time employment, and work schedule flexibility) in influencing absenteeism and stress.

The results do not clearly confirm the hypothesis that employees with no caregiving responsibilities experience less absenteeism than employees who are also caregivers. Interruptions during work is the only measure of time loss clearly associated with caregiving responsibility; however, on this measure, rates are two or three times as high for all the caregiver groups as compared with the no dependent care group. There are several possible explanations for this only partial confirmation of the hypothesis. Factors other than the caregiving responsibility itself that contribute to absenteeism may have eclipsed the effect of dependent care responsibilities, such as illness of the employee, the amount of care provided, flexibility of job requirements, and company sick leave policies. Also, each of the caregiver groups includes individuals with widely varying degrees of burden. It may be that the responsibilities of many caregivers are not overly burdensome and, therefore, with the exception of work interruptions, only minimally affect employees' absenteeism.

There is much stronger support for the hypothesis that those with no dependent care responsibilities experience less stress than those with caregiving responsibilities. All groups of caregivers report higher levels of stress in their family relationships and in combining work and family responsibilities than do noncaregivers. These findings are consistent with those of previous researchers who have studied the stressful effects associated with combining work and family roles (Brody et al., 1987; Enright & Friss, 1987; Rapaport & Rapaport, 1976). In general, our results indicate that employees with caregiving responsibilities, regardless of the type of dependent care provided, pay a price as measured by their perceived stress. The major spillover to work from these caregiving responsibilities occurs in the form of interruptions on the job. It appears, then, that the personal and home-related aspects of employed caregivers' lives, as opposed to their work lives, suffer most in relationship to their caregiving responsibilities.

The hypothesis that the three caregiver groups do not differ among themselves with respect to absenteeism and stress is not confirmed by these data. In fact, the results clearly show that employees with child care responsibilities have the greatest absenteeism. These employees are more likely to be interrupted at work, to arrive late, and to leave early. Employees with elder care responsibilities are least likely to experience such problems. The difference between these two caregiving groups may be partly attributable to the fact that all those in the child care group have children in their home and, therefore, have responsibility for constant supervision, whereas only a small proportion (9%) of the elder care group lives with their dependent elder. Also, child care involves helping children make transitions (from home to babysitter, home to school, school to home) that require a parent's physical presence or, at least, supervision over the telephone. This kind of responsibility, which can infringe on work time, may be less characteristic of most elder care situations.

There are also important group differences in relation to stress. Our data indicate that employees with child care and adult care responsibilities are the most stressed. Both groups experience financial stress, although perhaps for different reasons. The child care group may have higher household expenses as a result of the presence of children and the associated costs of child rearing. The adult care group may experience high financial stress because, as our analyses show, this group both has the lowest income and is the least likely to have an employed partner. The child care group also reports more difficulty with combining job and family responsibilities than does the elder care group. As with the absenteeism items, this difference may result from a more constant and different kind of responsibility held by employees with children as compared with employees caring for elderly relatives or friends.

Our results support the hypothesis that various socioeconomic and job characteristics differentially affect absenteeism and stress for the employee groups. These characteristics (partner status, income, full- vs. part-time employment, occupation, and job flexibility) can be conceptualized as resources that may make it easier for caregivers to combine their employment and caregiving roles. If these characteristics are considered as resources for caregiving, we would expect to find that they reduce absenteeism and stress for caregivers but have no effect for the group with no caregiving responsibilities, an expectation that is generally supported by these data. In addition, some resources have a consistently positive effect for all employee groups, as shown by the significant main effects relating: (a) higher occupational status with fewer work interruptions; and (b) higher income and more job flexibility with less difficulty combining employment and family.

These resources more consistently make a difference, however, for the employees providing adult care. Thus, being a professional or having more job flexibility is associated with fewer work interruptions for caregivers of adults than for the other three employee groups. Similarly, having a high income or being a part-time employee is associated with less difficulty combining work and family for caregivers of adults. One finding was in the opposite direction of the prediction: among caregivers of adults, those who have a nonemployed partner are the *most* likely to be interrupted at work, maybe because that partner is the disabled adult requiring care. Although Emlen & Koren (1984) have shown with respect to child care that income is not necessarily directly related to the amount spent for care or satisfaction with the quality of care, our research suggests that there may be a more direct relationship between employees' financial resources and their ability to manage adult care.

Resources also make it easier for caregivers of the elderly to cope, but less consistently across the types of resources. As with caregivers of adults, part-time job status is associated with less difficulty combining employment and family for caregivers of the elderly; being a professional or in management is associated with fewer work interruptions.

For employees who have minor children, partner status is closely related to times interrupted; that is, those lacking partner resources (having no partner or an employed partner) are more likely to be interrupted. It is only for this group that this relationship is in the direction hypothesized. Perhaps partners, and especially nonemployed spouses, are most likely to serve as a resource when the care-recipient lives in the household (all of the children, but only 26% of the adult disabled and 9% of the elderly lived in the household). It is particularly interesting to note that part-time job status does not appear to act as a significant resource for employees providing child care, although it is helpful to the other two caregiving groups. Perhaps it is more difficult to find, arrange, and manage part-time child care arrangements, especially if the part-time job has irregular hours (Emlen & Koren, 1984).

A final characteristic of the employee that was included as a factor in the two-way analyses of variance was gender. Although not directly a resource, gender may be thought of as being related to resources. Women generally assume the major responsibility for caregiving and appear less able to turn to their spouses for assistance (Pleck, 1985; Stone et al., 1987); thus, men, as a consequence of their gender, are more likely to have caregiving resources available to them. This interpretation is supported by the finding that across the employee groups, men reported fewer interruptions at work due to caregiving and less difficulty combining work and family. Male caregivers both for disabled adults and for children were particularly likely to show fewer job interruptions and less difficulty combining work and family than female caregivers. It is interesting to note that the gender differences in work interruptions disappear for employees with no caregiving duties. This suggests that the difference may be a consequence of caregiving responsibility rather than of gender *per se*.

Implications

The findings of this study have a number of implications for policy and practice. First, our data suggest that some form of response to the needs of employed caregivers is, indeed, called for to lessen the negative effects of caregiving on employees' personal, family, and work lives. The findings indicate that individuals who are both caregivers and employees experience significantly more interruptions at work to deal with family-related matters, stress in family relationships, and difficulty in combining work and family responsibilities. Other negative effects also are apparent for certain of the caregiving groups in comparison to employees having no dependent care responsibilities. Specifically, caregivers of children are more likely to arrive late at work or to leave work early or during the day. Also, caregivers of either elderly or adults experience more stress related to their personal health. Finally, caregivers of adults and caregivers of children experience more financial stress than employees who have no dependent care responsibilities. In sum, although most employees can manage their dual employment and caregiving responsibilities, they do so at considerable cost, that is, in increased stress and absenteeism.

Second, our findings suggest a need for a range of types of support for employed caregivers, flexibility in these supports, and different sources of support. The data indicate considerable diversity within and across the three groups of caregivers; this diversity has major impacts on absenteeism and stress. Important sources of diversity include level of responsibility for care (primary, secondary, or shared); the care recipient's level of need for care; the relationship of the care recipient to the employee (child, spouse, parent, or other); and place of residence (shared with the employee or separate). To address adequately the varied situations and needs of employed caregivers, a full range of types of services is needed.

Possible responses by employers to the needs of employees with caregiving responsibilities include the offering of flexible work schedules and flexible employee benefits, the hosting of educational seminars to provide information to employees about resources available in the community, and information and training specific to the type of informal care (elder, adult, child) the employee is giving. Also, individual and/or family counseling, perhaps through an existing Employee Assistance Program, as well as peer support groups, can be offered. Day care can be provided as an employee benefit or through a flexible spending account, in which pre-tax dollars are designated for use in paying for services. In some cases, respite care can also be offered in this fashion.

Employers who see direct effects of caregiving on productivity will be more likely to initiate programs and benefits to alleviate the difficulties of combining employment and caregiving. Although both stress and absenteeism can affect employees' productivity, the effects of stress sometimes are less readily apparent. Our findings indicate, however, that higher levels of stress are more likely to be manifest in caregivers than are higher levels of absenteeism. Furthermore, Emlen and Koren (1984) found a trade-off between absenteeism and child care stress; employees with very low levels of absenteeism pay a price in higher levels of stress, while employees with moderate absenteeism have lower levels of stress. This suggests the need for employers to examine the relationship to productivity of absenteeism, stress, and quality of work performance of employees who are attempting to deal with caregiving problems.

At the same time, it is unreasonable to expect employers to bear sole responsibility for supporting employed caregivers. As Kahn and Kamerman (1987) note in their analysis of corporate response to employees' child care-related needs, many companies have been unable or unwilling to respond sufficiently. Our data show that the relationship between adult care or elder care responsibilities and absenteeism is not as clear as that between child care responsibilities and absenteeism. As a result, companies may be even less willing to respond, at least through the commitment of financial resources, to the needs of employees who are caregivers to adults or elderly family members or friends. Also, our data indicate that much of the negative impact of caregiving is experienced by employees in their personal and family lives, as well as in the workplace. Thus, the need for response extends to the family and to the larger community.

Within the family, we believe it is essential that all members participate in carrying out caregiving and household responsibilities. The results of our study are consistent with the findings of others (Emlen & Koren, 1984; Pleck, 1985; Stone et al., 1987) that women are most adversely affected by the difficulties of combining employment and caregiving. Although we live in a society in which the majority of women have a paid job, family caregiving responsibilities still fall predominantly on women. One way to relieve the stress and absenteeism of primary caregivers is to encourage an equitable sharing of caregiving tasks among other members of the immediate and extended family, including spouses, children, and adult siblings. Changes within the family with respect to the sharing of responsibilities, however, hinge on changes in the workplace and also in the community service system.

As noted above, there is a need for an adequate range of community-based services to supplement the caregiving by family members. Examples of such services include child and adult day and evening care, home care services for the elderly and disabled adults, housekeeping services, and case management. In addition to responding to the needs of employed caregivers through the expansion of types of services available, consideration must be given to the accessibility and quality of these services if employees are to be able to fulfill their commitments to a job with a minimum of stress or interruption of their work schedule. One method for improving accessibility is expansion of the hours of service. Schools, health care organizations, and social service agencies can adapt their hours to be responsive to the situations of the majority of families, who do not have a caregiver available to attend to needs of care recipients during the workday. At present, for example, employees with children often must leave work early due to the early dismissal times of public schools, or miss work on school holidays. Employees caring for disabled adults or elders must miss work or make telephone calls on company time to make appointments for their family member or to take them to receive services.

Finally, in addition to responses on the part of employers, families, and community service systems, there is a need for a public policy response. While individual choice is involved in the decision to fulfill the dual roles of employment and caregiving, economic need and societal norms and expectations influence this choice. The difficulties that arise when individuals attempt to meet both domestic and job-related responsibilities affect not only the employed caregivers and their employers; those being cared for also are affected. The well-being of all of these groups affects the welfare of the community and, therefore, society as a whole. Moreover, only at the community, state, and/or federal level can issues related to the availability, accessibility, and coordination of social and health care services for caregivers and care recipients be addressed. In sum, response to the needs of employed caregivers is merited, and employers, families, community services, and various levels of government all have clear roles to play in the creation of this response.

Future Research

The study described here has been a first attempt to examine the effects of informal caregiving responsibilities on employees and the similarities and differences in impact experienced by employees with responsibilities for different groups of dependents, including children, disabled adults, and the elderly. Future research on employees and their caregiving responsibilities should take into consideration the diversity which exists within and across these groups of caregivers, as well as how caregiving changes over time.

Specifically, a number of variables related to the caregiving situation should be examined, including the level of responsibility for care, the level of dependency of the care recipient, the amount and type of care given, the caregiver's relationship to the care recipient, and whether or not the caregiver and care recipient reside together. Personal and social variables are important to examine, as well, such as race and ethnicity. Another such variable is the stage in the life cycle, since some groups are likely to be quite heterogeneous in this respect. For example, the group of employees with no dependent care responsibilities encompasses young singles, "empty nesters," and childless couples. Other family and household-related variables also should be considered. In the present study, employees whose children under the age of 18 did not live with them (e.g., noncustodial parents) were not considered as having child care responsibilities. Future research should include as caregivers those employees whose children do not live with them but for whom they continue to have responsibility.

Also requiring examination in future research efforts are several company and work-related variables and their differential impacts on the caregiver groups. For example, companies may have formal or informal sick leave or flex-time policies which are differentially applied to or used by employees who need to attend to children, disabled adults, or elderly relatives. This study found that members of the child care group who worked part-time did not report less difficulty combining work and family than those who worked full-time, while caregivers of adults and elderly who worked part-time did report less difficulty; is this due to differences in the kinds of part-time jobs held by parents (e.g., irregular on-call jobs), the different nature of the three groups' caregiving responsibilities, or to difficulties in arranging satisfactory child care on a part-time basis? More representation from employees who hold nonprofessional and nonmanagerial positions also would be beneficial in future research endeavors.

Finally, this chapter focused on various measures of stress and absenteeism from work as outcomes of caregiving. Other work-related outcomes, such as job turnover and leaving the workforce, productivity, and quality of work performed, as well as additional variables related to employed caregivers' physical and mental health, should be examined. Considerable work remains to be done in measurement and in exploration of the links among these various outcomes.

Conclusion

The relationship found in this study between caregiving responsibilities, absenteeism, and stress indicates that it is time to begin to address employees' dependent care responsibilities across caregiving groups. While there are differences among the groups with respect to work absenteeism and stress, our findings show that, regardless of the type of caregiving, those with caregiving responsibilities do experience somewhat more absenteeism (particularly work interruptions) and report considerably more stress than their noncaregiving counterparts. Since caregiver groups differ regarding which resources reduce absenteeism and stress, a variety of options for supporting employed caregivers is needed. To manage their caregiving responsibilities, employees need flexibility within their jobs, strategies within the family, and extensive, coordinated, and accessible community services that neither families nor employers can provide by themselves.

References

Allen, S. G. (1980). An empirical model of work attendance. *The Review of Economics and Statistics, 63*, 77-87.

American Association of Retired Persons. (1987). *Caregivers in the workplace: Survey results.* Washington, DC: American Association of Retired Persons.

Brody, E. M. (1980). Women in the middle and family help to older people. *The Gerontologist, 21,* 471-480.

Brody, E. M. (1985). Parent care as a normative family stress. *The Gerontologist, 25,* 19-29.

Brody, E. M., Kleban, M. H., Johnsen, P. T., Hoffman, C., & Schoonover, C. (1987). Work status and parent care: A comparison of four groups of women. *The Gerontologist, 27,* 201-208.

Crouter, A. C. (1984). Spillover from family to work: The neglected side of the work-family interface, *Human Relations, 37,* 425-442.

Emlen, A. (1987, August). *Child care, work and family.* Panel conducted at the annual meeting of the American Psychological Association, New York.

Emlen, A., & Koren, P. (1984). *Hard to find and difficult to manage: The effects of child care on the workplace.* (A report to employers). Portland, OR: Regional Research Institute for Human Services.

Enright, R. B., Jr., & Friss, L. (1987). *Employed caregivers of brain-damaged adults: An assessment of the dual role.* (Available from Family Survival Project, 44 Page Street, Suite 600, San Francisco, CA 94102).

George, L. K., & Gwyther, L. P. (1986). Caregiver well-being: A multidimensional examination of family caregivers of demented adults. *The Gerontologist, 26,* 253-259.

Gibeau, J. L., Anastas, J. W., & Larson, P. J. (1986). *Adult day health services as an employee benefit: Supporting workers who have elderly dependents.* (Executive summary Phase I: Exploratory summary). Washington, DC: National Association of Area Agencies on Aging.

Hewlett, S. A., Ilchman, A. S., & Sweeney, J. J. (1986). *Family and work: Bridging the gap.* Cambridge, MA: Ballinger.

Horowitz, A. (1985). Family caregiving to the frail elderly. In M. P. Lawton & C. Maddox (Eds.), *Annual review of gerontology and geriatrics, Vol. 5* (pp. 194-246). New York: Springer.

Jackofsky, E. F., & Peters, L. H. (1987). Part-time vs. full-time employment status differences: A replication and extension. *Journal of Occupational Behavior, 8,* 1-9.

Kahn, A. J., & Kamerman, S. B. (1987). *Child care: Facing the hard choices.* Dover, MA: Auburn House.

Karasek, R., Gordell, B., & Lindell, J. (1987). Work and non-work correlates of illness and behavior in male and female Swedish white collar workers. *Journal of Occupational Behavior, 8,* 187-220.

Klein, B. W. (1986). Missed work and lost hours: May, 1985. *Monthly Labor Review, 109*(11), 26-30.

Lebowitz, B. D. (1978). Old age and family functioning. *Journal of Gerontological Social Work, 1,* 111-118.

Oppenheimer, V. K. (1982). *Work and family: A study in social demography.* New York: Academic Press.

Patterson, J. M., & McCubbin, H. I. (1983). Chronic illness: Family stress and coping. In C. R. Figley & H. I. McCubbin (Eds.), *Stress and the family, Vol. II: Coping with catastrophy* (pp. 21-36). New York: Brunner/Mazel.

Pleck, J. H. (1985). Working wives/working husbands. Beverly Hills, CA: Sage.

Rapaport, R., & Rapaport, R. N. (1976). *Dual-career families re-examined: New integrations of work and family.* London: Martin Robertson.

Schorr, A. L., & Moen, P. (1979). The single parent and public policy. *Social Policy, 9*(5), 15-21.

Skinner, D. A. (1984). Dual-career family stress and coping. In P. Voydanoff (Ed.), *Work and family: Changing roles of men and women* (pp. 261-271). Palo Alto: Mayfield.

Steers, R. M., & Rhodes, S. R. (1978). Major influences on employee attendance: A process model. *Journal of Applied Psychology, 63,* (4), 393-407.

Stone, R., Cafferata, G. L., & Sangl, J. (1987). Caregivers of the frail elderly: A national profile. *The Gerontologist, 27,* 616-625.

Wagner, D. L., Neal, M. B., Gibeau, J. L., Scharlach, A., & Anastas, J. W. (1989). *Eldercare and the working caregiver: An analysis of current research* (Working paper). Bridgeport, CT: Center for the Study of Aging, University of Bridgeport.

Walker, K. E., & Woods, M. E. (1976). *Time use: A measure of household production of family goods and services.* Washington, DC: Center for the Family of the American Home Economics Association.

Whitbourne, S. K., & Weinstock, C. S. (1986). *Adult development.* New York: Praeger.

Winett, R. A., & Neale, M. S. (1980). Modifying settings as a strategy for permanent, preventive behavior change: Flexible work schedules and the quality of family life. In P. Karoly & J. J. Steffen (Eds.), *Improving the long-term effects of psychotherapy* (pp. 407-436). New York: Gardner Press.

8

Family Size and Caregiving of Aged Patients with Hip Fractures

T. MICHAEL KASHNER
JAY MAGAZINER
SHERI PRUITT

The popular myth that families tend to abandon functionally-impaired elder family members has been discredited (Brody, 1981; Brody, Johnsen, Fulcomer, & Lang, 1983; Comptroller General of the United States, 1977; Doty, 1986; Kovar, 1986; Shanas, 1979). Attention should now focus on the determinants of caregiving and the burden facing primary caregivers. "Burden" is defined as the physical and emotional strain, feelings of loss of control, and disruption of social relationships that the family experiences as it copes with an impairment of one of its members (Greene, Smith, Gardiner, & Timbury, 1982; Ory et al., 1985; Zarit, Reever, & Bach-Peterson, 1980).

The literature on the determinants of caregiving and caregiving burden generally has focused on the patient and the primary caregiver, in what may

AUTHORS' NOTE

This research was supported by a grant from the Health Care Financing Administration HCFA 17-C-98393/3. The authors wish to thank G. Richard Smith, M.D., Associate Professor of Psychiatry and Medicine, and Vice Chair for Research, Department of Psychiatry and Behavioral Sciences, University of Arkansas for Medical Sciences; and Frederick G. Guggenheim, M.D., Marie Wilson Howells Professor and Chair, Department Psychiatry and Behavioral Sciences, University of Arkansas for Medical Sciences; and an anonymous reviewer for their helpful comments and editorial suggestions. We also wish to thank Ms. Cindy Mosley, Ms. Martha Mobbs, and Ms. Dawn Neal for their technical assistance.

be called the two-person dyad model (Cantor, 1983; Caserta, Lund, Wright, & Redburn, 1987; Johnson & Catalano, 1983). In this study, we propose that members of the patient's family, rather than one or two designated members, collectively respond to the caregiving needs of an impaired family member. The existing literature provides some support that the family, in addition to designated hands-on caregivers, may play an important part in informal caregiving. Reliance on back-up support (Caserta et al., 1987; Morycz, 1985), frequency of family visits (Zarit et al., 1980), and consanguinity and living arrangements (Cantor, 1983; George & Gwyther, 1986) have been found to be good predictors of caregiver burden.

To test the importance of family characteristics in explaining informal caregiving, this study examined the relationship between one characteristic of the family, family size, and one component of informal caregiving, caregiving time. The theoretical relationship between family size and caregiving time is based on economic theory (Becker, 1981). The family, rather than an individual caregiver, is assumed to act as a small firm, producing assistance to the impaired member. Families are assumed to make collective decisions concerning how much and by what means assistance will be provided to the carerecipient. In making these decisions, families may consider the health of the patient as well as the resources available to the family. We hypothesized that larger families with more adult labor resources are expected to provide more caregiving than smaller ones. Larger families may give more assistance by: (a) using more than one caregiver to assist the impaired member; and (b) having noncaregiving members of the family lend emotional and activity support to those members actually caring for the impaired person. Such support may permit the caregiver more opportunity to assist the carerecipient. A supportive member need not physically be present to assist, as when money is sent by mail or emotional support is provided by telephone.

Very large families, however, may have difficulty coordinating their members to achieve important goals. With regard to caregiving, each member of a large family might expect others to provide assistance and take responsibility for the impaired member. Hence, we hypothesized that intermediate size families will provide more caregiving than very small or very large families after adjusting for all other factors.

The family size hypothesis is not necessarily inconsistent with the observation that informal hands-on caregiving tends to fall on only one or two family members (Horowitz & Dobrof, 1982; Stephens & Christianson, 1986). Household members have been noted to "specialize" in the performance of specific activities. For example, data from the 1982 Informal

Caregivers Survey (Stone, Cafferata, & Sangl, 1987) and the National Long-Term Care "Channeling" Demonstration project (Stephens & Christianson, 1986) revealed that male caregivers were more likely to assist with transportation and shopping than their female counterparts who, in turn, were more likely to assist with personal care. Green (1983) found that caregivers become more specialized in the types of caregiving they provided as formal sources of care were used.

Much of the previous research on caregiving has concentrated on patients with Alzheimer's disease (Morycz, 1985), dementia (George & Gwyther, 1986), mental illness (Safford, 1980), and the "frail" elderly (Stone et al., 1987). In this study, the sample is drawn from patients with a hip fracture (Silliman & Sternberg, 1988). A fracture of the hip is a serious problem among the aged. The National Center for Health Statistics (1985) reported that 241,000 elderly patients were discharged in 1985 with a hip fracture from a nonfederal short-stay hospital. An occurrence of a hip fracture leads to unanticipated and complete dysfunction of the patient, is usually diagnosed correctly, and requires immediate hospitalization. Unlike dementia, survivors of falls can expect to regain some of their former ambulatory state (Kreutzfeldt, Haim, & Bach, 1984; Miller, 1978; Moller, Lucht, Grymer, & Bartholdy, 1985). Hence, the motivation and type of care for a hip fracture patient may be different than the motivation and type of care for patients with dementia or Alzheimer's disease.

In addition to family size and caregiving time, we also examined how the duration of a disabling condition affects the patterns of informal caregiving over time.

Methods

The family size hypothesis was tested using data from a larger prospective study on the long-term care of aged patients with hip fracture. Eight hundred and fifty-eight patients with acute fracture of the hip were identified who were 65 years and over and who were admitted between October 1, 1984 and September 30, 1986 to one of seven Baltimore area hospitals from the community (ICD-9 Code section 820). Though not a random sample, the seven study hospitals reflected a broad range of practice settings, average costs, and average length of inpatient stays. These hospitals were responsible for providing the care for over half of all hip fracture patients age 65 and over in the Baltimore Standard Metropolitan Statistical Area during the study period. Persons in institutions at the time of their fracture were excluded to avoid biasing the sample with persons at high risk of returning to institutions.

Patients were identified through weekly calls to the orthopedic ward nurse or admissions officer. A subsequent study of discharge records indicated that 12.6% of potential study patients were missed by this method. Within one week following the admission, a trained interviewer contacted the patient to arrange for an interview. Interviewers also identified a proxy for each patient. This person was usually a frequent visitor who the interviewers felt would be knowledgeable about the patient's family.

After obtaining consent, the interviewer administered questionnaires both to the patient and to the proxy. Of the 858 patients identified, 10% refused and an additional 24% were too confused or too ill to participate. In these cases, the proxies were administered a longer questionnaire designed to obtain factual information about the patient. Ultimately, 21% of patients or proxies were unwilling or unable to provide information on pre-fracture circumstances and on hospitalization. Follow-up interviews were administered to the proxies of the remaining 677 patients at the end of the second month and sixth month following discharge. An additional 5% and 3% of the remaining sample could not be found or were unwilling to participate further in the study at the two-month and six-month follow-ups, respectively.

To test the family size hypothesis, caregiving time was defined to be the number of hours per week when family members provided assistance to the patient. Caregiving times were estimated for the week prior to the patient's fracture, and at two-month and six-month follow-ups. Types of assistance included: (a) personal care, such as assistance with dressing, bathing, grooming, feeding, and continuous supervision; (b) domestic care, such as preparing meals, housekeeping, doing laundry, and managing money; (c) medical assistance, such as supervising medications, changing of bandages, injecting medications, conducting rehabilitation services, and performing irrigations, enemas, catheters, and colostomy care; (d) arranging for medical services; (e) indoor mobility, such as walking, getting in or out of bed, and toileting; (f) outdoor mobility, such as shopping and transportation; and (g) emotional support, such as visiting, telephoning, and watching television with the hip fracture patient.

The family was divided into the patient's household, which is defined to include all members who live with the patient in a residential dwelling, and the patient's extended family, which is defined to include the children and siblings of the patient who do not live with the patient. Children and siblings were selected because of their high likelihood of providing direct caregiving to the patient (Soldo & Myllyluoma, 1983; Stephens & Christianson, 1986; Stone et al., 1987).

Linear regression was used to estimate the effects of household size and extended family size on caregiving time. Squared household size and squared family size variables were included to examine nonlinear relationships between size and caregiving time. Other nonlinear models were tested, and the one fitting the data best is presented here. The size of the household which produces the most caregiving can be determined from the estimated regression model.

The covariates included in the linear model were: demographic characteristics, functional health status, and use of formal caregiving services. Demographic characteristics included the patient's age, income, and number of years of formal education. Income spans all wages, pensions, interest, and social security and assistance benefits which the patient or spouse received during the month prior to the hip fracture. Dummy variables were also created and assigned a value of one if the patient was black, male, or had supplemental hospital insurance, physician insurance, or home care insurance. These dummy variables were assigned a value of zero otherwise.

The patient's functional status at pre-fracture and at two-month and six-month follow-ups were assessed by a 14-item questionnaire that had been adopted from the OARS instrument (Duke University, 1978). The physical activities of daily living (PADL) included eating, dressing, grooming, walking, transferring, bathing, and using the toilet. The instrumental activities of daily living (IADL) included taking medication, using the telephone, mobility, shopping, preparing meals, doing housework, and handling money. Patient functioning for each ADL was assessed on a 3-step scale. A summary PADL score and a summary IADL score were calculated by summing the scores over the individual items, as in Kane and Kane (1981) and Magaziner, Simonsick, Kashner, and Hebel (1988). Scores varied from 0 (no impairment) to 14 (complete impairment). Proxies were also asked to determine how often patients soiled or wet themselves for the week prior to the patient's fracture, and at two-month and six-month follow-ups.

Depression and cognitive skills of the patient were assessed during the initial hospital stay. Since these factors did not reflect differences in caregiving time at follow-up, they were excluded from the analyses.

Patients who obtain long-term care from paid home aides or nursing homes have less need for informal caregiving. For this reason, the list of covariates in the statistical model included: (a) number of hours per week of paid home care for the week prior to hospitalization and for the week prior to the two-month and the six-month follow-ups; and (b) dummy variables representing nursing home admissions for the two months following discharge and for the period between three months and six months following discharge. These dummy variables were assigned a value of one if the patient was admitted to a nursing home during the respective period, and zero otherwise.

Table 8.1 Characteristics of the Study Sample

Characteristic of Sample	% of Sample	Characteristic of Sample	% of Sample
Age		Household Size[1]	
65–74	24.5	0	41.4
75–84	44.2	1	38.4
85–94	29.0	2	10.6
95 +	2.3	3	5.8
Sex		4	2.4
male	19.5	5	1.5
female	79.5	Monthly Income	
Race		0–400	46.1
Black	6.2	401–800	31.3
Other	93.8	801–1200	10.4
Years Education		1201–1600	5.5
0–7	20.4	1601 +	6.7
8–11	35.7	Religion	
12	27.4	Catholic	31.7
13–15	7.2	Protestant	53.6
16	6.8	Jewish	11.3
17 +	2.5	Other	3.4
Extended Family Size[1]		Supplemental	
0	12.2	Health Insurance	
1–3	50.1	Hospital	83.0
4–6	24.8	Physician Care	79.7
7–9	9.9	Home Care	41.5
10–12	2.4		
13–15	0.6		

[1] Household and extended family size calculations did not include patient.

Results

A description of the study sample is provided in Table 8.1. Typical study patients were white females in their late 70s, with 10 years of formal education. Most patients had supplemental insurance to help pay the cost of hospital and physician care not covered by Medicare, though less than half of the study patients had supplemental coverage for home care. The average household contained one member in addition to the patient, while the extended family contained 2.6 members. Extended families included the children and siblings of the patient and members of their respective households.

Table 8.2   Mean Patient Physical and Instrumental Activities of Daily Living
Scores and Instances of Incontinence Per Week[1]

	Pre-Fracture Means	Two-Month Means	Six-Month Means
Physical Activities of Daily Living	0.96	3.9	3.0
Instrumental Activities of Daily Living	3.6	7.6	6.5
Instances of Incontinence Per Week	0.44	0.74	0.67

[1]Activities of Daily Living Scores range from 0 to 14, as described in the text. A score of zero represents complete independence, and a score of 14 represents complete dependence. An instance of incontinence includes occasions in which the patient soils him/herself.

Table 8.2 reveals the greater dependence for physical and for instrumental activities of daily living and the greater likelihood of suffering with incontinence that study patients experienced following a hip fracture. A slight improvement was observed after six months following discharge, though functioning continued to remain below pre-fracture levels.

The mean caregiving time per subject is equal to the product of the percent of patients who received care, or frequency of care, and the mean hours of care per week per recipient, or intensity of care. Table 8.3 contains the frequency and the mean intensity of total caregiving at pre-fracture and at two- and six-month follow-ups. The frequency of total caregiving tended to increase after the fracture, but returned to near pre-fracture levels within six months. Though not statistically significant, the intensity of total caregiving followed a similar pattern. That is, the intensity of informal caregiving increased after the fracture only to return to near pre-fracture levels within six months.

The frequency and intensity of care for different types of assistance are also described in Table 8.3. The frequency of caregiving for medical assistance and for arranging for services did not vary significantly between pre-fracture, two-month and six-month follow-ups. For other types of care, however, the frequency of care tended to increase between pre-fracture and two months, and to decrease between the two-month and six-month follow-ups. Exceptions include physical therapy, in which no change in frequency was observed between pre-fracture and two months, and outdoor mobility, in which the frequency of support declined after the fracture and remained

Table 8.3   Percent of Subjects Who Received Informal Caregiving and the Mean Hours Per Week Received among Recipients before Hospitalization for Hip Fracture and at Two Months and Six Months Following Discharge, by Type of Care

	Pre-Fracture		Two Months		Six Months	
	Percent Receiving	Number Hrs/Wk	Percent Receiving	Number Hrs/Wk	Percent Receiving	Number Hrs/Wk
Personal care	25.9	20.4	29.4	19.4	24.5[2]	17.7
Domestic	61.4	13.4	69.4[1]	13.4	59.9[2]	12.4
Medical assistance	17.1	5.1	14.4	4.3	12.9	6.3
Physical therapy	2.8	5.0	3.2	5.7	0.9[2]	5.2
Indoor mobility	11.1	8.4	14.3[1]	6.1	11.0[2]	7.8
Outdoor mobility	54.2	5.0	40.0[1]	5.1	42.7[3]	5.2
Arranging services	9.1	2.8	9.7	2.3	7.2	5.6
Emotional support	77.3	20.8	85.9[1]	23.6	80.2[2]	21.4
Total Support	81.8	41.4	87.6[1]	44.2	83.7	39.2

[1]Change from pre-fracture to two-month follow-up is statistically significant at $p<.05$ level.
[2]Change from two-month to six-month follow-up is statistically significant at $p<.05$ level.
[3]Change from pre-fracture to six-month follow-up is statistically significant at $p<.05$ level.

below pre-fracture levels during the six-month period following the hospital discharge. In contrast to the frequency of care, the intensity of care for each type of assistance did not significantly change over time. To summarize, caregivers tended to provide a greater variety of different types of care after the patient fell. A partial return to pre-fracture levels was observed within six months after the patient was discharged from the hospital.

The amount of formal caregiving the patient received during the study is contained in Table 8.4. Patients were more likely to receive formal care at the two-month follow-up than either at pre-fracture or at six-month follow-up. Patients used formal caregiving primarily to satisfy personal and domestic care needs. Between pre-fracture and the two-month follow-up, the hours per week declined and the cost per week increased for formal caregiving. Hence, average hourly wages for formal caregivers employed at the two-month follow-up were four times that of formal sources employed at pre-fracture.

The estimates of the partial relationships between household size, extended family size, and other covariates on caregiving hours per week are tabulated in Table 8.5. The estimates of the coefficients for the household

Table 8.4   Percent and the Amount of Formal Caregiving Received before Hospitalization for the Hip Fracture and at Two Months and Six Months Following Discharge, by Type of Care

	Pre-Fracture	*Two Months*	*Six Months*
Paid Caregiving			
Percent receiving	16.6	30.0	17.1
Hours per week	49.5	24.4	17.1
Cost per week ($)	94.0	182.0	88.0
Nursing Home or Rehabilitation Center			
Percent receiving	0.0	36.3	4.7

size and household size squared variables were significant and thus indicate an inverted U-shaped relationship between household size and the expected number of caregiving hours, as plotted in Figure 8.1. Here, caregiving time is adjusted for the characteristics of the average study patient. Caution is advised when predicting caregiving hours for extremely small or large families since the calculated values may be the result of the mathematical model which was used to plot the data. Figure 8.1 reveals that patients from households with more than two members tended to receive less caregiving after the fracture than before.

The extended family size was significantly related to caregiving time. The estimate of the extended family size squared coefficient was significant only for predicting caregiving time at the two-month follow-up. Hence, a significant inverted U-shaped relationship between expected caregiving time and family size was obtained only for the two-month follow-up (see Figure 8.2).

Figure 8.2 reveals that caregiving time was greater at the two-month than at pre-fracture or at the six-month follow-up. Patients with between six and seven children and siblings who do not live with the patient tended to receive a greater increase in caregiving time in response to the fracture than their counterparts with smaller or larger extended families.

Prior to the fracture, patients who were more dependent for IADLs tended to receive more caregiving hours. After two months following discharge, no significant IADL effect was observed. At six months following discharge, however, patients with severely impaired instrumental functioning began to receive more caregiving time. PADLs were not good predictors of caregiving

Table 8.5   Estimates of the Coefficients of the Linear Models on the Number of Hours of Caregiving Time Per Week Prior to Hospitalization, and at Two Months and Six Months Following Discharge

	Pre-Fracture Coefficients	Two-Month Coefficients	Six-Month Coefficients
Intercept	− 5.80	−33.11	10.60
Household size	23.45***	26.97***	18.18***
Household size squared	− 2.71***	− 5.84***	− 2.86**
Extended family size	4.37**	12.31***	4.59
Ex. fam. size squared	− 0.41	− 0.97***	− 0.45
Hospital insurance	32.27***	− 9.51	0.42
Physician insurance	− 19.98**	20.40	13.96
Home care insurance	− 7.71**	− 0.98	− 1.51
Physical ADLs			
Pre-fracture	0.69	–	–
at two months	–	− 0.48	–
at six months	–	–	− 1.46
Instrumental ADLs			
Pre-fracture	2.65***	–	–
at two months	–	1.76	–
at six months	–	–	4.24***
Incontinent			
Pre-fracture	2.51	–	–
at two months	–	− 0.10	–
at six months	–	–	− 4.62
Male	2.08	− 6.23	− 0.58
Patient income	0.00	0.00	− 0.00
Black	− 7.92	9.82	− 8.05
Years of education	− 0.55	− 0.68	0.27
Age	0.02	0.50	− 0.29
Paid home care			
pre-fracture	− 0.15***	–	–
at two months	–	− 0.12	–
at six months	–	–	− 0.16
Nursing home admission			
at two months	–	− 19.13***	–
at six months	–	–	− 22.84*
R^2	.381	.208	.155

*Significant at the .1 level. **Significant at the .05 level. ***Significant at the .01 level.

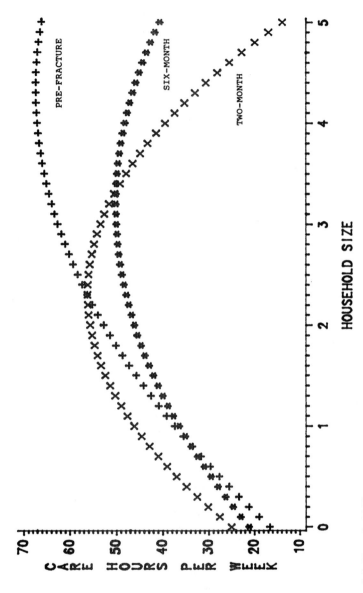

Figure 8.1 Household Size

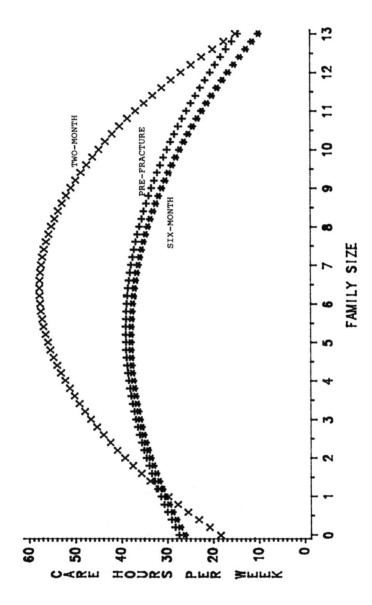

Figure 8.2 Family Size

time. Though not statistically significant, patients suffering with incontinence tended to receive less caregiving time at the six-month follow-up.
Patients with supplemental hospital but no supplemental medical insurance tended to experience more caregiving hours prior to the fracture. However, these effects were not replicated after the fracture.

Other patient characteristics, such as age, sex, income, and race, did not predict caregiving hours. Prior to the fracture, persons who received more hours per week of formal caregiving tended to receive slightly less informal caregiving. After the fracture, however, paid home care did not significantly affect the use of informal caregivers. In contrast to paid home care, patients who experienced a nursing home admission during the first two months following discharge, or the subsequent four months, tended to receive substantially less informal caregiving.

Discussion

The study subjects reported that they had received an average of 41 hours of caregiving per week from family and friends during the month prior to the fracture. This value contrasts with 48 hours per week of personal caregiving from family members as reported by Stephens and Christianson (1986) in the "Channeling" Demonstration project, and with 28 hours per week of caregiving as reported by Stone et al. (1987) in the 1982 nationwide Informal Caregivers Survey of the disabled, noninstitutionalized elderly.

The decrease in average caregiving hours per week by type of activity between pre-fracture and the two-month follow-up can be explained. Poorer functioning for many of these study patients after their fracture created need for assistance in a greater variety of areas of activities. Though caregivers did provide more total caregiving hours, broadening the scope of caregiving to include more types of activities could be accomplished with limited time resources only by rationing the number of hours that caregivers spent on any one activity. On the other hand, further analyses of the data on the use of formal caregiving revealed a different pattern for formal providers. After the patient's fracture, formal caregiving became limited to only a few types of care, mostly physical therapy and domestic care. The type of formal provider also changed after the fracture to those who earned substantially higher wages. Thus, as the patient experienced greater impairment after the fracture, informal caregiving became more generalized and formal caregiving became more specialized.

These data suggest that household and extended family sizes may be important to predict informal caregiving. Such a conclusion is consistent with the long-term care literature in which family characteristics have been found to be important determinants of nursing home use (Branch & Jette, 1982; Chiswick, 1976; Townsend, 1966). Our finding that large families with presumably more labor resources tend to provide more caregiving hours is consistent with Stephens and Christianson's (1986) finding that families with more caregivers provide more hours of caregiving. In contrast, Caserta et al. (1987) found no significant difference in the perception of need for formal supports between caregivers from large households and caregivers from small ones. Caserta's study, however, focused on the caregiver's perception of the need for formal supports and not the amount of caregiving assistance provided by the family.

Based on the estimated regression, the pre-fracture household of 4.3 members plus the patient is expected to provide the maximum hours of caregiving for the average patient in the study sample. At the two-month follow-up, the household size yielding the most caregiving was 2.3 members, and at the six-month follow-up, 3.2 members. We speculate that the disadvantages to very large households in coordinating its members may exceed the advantages of more labor resources. That larger households contain children and other impaired persons who compete for caregiving attention is not to be entirely ruled out as an explanation for these data. However, similar results were obtained when household size was determined by counting only persons over 15 years of age and who were in good or excellent health. Further research is needed to examine the effect of family composition on caregiving.

Caregiving hours per week continued to rise as extended families became larger over the entire range of family sizes at pre-fracture and at six-month follow-up. This is in contrast to households in which caregiving hours declined as households grew beyond some optimum household size. This may be the result of the different types of assistance provided by members of households and nonhousehold members of extended families. The extended family tended to assist the patient's emotional needs while household members tended to provide for personal and domestic care needs. Providers of emotional care may not require extensive coordination among participants and thus a downturn in caregiving as the family gets larger is not expected. By contrast, providers of domestic and personal care may require extensive cooperation to insure that adequate and timely support is provided. Further, providing for personal care needs may be distasteful to the caregiver. Thus, we speculate that the coordination of family caregiving may be more an issue among household members providing personal care services than among the members of the extended family who provide emotional support.

The data also suggest that the duration of the fracture affected family caregiving. After the fracture, patients from households of fewer than three members tended to receive more caregiving, while patients from larger households tended to receive less care. We speculate that after the patient suffers a hip fracture, relationships among household members are disrupted as the family responds to the increased demands of the patient. The advantages of more members may be offset by the inability of very large families to coordinate effort and assign responsibilities to care for the patient's sudden injury. This speculation also receives support when one observes changes over time in the relationship between caregiving time and extended family size. At pre-fracture and at the six-month follow-up, the larger the extended family, the more caregiving the patient received. At the two-month follow-up, however, larger extended families provide more caregiving but only up to an average of 6.3 members. The downturn in caregiving hours at the two-month follow-up suggests that problems with coordination of care that arise after the patient breaks a hip may interfere with caregiving even at the extended family level.

To support our speculation, we calculated the difference in weekly caregiving hours between a three-member and a two-member household. After adjusting for patient and family characteristics, the additional member to the household adds, on the average, 9.9 hours per week of caregiving at pre-fracture. At two months following the fracture, the additional member actually subtracts from the total caregiving hours by 2.2 hours. At the six-month follow-up, productivity of the additional member increases to 3.9 hours per week. The decline in caregiving hours attributed to the additional person at two-month follow-up may reflect disorientation among household members responding to the patient's fracture. The increase in caregiving hours attributed to the additional member at the six-month follow-up may reflect a household which, since the fracture, has begun to learn how to manage the caregiving needs of the patient.

These data predict that an additional member to an average family of three will provide additional caregiving hours per week of 1.5 hours at pre-fracture, 5.5 hours at the two-month follow-up, and 1.4 hours at the six-month follow-up. Two points are worthy of note. First, productivity of an additional household member to an average size household of one member tended to be greater than the productivity of an additional member to an average size extended family. This may reflect the fact that household members are proximate to the patient's residence. Such a conclusion is consistent with the findings that proximity of the family member to the patient's residence has a positive influence on the frequency of family contacts with the patient (Krout, 1988) and on caregiving time (Stephens & Christianson, 1986). A second observation is that the productivity of an additional member to the extended family increased after the fracture, while the productivity of an additional household member declined. This provides further evidence to our speculation that members of the patient's family who provide emotional support may be more responsive to the increased demands of the fracture than the members of the patient's household who provides personal care and thus must coordinate their efforts to provide adequate and timely care.

The relationship between functional impairment and caregiving time provides further evidence that the duration of an impairment may influence patterns of caregiving. Though caregiving hours increased after the patient fell, there was no significant difference at two months in the caregiving hours received by patients with different levels of functioning. This is disturbing because it suggests that caregiving may not be related to needs after the patient's hip fracture. This compares with the failure of Zarit et al. (1980) to find a relationship between frequency of family visits to patients suffering with senile dementia and the capacity of these patients to perform physical or instrumental activities of daily living. However, the amount of caregiving at six months after discharge was associated with patients who suffered greater impairment with IADLs. Furthermore, patients suffering with incontinence tended to receive more caregiving before the fracture and less caregiving after the fracture than their continent counterparts. Though the relationships were not significant, we speculate that hip fractures may exacerbate problems with incontinence and thus make it more unpleasant for members of the family to provide care. This speculation is consistent with Sanford's (1975) finding that caregivers do not tend to tolerate fecal incontinence. Therefore, the type of illness, the duration of that disease, and the experience the family has with it may play important roles to determine how families respond to the needs of their impaired members.

That duration and type of underlying illness affect patterns of caregiving may help explain the inconsistent findings on the determinants of caregiving burden. For example, disruptive behavior and confusion of the elder were important determinants of caregiver burden among the community-based aged (Deimling & Bass, 1986), among aged psychiatric patients (Grad & Sainsbury, 1968; Pearson, Verma, & Nellett, 1988), but not among the aged with dementia of the Alzheimer's type or senile dementia (Ory et al., 1985; Zarit et al., 1980; Zarit, Todd, & Zarit, 1986). In contrast, the literature suggests that caregiver burden tends to be greater when the elder has limitations in ADLs, such as eating, dressing, or walking (Deimling & Bass, 1986; Morycz, 1985; Pearson et al., 1988); in social functioning (Deimling & Bass, 1986); or in performing self-care (Grad & Sainsbury, 1968; Sanford, 1975). However, caregiving burden is not necessarily greater for patients with physical impairments (Gilhooly, 1984; Zarit et al., 1980); with limitations in IADLs, such as doing housework, preparing meals, or going shopping (Pearson et al., 1988; Zarit et al., 1980); or with elders who have generally poor health (Cantor, 1983). Further research is needed to explain how the underlying cause of the dysfunction influences the patterns of caregiving.

From our data, we calculated that caregiving time will be reduced by 15 minutes per week for every hour purchased from a formal caregiver. This result compares to a reduction in informal caregiving of 12 to 30 minutes (Christianson, 1988) for every hour purchased from a formal caregiver. Hence, the use of formal care services is not offset by a substantial reduction in informal caregiving so that there is an overall increase in caregiving hours from both formal and informal sources. This conclusion is also consistent with Stone et al. (1987), who used a national sample of noninstitutionalized disabled elderly to find that primary caregivers who used paid assistance will provide more care time, though no correction was made for the greater disability associated with persons who use paid assistance.

The failure to obtain significant associations of age, sex, income, and education on caregiving time is inconsistent with the findings by Krout (1988) and Kashner, Krompholz, & McDonnell (1982). However, both reports failed to control for the patient's supplemental medical insurance which is correlated with patient income, education, and race.

Generalizing from these results should be done with caution. Total hours of caregiving per week measures only one component of caregiving. These analyses do not reflect differences in the content (Green, 1983), the quality, or the number of contacts (Krout, 1988) of caregiving. We also do not have information that directly measures the ability or willingness of the caregiver to assist the elder family member. The sample was limited to hip fractures in Baltimore and thus may not reflect patterns of assisting patients in other localities (Kashner, Magaziner, & Kiser, 1987) with other types of health conditions. Furthermore, information was obtained from a proxy whenever the patient was unable or unwilling to respond (Magaziner et al., 1988).

The policy implications of this research are that providers of mental health care, long-term care, case management, and discharge planning need to consider family management, rather than stress management, of one or two primary caregivers or case management of single patients. Larger families can and do provide more caregiving than smaller ones, but only if the family can coordinate its members. Families who care for an aged member who suddenly becomes functionally impaired may find it difficult to adapt quickly to the patient's impairment and to coordinate its members to provide the needed assistance with ADLs. Though families may eventually learn how to care for the patient, we advise that professionals help families to manage the patient's care by: (a) teaching members of the family, not merely a designated primary caregiver, about the patient's illness and about the resources and commitments necessary to manage the patients ADLs; (b) evaluating how members of the family intend to work together to respond to the needs of the aged member and the needs of each other as the impact of the impairment ripples through family life; and (c) intervening, when appropriate, to help the family coordinate its members to achieve its desired goals. Family management may help families to designate what activities need to be done and by whom. Encouragement should also be directed to members who can help the lay-on-of-hands caregivers, such as helping with child care for caregivers with dependent children.

Agencies responsible for financing long-term care should also take notice of the importance of the dynamics of the entire family in the caring process, and not be concerned only with the lay-on-of-hands caregivers. Financial inducements to caregivers will probably be inaffective if families do not know how to coordinate their resources to manage all of their responsibilities. By educating as to how adequate and timely caregiving can be provided, family management may preclude costly admissions to the hospital or nursing home.

References

Becker, G.S. (1981). *A treatise on the family*. Cambridge, MA: Harvard University.

Branch, L.G., & Jette, A.M. (1982). A prospective study of long-term care institutionalization among the aged. *American Journal of Public Health, 72*, 1373-1379.

Brody, E. (1981). Women in the middle. *The Gerontologist, 21*, 19-29.

Brody, E. (1985). Parent care as a normative family stress. *The Gerontologist, 25*, 19-29.

Brody, E. (1986). *Mental and physical health practices of older people: A guide for health professionals*. New York: Springer.

Brody, E.M., Johnsen, P.P., Fulcomer, M.C., & Lang, A.M. (1983). Women's changing roles and help to elderly parents: Attitudes of three generations of women. *Journal of Gerontology, 38*, 597-607.

Cantor, M.H. (1983). Strain among caregivers: A study of experience in the United States. *The Gerontologist, 23* (6), 597-604.

Caserta, M.S., Lund, D. A., Wright, S.D., & Redburn, D.E. (1987). Caregivers to dementia patients: The utilization of community services. *The Gerontologist, 27*, 209-214.

Chiswick, B.R. (1976). The demand for nursing home care: An analysis of the substitution between institutional and noninstitutional care. *Journal of Human Resources, 11*, 295-316.

Christianson, J.B. (1988). The effect of channeling on informal caregiving. *Health Services Research, 23*, 99-117.

Comptroller General of the United States. (1977). *Report to Congress on home health: The need for national policy to better provide for the elderly.* Washington, DC: General Accounting Office.

Deimling, G.T., & Bass, D.M. (1986). Symptoms of mental impairment among elderly adults and their effects on family caregivers. *Journal of Gerontology, 41*, 778-784.

Doty, P. (1986). Family care of the elderly: The role of public policy. *Milbank Quarterly, 64*, 36-75.

Duke University Center for the Study of Aging and Human Development. (1978). *Multidimensional functional assessment: The OARS methodology.* Durham, NC: Duke University.

George, L.K., & Gwyther, L.P. (1986). Caregiver well-being: A multidimensional examination of family caregivers of demented adults. *The Gerontologist, 26*, 253-259.

Gilhooly, M. (1984). The impact of caregiving on caregivers: Factors associated with the psychological well-being of people caring for a dementia relative in the community. *British Journal of Medical Psychology, 57*, 35-44.

Grad, J., & Sainsbury, P. (1968). The effects that patients have on their families in a community care and a control psychiatric service—a two year follow-up. *British Journal of Psychiatry, 114*, 265-278.

Green, V.L. (1983) Substitution between formally and informally provided care for the impaired elderly in the community. *Medical Care, 21*, 609-619.

Greene, J.G., Smith, R., Gardiner, M., & Timbury, G.C. (1982). Measuring behavioral disturbance of elderly demented patients in the community and its effects on relatives: A factor analytic study. *Age and Aging, 11*, 121-126.

Horowitz, A., & Dobrof, R. (1982). *The role of families in providing long-term care to the frail and chronically ill elderly living in the community.* (Final Report). Washington, DC: Health Care Financing Administration.

Johnson, C.L., & Catalano, D.J. (1983). A longitudinal study of family supports to impaired elderly. *The Gerontologist, 23*, 612-618.

Kane, R.A., & Kane, R.L. (1981). *Assessing the elderly: A practical guide to measurement.* Lexington, MA: Rand Corporation.

Kashner, T.M., Krompholz, B., & McDonnell, C. (1982, November). *The demand for respite care and caregiver's time by families with impaired elderly persons.* Paper presented at the meeting of the American Public Health Association, Montreal, Canada.

Kashner, T.M., Magaziner, J.S., & Kiser, S.M. (1987, October). *The impact of for-profit medical care on aged hip fracture patients,* Paper presented at the meeting of the American Public Health Association, New Orleans, LA.

Kovar, M.G. (1986). Aging in the eighties: Preliminary data from the supplement on aging to the national health interview survey, United States, January-June 1984. *Advanced data from vital and health statistics* (DHHS Publication No. PHS 86-1250). Washington, DC: U.S. Government Printing Office.

Kreutzfeldt, J., Haim, M., & Bach, E. (1984) Hip fracture among the elderly in a mixed urban and rural population. *Age and Ageing, 13*, 111-119.

Krout, J.A. (1988). Rural versus urban differences in elderly parents' contact with their children. *The Gerontologist, 28*, 198-203.

Magaziner, J., Cadigan, D.A., Hebel, J.R., & Parry, R.E. (1988). Health and living arrangements among older women: Does living alone increase the risk of illness? *Journal of Gerontology: Medical Sciences, 43*, 127-133.

Magaziner, J., Simonsick, E.M., Kashner, T.M., & Hebel, J.R. (1988). Patient-proxy response comparability on measures of patient health and functional status. *Journal of Clinical Epidemiology, 41*, 1065-1074.

Miller, C.W. (1978). Survival and ambulation following hip fracture. *Journal of Bone and Joint Surgery, 60A:7*, 930-933.

Moller, B.N., Lucht, U., Grymer, F., & Bartholdy, N.J. (1985). Early rehabilitation following osteosynthesis with the sliding hip screw for trochanteric fractures. *Scandinavian Journal of Rehabilitative Medicine, 17*, 39-43.

Morycz, R.K. (1985). Caregiving strain and the desire to institutionalize family members with Alzheimer's disease. *Research on Aging, 7*, 329-361.

National Center for Health Statistics. (1985). *Utilization of short-stay hospitals* (DHHS Publication No. PHS 87-1751). Washington, DC: U.S. Government Printing Office.

Newman, S.J. (1976). *Housing adjustments of older people*. Ann Arbor: University of Michigan, Institute for Social Research.

Ory, M.G., Williams, T.F., Emr, M., Lebowitz, B., Rabins, P., Salloway, J., Sluss-Radbaugh, T., Wolff, E., & Zarit, S. (1985). Families, informal supports, and Alzheimer's disease. *Research on Aging, 7*, 623-644.

Pearson, J., Verma, S., & Nellett, C. (1988). Elderly psychiatric patients status and caregiver perceptions as predictors of caregiver burden. *The Gerontologist, 28*, 79-83.

Safford, F. (1980). A program for families of the mentally impaired elderly. *The Gerontologist, 20*, 656-660.

Sanford, J.R.A. (1975). Tolerance of debility in elderly dependents by supporters at home: Its significance for hospital practice. *British Medical Journal, 3*, 471-473.

Shanas, E. (1979). Social myth as hypothesis: The case of the family relations of old people. *The Gerontologist, 19*, 3-9.

Silliman, R.A., & Sternberg, J. (1988). Family caregiving: Impact of patient functioning and underlying causes of dependency. *The Gerontologist, 28*, 377-382.

Soldo, B.J., & Myllluoma, J. (1983). Caregivers who live with dependent elderly. *The Gerontologist, 23*, 605-611.

Stephens, S.A., & Christianson, J.B. (1986). *Informal care of the elderly*. Lexington, MA: Lexington Books.

Stone, R., Cafferata, G.L., & Sangl, J. (1987). Caregivers of the frail elderly: A national profile. *The Gerontologist, 27*, 616-626.

Townsend, P. (1966). The effects of family structure on the likelihood of admission to an institution in old age: The application of a general theory. In E. Shanas and G. Streib (Eds.), *Social Structure and the Family*. Englewood Cliffs, NJ: Prentice-Hall.

Zarit, S.H., Reever, K.E., & Bach-Peterson, J. (1980). Relatives of the impaired elderly: Correlates of feelings of burden. *The Gerontologist, 20* (6), 649-655.

Zarit, S.H., Todd, P.A., & Zarit, J.M. (1986). Subjective burden of husbands and wives as caregivers: A longitudinal study. *The Gerontologist, 26*, 260-266.

9

Linguistic Strategies Used by Normally Hearing Caregivers in Conversations with Elderly Hearing-Impaired Spouses

TAMY S. CHELST
CHARLES A. TAIT
TANYA M. GALLAGHER

To interact conversationally on a daily basis with a hearing impaired older person presents a challenging responsibility for the family member, be it the spouse, child, or sibling. Family caregivers often need to assume the role of intermediary between the hearing impaired individual and those who are unaware of his or her hearing loss. This role may be particularly crucial in difficult listening situations in which the hearing impairment places the affected adult in communicative stress, such as in telephone conversations or in the presence of environmental background noise. A more prominent effect of hearing loss on the family member–caregiver relationship, however, is the demand placed on the normally hearing conversationalist to change his or her speaking and listening "style" when addressing a hearing impaired relative.

Forty-five percent of all individuals over the age of 65 suffer from hearing impairment sufficient to reduce normal speech understanding (Fein, 1983). The most prominent manifestation of hearing loss due to aging is the reduction in speech understanding. As a result, the hearing impaired individual must depend on others to make adjustments in conversation to reduce communication failure.

Blesser (Stark, 1974) emphasized the need for long-term practice with an intimate or interested partner in order to improve the impaired listener's comprehension. He found that, when he was listening through headphones that distorted incoming speech stimuli, people addressed him in "too chopped or quick a manner," suggesting that most people were not used to addressing listeners who suffer sensory deficits. Blesser underscored that what he lacked was a symbolic "mother figure," a caregiver or significant other, to assist him in achieving linguistic comprehension. The present study focused on syntactic and pragmatic linguistic strategies utilized by individuals who regularly engage in conversation with elderly hearing-impaired relatives as they assume the role of linguistic "mother figure."

Significant others who find it necessary to assume the role of linguistic "mother figure" may face considerable sociolinguistic stress during dialogue with the hearing impaired "dependent figure." Mishler (1976) has suggested that "specific features of dialogue convey social meaning." If each speaker's conversational turn taking can be viewed as an exercise of dominance in the time domain of dialogue similar to the concept of territoriality in the space domain (Jaffe & Feldstein, 1970), the progress of speaker–listener roles in conversation can have considerable impact on the relationship between the normally hearing caregivers and the elderly hearing-impaired patient or other family member whom they support.

To decrease his or her vulnerability to communication mishap, the elderly hearing-impaired family member may choose to increase his or her own verbal output (Toscher & Rupp, 1974), attempting to convert dialogue into a monologue. When he/she is the information provider instead of the information recipient, topics can be set in advance. The hearing impaired person does not need to listen and, thereby, risk the possibility of communication failure. Unfortunately, this loquaciousness can be perceived by the others as controlling or aggressive behavior. To the spouse or child caregiver, this talkativeness may seem to be an attempt to exercise dominance. In fact, adults often ask children questions to usurp authority within discourse (Mishler, 1976). Similarly, the elderly care-recipient's attempt to control conversation may be interpreted as an attempt to initiate role reversal.

Even when the hearing impaired individual functions primarily as an information recipient, his or her linguistic behavior can be subject to misinterpretation and may precipitate tension in the caregiver–care-recipient relationship. When the hearing impaired individual does not respond to his or her "mother figure," this lack of response can be perceived as a violation of the Summons-Answer (SA) sequence which is normative in dialogue (Schegloff, 1968). The caregiver may be unsure as to whether the hearing-impaired person's lack of response is due to his or her sensory deficit or attributable to lack of interest. "No response" may be misconstrued as an insult or a "cold-shouldering" that was never intended. It is not uncommon for family members to complain that an elderly hearing-impaired relative "hears what he or she wants to hear." Communication failure or success is interpreted as a function of the elderly hearing-impaired person's choice rather than his or her misfortune. Furthermore, an inappropriate response may be misinterpreted by conversational partners as an indication of the elderly individual's cognitive as opposed to sensory decline.

Little experimental attention has been paid to the course of natural dialogue between conversational partners when one speaker is adventitiously hearing impaired. Instead, clinical hints based on intuition and experience are aimed at increasing the effectiveness of communication. Advice often takes the form of professional "prescriptions" for hearing impaired individuals and those who share intimate and frequent association with them— either family members or nursing home personnel. Hull's (1980) "Thirteen Commandments for Talking to Hearing Impaired Older Persons" provides an excellent example of this trend. Because of the lack of experimental data, the variables in these prescriptions are neither clearly nor operationally defined.

Studies of child language have demonstrated that mothers generally adjust their linguistic styles, depending on the child's age and linguistic ability, by reducing their length of utterance (Moerk, 1974), by simplifying grammatical structure, and by reducing rate of speaking (Cramblit & Siegel, 1977; Snow, 1972).

Examining communication between persons when listeners received a systematically interrupted message, Longhurst and Siegel (1973) found that speakers favored three strategies when listeners experienced communication failure: (a) increased conversational length; (b) reduced talking rate; and (c) increased redundancy. For those addressing the hearing impaired, Picheny, Durlach, and Braida (1985,1986) examined the characteristics of increasing speech "clarity." They found that the primary differential between clear or exaggerated speech and natural speech was the considerably slower talking rate of the former mode. Unfortunately, conversational research to date has focused only on young adult participants. These studies have not addressed the elderly who experience a high incidence of hearing loss nor the caregiver–care-recipient relationship. The present study investigated a conversational data base, focusing on elderly conversationalists with particular emphasis on the role of the normally hearing caregiver as a hypothetical "mother figure" who would adjust her dialogue in order to improve the hearing impaired listener's comprehension.

Methodology

Subjects

Participants were six elderly (age 60–76) married couples. All were native speakers of English. All subjects were normally hearing for their age group (audiometric screening levels were 20dB HTL at 500, 1000, and 2000 Hz and 35dB at 4000 Hz). To avoid interference from past experience, they presented no history of otitis or hearing loss over any extended period of time and had no regular close personal contact with any hearing impaired persons. Subjects were in relatively good health with no previous history of stroke or central impairment. Husbands were all retired middle class professionals, and wives were homemakers. All participants had a junior high school education or greater.

Materials

Twenty-four passages were selected from the Comprehension Skill Series, Middle Level (1976), reading materials designed for junior high school students in preparation for standardized achievement tests. They ranged in reading level from grades 5 to 8 and were from 125 to 175 words long. All passages chosen had been given high interest judgment ratings by five female readers matched in age and background to test subjects. Passage content covered a wide variety of nonfiction and fictional topics. (See Appendix A for sample passage.)

In order to motivate subject participation in conversations, the husband completed a comprehension quiz at the end of each conversation with monetary compensation (up to a maximum of $76/husband) offered for correct answers.

Procedures

Information flow was directed from the normally hearing wife, the information provider, to the adventitiously hearing-impaired husband, the information recipient. For eight 1½ hour long sessions over a period of one month, the couples met with the experimenter in their homes. The topics of conversations were set by the content of each of the 24 passages presented to the wife to read. Wives then related passage details to their husbands. A 10-detail key phrase outline was given to each wife to assist her with information recall. A barrier eliminated the input of visual nonverbal cues between speakers during conversations. Couples were urged to discuss the passage content in order to insure the husband's comprehension of all included information and to maximize his performance on the postconversational quiz. No time limit restricted conversational length. All 24 conversations, 3 per session, were auditorily recorded.

For 16 experimental conversations, 2 per session, each husband was outfitted with earplugs and circumaural earphones to simulate a hearing loss. This combination of ear protective devices was previously demonstrated to shift thresholds for pure tones an average of 40, 55, 45, and 60 dB at 500,

1000, 2000, and 4000 Hz, respectively. In this study, recorded CID sentence lists (Davis & Silverman, 1970) were presented to insure that placement of protective plugs and ear muffs reduced discrimination levels to the 60–70% range. The remaining eight conversations, one per session, served as controls. Husbands participated in these without hearing protective devices.

The simulated hearing loss was limited to the interview sessions. This allowed for control of the subjects' hearing impairment, holding constant across all six subject pairs the degree of the husbands' hearing impairment, the onset and duration of loss, and experiential environments.

Tape recorded conversations were transcribed and utterance boundary guidelines adapted from Brinton and Fujiki (1984), Duncan (1973), Johnson, Darley, and Spriestersbach (1963), and Roy (1981). T-tests for repeated measures contrasted control and experimental conditions. Reliability judgments for both control and experimental conditions ranged from 92.4% to 100% for transcription, including word count, word assignment, and turn allocation.

Results

Results contrasted experimental and control conversations over all subject pairs and for all eight sessions. For the normally hearing wife information providers, two major linguistic strategies in experimental conditions were identifed: (a) elongation; and (b) simplification. When total conversation length was measured in mean total turns across conditions, experimental conversations ($\bar{x}$ = 56 turns) were significantly longer than control ($\bar{x}$ = 36 turns) conditions (t = 5.65, df = 10; $p<.001$). The wives' "elongation" trend is demonstrated in Table 9.1 by a significant increase in conversation length from $\bar{x}$ = 55 utterances per conversation in control conditions to $\bar{x}$ = 75 in experimental conditions (t = 3.90; df = 10; $p<.01$). This difference parallels the adventitiously hearing-impaired husbands' significantly (t = 3.59; df = 10; $p<.01$) increased conversation length ($\bar{x}$ = 28 control utterances to $\bar{x}$ = 41 experimental utterances), which is largely attributable to the husbands' incidences of communication failure.

In experimental conditions, the adventitiously hearing-impaired husband, often faced with uncertainty about information received, embarked on a course of turns and utterances revealing his difficulties to his wife and requesting her assistance in effecting resolution of his problems. These utterances were termed "signals of communication failure." (See Appendix B.) As shown on Table 9.2, these signals of communication failure were significantly more prevalent in experimental ($\bar{x}$ = 8.4 utterances) than in control ($\bar{x}$ = 1.5 utterances) conversations (t = 6.07; df = 10; $p<.001$).

Table 9.1 Mean Number and Percentage of Utterances
Per Conversation for Husband and Wife Speakers in
Control and Experimental Conditions

		Utterances	
Speaker	Subject Pair	Control x (%)	Experimental $\bar{x}$ (%)
Wife	I	40 (74)	80 (72)
	II	50 (83)	74 (73)
	III	73 (62)	77 (60)
	IV	62 (60)	83 (56)
	V	63 (66)	72 (69)
	VI	42 (63)	65 (63)
	Mean	55 (66)	75 (65)
Husband	I	14 (26)	31 (28)
	II	10 (17)	28 (27)
	III	45 (38)	51 (40)
	IV	41 (40)	66 (44)
	V	32 (34)	32 (31)
	VI	25 (37)	38 (37)
	Mean	28 (34)	41 (35)

A total of 70% of the wives' increased utterances are attributable directly to adventitiously hearing-impaired husbands' increased incidences of communication failure. These utterances include wives' revisions (55%) and confirming repetitions after husbands' resolutions of incidents of communication failure (15%).

In order to respond to husbands' communication failures in experimental conditions, wives increased revision utterances in which they restructured or rephrased misunderstood target words or utterances (see Table 9.2). The revision utterances increased significantly from $\bar{x} = 2.7$ utterances in control to $\bar{x} = 13.8$ revisions utterances ($t = 5.24$; $df = 10$; $p<.001$).

After the adventitiously hearing-impaired husbands resolved incidents of communication failure and indicated that they had achieved accurate comprehension of the originally misunderstood word or phrase, the wives often repeated the target word or phrase in question. These confirming repetitions, defined as a subset of Gallagher's (1981) Resumption at Speaking Turn (RTAS) category, ranged from $\bar{x} = .8$ utterances in control to $\bar{x} = 3.8$ in experimental conditions.

Table 9.2   Mean Number of Wives' Revision Utterances Per Session and Ratio of Revisions to Mean Utterances in Both Control and Experimental Sessions Versus Mean Number of Husbands' Signals of Communication Failure and Ratio or Signals to Mean Utterance

| | | Conditions | | | |
| | | Control | | Experimental | |
Speaker	Subject Pair	$\bar{x}$	Ratio	$\bar{x}$	Ratio
Wife	I	2.1	(.05)	15.8	(.20)
	II	*	*	8.2	(.11)
	III	3.9	(.05)	16.9	(.22)
	IV	3.6	(.05)	22.2	(.27)
	V	2.9	(.05)	7.4	(.10)
	VI	1.0	(.02)	11.9	(.18)
	Mean	2.7	(.05)	13.8	(.18)
Husband	I	1.4	(.10)	9.0	(.29)
	II	0	(0)	5.3	(.19)
	III	2.4	(.05)	10.3	(.20)
	IV	2.3	(.06)	13.4	(.20)
	V	2.0	(.06)	4.8	(.15)
	VI	.8	(.03)	7.4	(.19)
	Mean	1.5	(.05)	8.4	(.20)

*There are no revisions nor signals of communication failure in this control condition.

The remaining 30% of increased utterances represents an increased sensitivity of wives to adventitiously hearing-impaired husbands' potential difficulty. These do not follow nor are directly related to signals of communication failure or revisions. Several low incidence strategies distinguish the wives' performance in experimental from control conversations. Among these were turn-yielding devices such as questions probing adventitiously hearing impaired husband's hearing or comprehension. These increased from $\bar{x} = .6$ in control conversations to $\bar{x} = 1.8$ in experimental conversations. Furthermore, requests soliciting questions from the husbands increased from $\bar{x} = .5$ in control to $\bar{x} = .8$ in experimental conditions. Some of the strategies used to elongate the wives' verbal output served specifically to increase semantic redundancy. These included the spontaneous spelling out of words and usage of similes.

One measure of linguistic diversity which probes redundancy is the Type Token Ratio (TTR) (Johnson, 1944). The TTR is defined as the proportion of different words (types) to the total number of words (tokens) in a given sample. The higher the TTR, the more diverse the conversational sample. The lower the TTR, the less diverse and, therefore, more redundant the sample. Unfortunately, this measure was not applicable to much of the present conversational data because a minimum verbal corpus for such analysis requires a turn at speaking of at least 100 words in order to provide a valid measure of diversity. Only for wives in subject pairs I and V were turns sufficiently long to allow for comparison of differences between control and experimental conditions. These TTRs demonstrated reduced linguistic diversity in experimental conditions. For subject wives I and V, mean TTR was reduced from .60 and .72, respectively, to .57 in control and to .65 in experimental turns. This additional measure of linguistic redundancy demonstrated yet another manifestation of an "elongation" strategy, that of repeating information to increase the probability of listener comprehension.

Attention-getting strategies also accounted for increased conversation length. They were more prevalent in experimental than in control conversations. In fact, some wives evolved quite complex styles of address to begin conversations and signal the onset of an experimental versus a control conversation.[1] Another strategy utilized by wives when addressing adventitiously hearing-impaired spouses can be explained as a "simplification" trend. This simplification strategy was revealed in the wives' reductions of utterance length in experimental conditions from control conditions while husbands' utterance length remained unchanged.

Beyond the intrinsic conversational analysis of speakers' performance, it is noteworthy that husbands maintained relatively high scores on the postconversational comprehension quizzes for all conversations ($\bar{x} = 83\%$ in control and $\bar{x} = 88\%$ in experimental conditions). Therefore, despite the husbands' hearing loss, subject pairs successfully maintained information transmission by utilizing the above noted linguistic strategies.

Couples occasionally expressed awareness of the wives' changed conversational styles. Wives encouraged further expressions of communication failure. As one noted: "If there's a question while I'm talking, stop me." Others discouraged topical changes or digression, for example, "You're not supposed to be talking while I'm telling a story." One described her change in speaking style, for example, "I want to pronounce clearly and distinctly. I like to pause and speak deliberately and slowly." One husband labelled this speaking style as "lecturing." Likening his wife's experimental utterances to those addressed to children, he playfully remarked, "Go over the content. Make sure about the 4 and 5-year-olds."

Discussion

The normally hearing wives displayed considerable sensitivity to their spouses' adventitious hearing loss through a variety of linguistic strategies that can be characterized essentially as "elongation" and "simplification." The elongation strategy exercised by the normally hearing spouses is comparable to mothers' speech to children, which is more redundant than commonly found in adult-to-adult utterances. Revision behavior of caregiver wives is also highly comparable to that of mothers in response to child communication failure. When a child does not respond, mothers either repeat themselves (Berko-Gleason, 1974) or revise their utterances (Nelson, Carskaddon, & Bonvillian, 1973) to increase the likelihood that the child will comprehend at least one of the utterances.

The simplification, or utterance length reduction strategy, shares with other research that reports reduced utterance complexity and speaking rate (Longhurst & Siegel, 1973; Picheny et al., 1985) a common goal of listener stress reduction. Bergman (1980) found that elderly listeners processed simple short sentences in noise better than complex long ones. A generative approach to language grammar (Slobin, 1971) would explain that the more transformations necessary to attain sentence surface structure, the harder the task of listening.

Normally hearing caregivers, therefore, respond much as mother speakers who simplify their linguistic styles depending on the age of the child to whom they are talking (Broen, 1972; Phillips, 1973; Snow, 1972). In fact, mothers also reduced their length of utterance to match that of the child (Moerk, 1974). Furthermore, they downgraded their speaking rate to the slower pace of the child conversational partner.

Both elongation and simplification strategies that characterized the normally hearing wives' role in this study may be generalized to a caregiver style of address. This style may be applicable to a wide range of substandard conversationalists with linguistic handicaps or limitations. Among these may be children, nonnative speakers of a language, the hearing impaired, and cognitively impaired adults (e.g., poststroke or Alzheimer's disease) or children (e.g., mental retardation or autism). The literature also suggests that these strategies may assist information transmission under distorted listening conditions (e.g., interrupted speech or environmental and babble noise). Based on strategies identified herein, future applied research might focus on the development of training protocols directed both to family caregivers and to other service providers who need to interact more effectively with the hearing impaired elderly or other conversational partners who suffer linguistic limitations.

Such protocols would utilize model conversations to encourage strategies that increase communicative success. Conversations varying in amount of caretaker verbal output would be contrasted. These would be elongated both by repetition of words and phrases and by revision or rewording of words and phrases. Furthermore, caregivers would be trained to yield turns to their conversational partners by questioning communicative success or failure. Additionally, exercises contrasting sentences of varying length and rate of speaking would focus on the simplification strategy. Another training approach asks caregivers to simulate a hearing loss in order to increase their sensitivity to hearing impaired conversational partners (Chelst & Figurski, 1989). In model conversations, the temporarily hearing-impaired caregivers assume the roles of information recipients who suffer hearing handicaps. Caregivers can thus be given the opportunity to weigh the effectiveness of various elongation and simplification strategies in increasing their own comprehension.

In this study, the adventitiously hearing-impaired husbands achieved excellent comprehension scores on postconversational quizzes. This performance may be attributed to the linguistic efforts of both the wives as information providers and the husbands as information recipients. The wives' consistently high motivation to provide and transmit passage details to their spouses and their spouses' equivalently high motivation to receive information underlied their successful information transmission. Both wives and husbands strove to increase husbands' remunerated performance on postconversational quizzes. Increasing the motivation of normally hearing caregivers to provide information to hearing impaired conversational partners despite incidents of communication failure should, therefore, become an integral part of training protocols that strive to facilitate effective communication.

It should be underscored that, in this study, spouses may have been uniquely sensitive and aware of their husbands' hearing loss given its emphasis in the experimental design. Furthermore, because speakers were not given any particular time limitations, wives were under no particular time pressure to complete their information transmission as quickly as possible. Additionally, the monetary compensation received for successful performance offered husbands a special incentive to seek as much information as possible to increase comprehension. In more natural real-world settings, a similar high level of motivation may not be present.

Given its structure, likened to an "orchestral arrangement built on synchronized deviations," the dialogue between normally hearing caregivers and hearing impaired care-recipients can be characterized as a dialogical chain built on the systematic alternation between two participants and a shared code between them (Riegel, 1977). As in the Longhurst and Siegel (1973) research, conversational performance of information providers in this study showed a close relationship with the communicative successes or failures of the information recipients'. The husbands' feedback as to communicative success, their signals of communication failure, were instrumental in encouraging their wives' revisions. Furthermore, the husbands' signals of communication failure were also related to an increase in turn-yielding and attention-getting strategies utilized by wives to preclude future incidents of communication failure.

Despite the linguistic changes introduced during experimental conversations, the wives maintained their roles as principal information providers throughout the entire study, providing over 60% of utterances both in experimental and in control conditions. Given their consistently high motivation to transmit information, the linguistic adjustments made by the wives during experimental conditions did not reflect a role change from information provider to information recipient. Instead, strategies indicated a heightened awareness of the speaker's role as an information provider and increased sensitivity to the listening needs of the hearing impaired information recipient.

This heightened awareness of speaking role is probably attributable to both spouses' motivation to effect successful information transmission. The quality of a close personal relationship increased both conversationalists' sensitivity to each other's role. Unfortunately, in the real world, hearing loss is often a silent handicap; and the information provider may be unaware of his or her conversational partner's hearing loss. Furthermore, the hearing impaired partner may strive to hide this handicap by denying the loss and projecting the blame for comprehension failure on his or her conversational partner's poor speaking style. He or she may feign comprehension even when information has not been accurately received (Rupp & Heavenrich, 1982). In such situations, interactions between normally hearing speakers and their conversational partners may become quite strained. It would, therefore, be of paramount importance to caretakers both to identify conversational partners' hearing losses and to strive to encourage the hearing impaired individuals to face their disability head on by admitting their sensory loss.

Strategies used by the normally hearing caretakers in this study were quite successful in maintaining a high level of comprehension. Further research should also seek to examine the psychosocial effects of these strategies on the interpersonal dynamics between conversationalists. It is possible that some of these comprehension aiding devices may be perceived as interactionally "offensive" either by information providers or by recipients. The similarity between caregiver strategies and those utilized by individuals interacting with children may strain interactive dynamics. Hearing impaired information receivers may resent being placed into a "child-like" role (Mishler, 1976). The examination of the psychosocial impact of each of the caretaker information providing strategies identified in this study would be of considerable importance in enhancing the well-being of caretakers and hearing impaired care recipients.

Conclusion

In conclusion, the linguistic strategies of elongation and simplification form a "lecturing style" which reflects a caregiver's heightened role awareness when given the responsibility of information transmission to another conversationalist with linguistic limitations. These strategies, along with the information recipient's increased readiness to express communication failure, seem to be quite successful in assisting the information recipient in the information processing task and in effecting successful comprehension between caregivers and elderly hearing-impaired care-recipients.

Note

1. One couple began experimental conversations in the following manner:
     W: Honey, Dad.
     H: Yeh.
     W: Hi. You there? How you doing?
     H: Alright.
   This was distinguished from the control style:
     W: Dad. This is a story about a fox.

References

Bergman, M. (1980). *Aging and the perception of speech.* Baltimore: University Park Press.

Berko-Gleason, J. (1974). *Talking to children: Some notes on feedback.* Paper presented to the Conference on Input Language and Acquisition, Boston, MA.

Brinton, B., & Fujiki, M. (1984). Development of topic manipulation skills in discourse. *Journal of Speech and Hearing Research, 27,* 350-358.

Broen, P. (1972). *The verbal environment of the language learning child.* (Monograph # 17). Washington, DC: American Speech & Hearing Association.

Chelst, T.S., & Figurski, T.J. (1989). *Teaching students sensitivity to the everyday life experiences of the elderly hearing impaired through a simulation task.* Paper delivered at the annual meeting of the Association for Gerontology in Higher Education, Tampa, FL.

Comprehension Skill Series, Middle Level, CB 4M-8M. (1976). Providence, RI: Jamestown Publishers.

Cramblit, N.S., & Siegel, G.M. (1977). The verbal environment of the language-impaired child. *Journal of Speech and Hearing Disorders, 42,* 474-482.

Davis, H., & Silverman, S.R. (1970). *Hearing and deafness.* New York: Holt, Rinehart & Winston.

Duncan, S. (1973). Toward a grammar for dyadic conversation. *Semiotica, 9,* 29-46.

Fein, D. (1983). Projections of speech and hearing impairment to 2050. *ASHA, 25,* 31.

Gallagher, T.M. (1981). Contingent query sequences within adult–child discourse. *Journal of Child Language, 8,* 51-62.

Hull, R.H. (1980). Hull's thirteen commandments for talking to the hearing impaired person. In Interview: Conversation: the aging speaker. *ASHA, 22,* 423-428.

Jaffe, J., & Feldstein, W. (1970). *Rhythms of dialogue.* New York: Academic Press.

Johnson, W. (1944). Studies in language behavior: I. A program in research. *Psychological Monographs, 56,* 1-15.

Johnson, W., Darley, F.L., & Spriestersbach, D.C. (1963). *Diagnostic methods in speech pathology.* New York: Harper & Row.

Longhurst, T.M., & Siegel, G.M. (1973). Effects of communication failure on listener and speaker behavior. *Journal of Speech and Hearing Research, 16,* 128-140.

Mishler, E.H. (1976). Studies in dialogue and discourse: II. Types of discourse initiated by and sustained through questioning. *Journal of Psycholinguistic Research, 5,* 355-375.

Moerk, E. (1974). Changes in verbal child-mother interactions with increasing language skills of child. *Journal of Psycholinguistic Research, 3,* 101-116.

Nelson, E.E., Carskaddon, G., & Bonvillian, J.D. (1973). Syntax acquisition: Impact of experimental variation in adult verbal interaction with the child. *Child Development, 44,* 497-504.

Phillips, J.R. (1973). Syntax and vocabulary of mothers' speech to young children: Age and sex comparisons. *Child Development, 44,* 182-185.

Picheny, M.A., Durlach, N.I., & Braida, L.D. (1985). Speaking clearly for the hard of hearing: I. Intelligibility differences between clear and conversational speech. *Journal of Speech and Hearing Research, 28,* 96-103.

Picheny, M.A., Durlach, N.I., & Braida, L.D. (1986). Speaking clearly for the hard of hearing: II. Acoustic characteristics of clear and conversational speech. *Journal of Speech and Hearing Research, 29,* 434-446.

Riegel, K.F. (1977). The temporal structures of dialogue. Unpublished manuscript. University of British Columbia.

Roy, A.M. (1981). Identifying and counting utterances. *Semiotica, 37,* 15-25.

Rupp, R.R., & Heavenrich, A.Z. (1982). Positive communicative game rules. Part III: Self-defeating behaviors. *Hearing Instruments, 33,* 20, 22.

Schegloff, E.A. (1968). Sequencing in conversational openings. *American Anthropologist, 70,* 1075-1095.

Slobin, D. (1971). Developmental psycholinguistics. In W.C. Dingwall (Ed.), *A survey of linguistic science.* College Park: University of Maryland, Linguistic Program.

Snow, C.E. (1972). Mothers' speech to children learning language. *Child Development, 43*, 549-565.

Stark, R.E. (Ed.). (1974). *Sensory capabilities of hearing-impaired children*. Baltimore: University Park Press.

Toscher, M., & Rupp, R.R. (1974). A philosophical review—The psychological implications of deafness: The human factor. *Michigan Speech and Hearing Association Journal, 10*, 60-67.

Appendix A: Sample Passage

How would you like to have been born without any ability to feel pain? There are such people. One of them is being studied by doctors at a hospital in New York City. He is a 22-year-old clerk who really does not know the meaning of pain. But he wishes he did.

Not long ago a packet of matches flared up in his hand. Luckily the burn was not serious. It caused large blisters but still did not bother him. He said the burn felt like a fly crawling on his fingers. It has been the same story as far back as he can remember. He has never had headaches or sore muscles. Bee stings, cuts, and bruises do not hurt.

Being free from pain is not as wonderful as you may think. The young man has had to have rotted teeth pulled because he never felt toothache warnings. A sudden attack of appendicitis could be deadly. Life without pain is as risky as trying to run a cruise ship without fire alarms.

Appendix B: Classification of Signals of Communication Failure

I. *Directives—Time Out* (TO)—e.g., "wait a minute"; *Request for Rate Reduction* (RR)—e.g., "slow down"; and *Request for Increased Loudness* (IL)—e.g., "speak up."

II. *General Admission of Comprehension Problem* (Adm)—e.g., "I can't hear you," "I don't understand"; and *Requests for Repetition* (RP)—e.g., "repeat that."

III. *Specific Requests for Repetition* (RP-sp)—e.g., "tell me the last part of what you said"; and Specific Admissions of Comprehension Problems (Adm-sp)—e.g., "I didn't hear the beginning," "I don't understand the three days and one month."

IV. *Requests for Spelling* (RSP)—e.g., "how do you spell it?"

V. *Nonspecific Requests* (NSR)—e.g., "huh?" "pardon?" "what?"

    VI. *What questions*—e.g., "what are they?" "why do they play it outdoors?"— including *Requests for Specific Constituent Repetition* (SCR)—e.g., "about what?" "he was what?" "they had diamonds and what?"

    VII. *Yes–no questions*—e.g., "is that a driver?" "is that the Sumerians?"—including *Requests for Confirmation* (RC)—e.g., "eighteen on a team?" "a human piece of ice?" or a spelling attempt—e.g., "F-O-X?" and RC-like questions—e.g., "did you say diving bells?" "you mean the Titanic looked like that?" "did you say they were not for them?"

    VIII. *Definitions*—e.g., "stones?" following the yes–no question "are you talking about boulders?" (with target word "boulders"); or "motorcycle?" following the SCR "about the what?" (with the target word "Honda").

PART III

Public Policy Perspectives

10

Women as Caregivers of the Elderly

Implications for Social Welfare Policy and Practice

NANCY R. HOOYMAN

Long-term care of the elderly by family members is central to the functioning of current social and health care systems and therefore a critical policy issue. It is also an issue for feminist practice within the social work and other human service professions, since women caregivers predominate both as clients and as service providers. Given the growing proportion of our older population with long-term disabilities, along with reduced public support of resources for care (Moroney, 1980), our society is confronting fundamental policy dilemmas regarding who should provide what types of long-term care and at what costs. With the current focus on cost containment and service reduction, policy makers face critical decisions for determining the conditions under which the elderly will live, and women's caregiving choices will contract or expand.

This chapter examines how the "new conservatism" of the past decade, by its emphasis on privatization, fiscal restraints, cost-effectiveness, and efficiency, combined with the ideology of community care, has overlooked equity issues and intensified burdens faced by family caregivers, particularly women. Two underlying trends that have served to make female caregivers hidden victims of our social and health care policies are discussed: (a) historically, an ideology of separate spheres between men's and women's work has perpetuated the expectation that women's major role is to provide uncompensated care to dependents; and (b) the welfare of family caregivers has not been a goal of public policy. Current policy changes to support family caregivers of the elderly are also examined; many of these have incrementally reduced caregiver burdens, but have nonetheless failed to alter the gender imbalance of care responsibilities. A major theme is that health and social service professionals must carefully examine their policy objectives and strategies to avoid inadvertently perpetuating such inequities and increasing caregiver stress.

Throughout this analysis, caregiving values per se are not under attack. The importance and necessity of caregiving work are taken as givens. For many women—and some men—family caregiving is their preferred and chosen life's work. Rather, the critique is directed at the socially constructed assumption that caregiving is women's natural role, an assumption that blocks their access to socially valued marketplace resources and thereby perpetuates their powerlessness.

The chapter concludes by arguing that human service professionals must challenge the normative designation of women as the primary carers faced with the moral imperative to care. It is the isolation of women under current social structures that must be changed, not the activity itself—the humanizing imperative of caring. In the long run, fundamental solutions are needed to reintegrate women's and men's personal and work lives so that caregiving of the elderly is a shared public and private, male and female, responsibility, rather than divided along gender and economic lines as a low-cost alternative to public responsibility.

The "New Conservatism" and Care of the Elderly

Who provides uncompensated custodial care for the elderly is a growing policy and practice issue because of demographic, social, and political trends, including: longer life expectancy; technological medical advances, improved care, and nutrition which allow children and adults to survive diseases that were previously fatal; the resultant financial pressures incurred by the growing social burden of disability; the declining pool of younger family members available to provide care; and the increasing numbers of women, traditional providers of care, who are now in the paid labor force. Contrary to stereotypes, the increase in the nursing home population within the past two decades does not reflect familial disregard for elders, but rather the growing numbers of elderly and the improved survival rates among victims of chronically incapacitating illness.

As a result of these oftentimes conflicting trends, the answer to who cares for older relatives is frequently based on filial love and responsibility combined with political and fiscal considerations. Filial love and responsibility translate into the fact that families provide over 80% of in-home care to elders. In fact, 10% of the elderly who live in private homes would require nursing home placement without the family support they receive, thereby tripling the number of elders in institutions (Brody, 1981, 1985). Yet such family care is usually taken for granted as a labor of love. As an example, the United States is one of the few industrialized nations that does not uniformly provide a stipend to family caregivers of the elderly, although over 20 states now have direct payment programs to caregivers. Despite the reality of family care, a myth of uncaring families persists, reflecting a romantic and naive understanding of what it means to be unpaid caregivers to older people.

Political and fiscal factors, producing cutbacks in social and health services, mean that many families have no alternatives to providing custodial care, often on a 24-hour basis and at great stress to themselves. The "new conservatism" has also spawned an ideology, most visibly reflected in deinstitutionalization policies, that community care is preferable and, in fact, optimal for the older person (Briar & Ryan, 1986). Uncompensated care by the family is viewed as being more kind, sensitive, attuned to individual needs, and compatible with traditional values than that provided by paid caregivers. However, the underlying rationale for this perspective, espoused by both policy makers and service providers, is not necessarily quality of care. Rather, family care is often viewed as less costly than institutional care, and the cost-effectiveness imperative assumes that the lower the financial cost of a service, the more efficient it is (Pilisuk & Park, 1988; Waerness, 1985; Walker, 1985; Wood & Estes, 1986-87). Yet maintaining an older person with chronic care needs within the community, frequently in a relative's home, may place tremendous physical, financial, and emotional pressures on family members and conflict with their best interests. An additional pressure on families is our health care system's focus on the cure of acute illnesses and on only the older individual rather than the total family system; this means that providers' care plans often fail to consider the elder's maintenance needs as well as the family and environment from which an older person has come and hopes to return (Briggs & Oliver, 1985).

The current public policy option of transferring caregiving work from the public to the private sphere is apparently based on the erroneous assumption that informal structures for providing care (e.g., the family) are underutilized and simply need to be activated (Briggs & Oliver, 1985; Waerness, 1985)—a viewpoint vividly expressed by the acting administrator of the U.S. Health Care Financing Administration on prime time television in 1985:

> We believe strongly that the strength of America is in the family unit, and if we encourage and send the strong signal to those family members that we are not going to accept that responsibility, they will rise to the occasion and provide the necessary levels of support for elderly family members (Haddow, 1985).

Policies for the elderly thus often assume the total availability of the family's free domestic labor and time—that someone is at home, willing to provide care, and simply waiting to be called upon.

Closely related to the trend of fiscal conservatism and community-based care is the current fashionability of research on social supports and official interest in appeals to natural helping networks (Guberman, 1988; Walker, 1985). Such research is extremely important and has expanded our knowledge about the types, extent, and limits of care provided by families, friends, and neighbors. Nevertheless, research on informal supports has flourished in a conservative era, in part because such analyses can be utilized by policy makers as a rationale for strengthening the informal system's capacity to do even more (Walker, 1985). Largely because of the fiscal crises in social and health services, revitalizing the family has become an important economic and political objective in the 1980s (Biegel & Naperstek, 1982; Briggs & Oliver, 1985; Brody, 1985). As Brody has so vividly documented, the informal helping network—frequently one person—has always been there, but policy makers oftentimes act as if it has just been discovered. Yet, as Biegel and Naperstek (1982) have so eloquently argued, informal support cannot—and should not—be viewed as a universal panacea to the costs of social and health care.

Fortunately, recent research on informal helping networks has documented the need to support families in their care responsibilities. But even those who advocate increased public resources for family caregivers often frame their arguments in terms of the cost-effectiveness of reducing institutional placements by preventing caregiver burnout (Gallagher, Lovett, & Zeiss, 1988; Lewis & Meredith, 1988). Rather than legitimating increased public responsibility for elder care, proponents of "supporting the supporters" are quick to claim that they are complementing, not replacing, family care (Perry, 1987). The focus on sustaining families' capabilities to provide care suggests that policy makers may view family members as unpaid helpers who, in Brody's (1985) words, simply need to be "cheered on in their caregiving work." In such instances, caregiver self-sacrifice is implicitly expected.

Such public expectations have persisted despite extensive documentation of the social, emotional, physical, and financial costs incurred by family caregivers. Physical costs result from the daily grind of personal care, the wearing routine servicing of basic functions, the strain of backbreaking lifting, of interrupted sleep, night after night, year after year, with no prospect of any reduction in the work (Finch & Groves, 1983). Physical stress often manifests itself in health problems—generalized fatigue, gastrointestinal disturbances, headaches, weight changes, and, in some instances, higher morbidity rates of the caregivers (Haley, Levine, Brown, Berry, & Hughes, 1987; Shapiro, 1983). These physical costs affect not only the caregiver, but also the provision of social and health care services. For example, the family caregiver's serious illness or death is the single most prevalent reason cited by families seeking nursing home placement of an older relative (Teresi, Toner, Bennett, & Wilder, 1980). Financial costs include not only the direct expenses of medical care, modifications to the home, or hiring help, but also the indirect opportunity costs of lost income or foregone promotions (Finch & Groves, 1983). Family members may be forced to choose between their jobs and caregiving; those who attempt to juggle both often face stress, fatigue, lower productivity, and more absenteeism (Grassi, 1988).

The emotional burdens of caregiving appear to be the greatest: feeling alone and in "second place," without anyone to help or talk with, lacking privacy, sacrificing leisure and recreation, and experiencing a narrowing of one's life to the point where some caregivers, who feel imprisoned and increasingly isolated in their own homes, describe the "sheer inescapable boredom of care" (Briggs & Oliver, 1985; Brody, 1981; Fengler & Goodrich, 1979; Horowitz & Dobrof, 1982). Faced with such strains, caregivers may experience depression and mood swings; feel entrapped, bitter, resentful, and antagonistic toward their older relatives in a "tangled web" of emotions (Birenbaum & Re, 1983; Briggs & Oliver, 1985); and postpone or avoid seeking help.

The nature of the caregiving role may underlie the emotional burdens. Few people enter the caregiving role fully understanding its consequences. Instead, they often react to a crisis or emergency that requires quick decision-making. Many families find themselves suddenly caught in circumstances beyond their control, victims of capricious and inexplicable bad luck. They assume a caregiving role with the hope that they can help their loved one get better and that the situation will improve, only to find that caregiving tends to be all-consuming and progressive. Caregivers of the elderly, especially those diagnosed with dementia, face a future that promises little relief—only increasing dependence, decline, and relentless physical care tasks (Brody, 1985; Moroney, 1980). Combined with the unpredictability of tasks and the uncertainty of prognosis, family caregivers must redefine a normal life and future options (Moroney, 1980).

In some situations, lack of social support is a predictor of the stress of caregiving (George & Gwyther, 1986; Zarit, Reever, & Bach-Peterson, 1980). Not surprisingly, caregivers frequently feel they lack such support.

One reason for this may be the low status of caring for the elderly, who are accorded low regard in our society. Another factor contributing to the low status of caregiving tasks is that they are performed in relative isolation from others. Generally not visible, such tasks often go unrecognized. Instead, caregiving work is more likely to be noticed by others when performed poorly—particularly in instances of abuse and neglect—than when it is done well. Families, especially women, are expected to know automatically how to be long-term caregivers, and blamed for failing to meet societal expectations if their older relatives are neglected, abused, or institutionalized. Although the number of educational and training programs for caregivers has increased in the past decade, our society traditionally has done little to prepare families or to provide models for long-term care. The lack of rewards for caregiving is also intensified by the nonreciprocal nature of care, with the caregiver often giving more support than he or she receives and thus experiencing a "support gap" (Belle, 1982).

Caregiving as a Growing Feminist Issue

Within the current context of shifting responsibilities from the public to the private sphere, the term "family caregiving" is misleading, since family members rarely share the work of caregiving. Rather, it is usually performed by one person, and 70 to 80% of the time that person is a woman—mother, daughter, wife, granddaughter (Cantor, 1983; Daatland & Sundstrom, 1985; Johnson & Catalano, 1983; Nygard, 1982; Stone, Cafferata, & Sangle, 1986; Sundstrom, 1983). The probability is also great that the person receiving care will be a woman, typically a widow over age 80 with at least one chronic illness. Although some men are "unsung heroes" as caregivers, they are less likely to be involved in direct "hands-on" care (Brody, 1985; Lang & Brody, 1983). For example, men generally provide indirect assistance to the elderly, such as financial management and home maintenance, and assume primary responsibility only when a female relative is unavailable (Brody, 1985; Brody, Johnson, & Fulcomer, 1984; Horowitz & Dobrof, 1982; Waerness, 1985).

Because social and health care of older relatives depends on women's invisible and unpaid labor, it is a growing feminist issue. Increasing expectations of families create intractable dilemmas for women who are being told, and who often genuinely feel, that they really ought to provide care and, on the other hand, are touched by the women's movement's emphasis on economic independence and choice of lifestyles. Brody's research (Brody, 1981; Brody, Johnson, & Fulcomer, 1984) with three generations of female family members indicates that today's young women have both a very strong commitment to care and a strong preference for equal opportunities in the public sphere. Such conflicting objectives are intensified by the fact that, for most women, caregiving for dependents is not a single time-limited episode, but spans the life course (Rossi, 1985). Many women experience a career of presumably "natural" stages of caregiving, beginning with motherhood, then middle-age responsibilities for an older relative, and extending into old-age responsibilities of caring for disabled husbands. In addition, women often care for more than one generation (Brody, 1985). Such multiple responsibilities become even more complicated when women within remarriages are caring for extended blended families and former in-laws. Although the particular constellation of caregiving demands varies by generations and family structure, the societal denigration of caregiving services can lock women into socially powerless positions throughout their lives, thereby creating tremendous costs for them.

Therefore, behind the public debate of formal versus informal care is a debate over whether and how women will care for dependent persons in our society. It is a debate over whether caregiving should be a salaried (albeit low salary) market activity, or whether it should be assumed by the non-market private sector of volunteers and free domestic labor. Along with this debate is increasing public concern about the shortage of caregivers created by the growing entry of women into the paid labor force. Such concern apparently stems more from considerations with costs than with the caregiver's well-being. For example, a number of states have instituted programs, financed by Medicaid, to provide in-home care to low-income elders who would otherwise reside in nursing homes at government expense. Under such programs, relatives who meet program restrictions can be paid as providers of in-home care. However, these programs may not necessarily promote caregiver welfare, but rather serve cost containment goals, since in-home care is assumed to be less expensive than nursing home placement.

Failure to analyze critically the effects of social and health policies on caregivers' well-being can obscure the issue of who is burdened, who is at risk, and who benefits at another's expense (Stober, 1982). Questions that need to be addressed include the following: Why in the development of long-term care policies are family caregivers, primarily women, treated as unpaid service providers rather than rewarded as beneficiaries of policies? Why is the "informal network" preferred over professional care, even though family members, faced with inadequate support options, may have to alter radically their lives to provide care? Why is family caregiving romanticized and institutional care seen as an undesirable last resort, even in instances of family histories of abuse, neglect or abandonment, or current situations of caregiver stress? Why are issues of justice and equity ignored, by expecting sacrifice of an individual who simply has the misfortune of a relative becoming ill? Part of the answers to these questions lies in how social welfare policy in the United States and the societal expectations of women as caregivers of dependents have developed. Both of these factors are examined below.

Historical Development of Societal Expectations for Caregivers

The caregiving responsibilities traditionally assumed by women did not become social norms and central to their life's work until after the Industrial Revolution, which spawned an ideology of separate spheres (Ehrenreich, 1983). This ideology, which held caregiving to be women's mission to save civilization from moral ruin in the new industrial age, had major consequences for the ways in which caregiving is viewed in our society (Hooyman & Ryan, 1987). It accepted profit as the sole operating principle of the marketplace and exonerated the public sphere from obligations of social responsibility. Caregiving values, thus removed from the mainstream of public life, were sequestered in the home as an antidote to the public sphere rather than a central force in shaping it. Although the ideology of separate spheres elevated caregiving to new importance as a function of family life, caregiving nevertheless remained a private activity to be performed in isolation, behind closed doors. Nonmonetized and nontechnological, caregiving became devalued in a society that increasingly defined work in terms of measurable output and wages rather than nurturance and maintenance (Bernard, 1983).

In the most basic sense, the ideology of separate spheres took two conflicting philosophies—the old one of community, responsibility, and duty, and the new one of individualism—and resolved the conflict along the lines of gender: women would nurture, men would achieve; women would be the carers, men the breadwinners. The domestic sphere (of women) became culturally linked to expressivity, nurturing, and emotion, while the public sphere (of men) became characterized as instrumental, competitive, and rational (Chodorow, 1978). Accordingly, women have frequently been socialized to a value system of responsiveness and care that is antithetical to the marketplace norms of competition and financial gain. Even when women moved into the marketplace through professional caregiving roles, such as nursing, education, and social work, these were low-status poorly-paid professions. The same myth—that women should give rather than be compensated for their giving—has been operative even for women trained as professionals. In sum, women are expected to perform unpaid and underpaid work that underpins the economy, yet is peripheral to the economy as defined by men. Their life's work is thus regarded as nonwork, unrecognized and undervalued in our society.

This dual nature of caregiving serves to perpetuate the powerlessness of those for whom caregiving is primary (Graham, 1983). One example of this dual nature is how caregiving is viewed with ambivalence in our society. It is romanticized and honored for meeting fundamental needs for affection within the family, needs which presumably cannot be met by paid caregivers. Yet caregiving is also viewed with contempt, in part because it does not resemble the time-regulated tasks of the industrial marketplace (Cott, 1977). In contrast to the production of tangible goods, caregiving involves maintenance services—being present on 24-hour call to give time and attention to others. In fact, caregiving services are costly precisely because large expenditures of time are involved. The dual nature of caregiving also intertwines the physical drudgery of providing personal services with concern for a loved one's well-being, emotionally tying women to those they assist (Graham, 1983; Waerness, 1983). A woman cannot simply walk away from an incontinent parent or a paralyzed husband as she might from a poorly paid job. In sum, caring for older family members is unpaid, low status, and emotionally binding work. The burdens for women as caregivers of the elderly are thus best understood within the broader context of the costs created by the primacy and nature of women's caregiving roles throughout their lives, which serve to isolate them from mainstream activities, values, and rewards.

One way in which the costs of elder care for women are intensified is by their socialization to form empathic relationships and respond to others' needs. Women have tended to develop a responsibility orientation—the capacity and the need for close interpersonal connections and responsiveness to others' needs, while men have generally formed a rights orientation—the capability and the need for separation and instrumentality (Lyons, 1983). Internalizing an injunction to care, women often have difficulty setting limits on others' expectations, as well as their own, about how much care to provide (Lewis & Meredith, 1988). They may believe they should be able to perform all caregiving tasks themselves, as proof of their love, competence, or marriage vows. Accepting others' help may be viewed as an admission of weakness or failure. Chodorow (1978) has elaborated on the ways in which the social division of labor in the family (child care and nurturing vs. breadwinning) reproduces the domestic/public split, and thus recreates gender inequity in care. This translates into each generation of women developing the capacity and need for close interpersonal connections while men form the capability and need for separation and instrumentality. As a result, women who find it hard to accept help and set limits on care responsibilities may nevertheless feel burdened and may fall into the "martyr" role, complaining that no one helps, while simultaneously refusing offers of assistance.

This gender difference, whereby women are frequently socialized to set their priorities in terms of others' needs, also means that they are more likely than their male counterparts to find care demands stressful, even when care tasks are equally shared (Horowitz & Dobrof, 1982). Likewise, men have been found less likely than women to feel personally responsible for their parents' emotional well-being or to experience guilt from not doing more (Robinson & Thurnher, 1979). A number of factors may explain these variations. In general, men are less involved with others' emotional needs than women (Wethington, McLeod, & Kessler, 1987). Men's concern for others may show itself in particular relationships but, compared to women's concern, does not extend as far into their social relationships. Likewise, men appear better able to distance themselves physically and emotionally from the care-recipient, focusing primarily on economic responsibilities and concrete assistance (Gilligan, 1982). In contrast, given the ideology of separate spheres, responsiveness to others is the "work" of women, both at home and on the job. Women may also judge themselves by their capacity to care, so that failure to do so, for whatever reason, commonly induces guilt (Lewis & Meredith, 1988). Therefore, women are more affected emotionally than men, not only by their own stressful experiences but also by those of people they care about. Accordingly, women's networks are not necessarily ones with mutual benefits. In fact, women's greater embeddedness in social networks may itself be stressful, by exposing them to events that are outside their control but demand a response (Fischer, 1982). Women's relationships with older dependent relatives are thus characterized by an identification of caring *about* with caring *for*—between love and labor (Lewis & Meredith, 1988).

The ideology of separate spheres also means that women who do not regard the domestic sphere as primary, but try to set limits by seeking institutionalization or in-home help for their older relatives, may be labelled by others as unloving and selfish, and instilled with guilt and self-doubt. In fact, the husband or son of an older person is more likely to be provided with in-home services or encouraged to seek nursing home care than is his female counterpart, partially because caregiving is not presumed to be his inherent responsibility (Guberman, 1988). Similarly, single sons have been found to receive home help services more often than daughters. In addition, mothers living with sons are more likely to participate in cooking and cleaning activities than those living with daughters (Wright, 1983). Accordingly, hospital discharge planners have been found to assume the ability and willingness of wives, daughters, and daughters-in-law to provide care and to contact them first (Polansky, 1985). The ideology of separate spheres means that while caregiving is an expected duty for women, it is more likely to be regarded as an unexpected expression of compassion by men. Therefore, when human service professionals follow the path of least resistance and shield men from caregiving, they perpetuate traditional gender-based inequities in care.

A more severe, long lasting, cost of care is the structural economic inequality that results from women assuming the socially expected caregiving role as primary. Society's denigration of the invisible work of caregiving is played out in women's lower economic status throughout life, and especially in old age. Years spent out of the full-time paid labor force to care for others are not compensated by private pensions or social security, even though caregiving services are essential to the economy and to the family. After devoting her life attending to others' needs, a woman, particularly upon divorce or her husband's death, may face years of living alone on a low income, with inadequate medical care, and with her welfare resting on the presence, willingness, and ability of younger female relatives (Older Women's League, 1986). Likewise, women who outlive their caregivers predominate in nursing homes, part of a woman's industry, with poor women as attendants and as residents (Minkler & Stone, 1985; Older Women's League, 1988). Many women thus are forced to choose between performing their caregiving obligations at the cost of economic security, or deviating from societal expectations to pursue employment-related stability as their primary goal, generally without professional, familial, or public support for the latter choice.

While older female caregivers face poverty and powerlessness, younger women who attempt to bridge the separate spheres and work outside the home, in addition to caring for family members, are confronted with the expectation to be "superwomen" and to "do it all" (Brody, Kleban, Johnson, & Hoffman, 1984). Whether entering the paid labor force from career choice or out of economic necessity, most women find their domestic responsibilities have not diminished. Instead, double duty becomes the norm, with their leisure or discretionary time shrinking but not their other obligations (Bernard, 1983; Robinson & Thurnher, 1979). A model of progress prevails that places increasing economic responsibility on women without reducing their role as the mainstay of family life in the home, even though women's jobs rarely provide the flexibility or income to cushion the effects of caregiving demands (Stoller, 1983). For example, both employed and unemployed women have been found to provide nearly equal amounts of care to their dependent mothers (Brody, Kleban, Johnson, & Hoffman, 1984). In other words, the gender-based division of labor has eroded in a lopsided fashion, with more women becoming economic providers, often the sole provider, but fewer men assuming care responsibilities (Vanek, 1983). As a result, many women end up physically and/or emotionally exhausted. In addition, women are more likely than men to quit their frequently poorly compensated jobs in order to provide care to older relatives, not only because of gender-based pay inequities, but also because most men simply do not perceive caregiving as their work (Waerness, 1983). Unlike many women, most men have not bridged the separate spheres of work and home.

In sum, women experience the costs of care because of a variety of factors: internalized sex-role and filial obligation ideology; external pressures from other family members and professionals; material conditions related to the gender division of labor in the public and private spheres; lack of service supports and options; and professional practices whereby there is differential access to services if a female relative is available. These costs, inherent in the gender-based distribution of caregiving responsibilities, have also been perpetuated by social and health care policies.

Social Policy and Caregiving Inequities

Such gender inequities persist because promoting the well-being of family caregivers of the elderly has not been a policy goal. Nor have caregivers' rights to public support been legitimized within social and health policies. Instead, the interests of family caregivers are accorded a low priority in the distribution of scarce resources. Social and health benefits are generally allocated on the basis of the older person's needs, not the family care system (Briggs & Oliver, 1985). As examples, Medicaid and Medicare, the major health care reimbursement mechanisms, fund primarily institutional care, not in-home services, respite, and day care that could support both family caregivers and their older relatives. Private insurance schemes are also biased toward institutionalized care, a bias that leaves many responsible family members feeling that they have no options but to provide care themselves. Only recently have nursing homes been offering more flexible and part-time relief rather than an "all or nothing" approach.

Historically, United States social welfare policy has been organized on the premise of private responsibility, specifically that the family is primarily responsible for the care of dependent persons and that it is natural for the family to provide care. The state has generally intervened only after family resources have been exhausted, or the family has proven itself incapable of meeting certain care standards, as in instances of abuse and neglect. Community care services have, at times, been limited to crisis or casualty intervention, thereby putting a penalty on caring while rewarding the break-down of a caring relationship (Moroney, 1980; Walker, 1985). The concept of privatization was institutionalized around the 1930s in the filial responsibility laws of 25 states (Kane, 1985). In the current conservative context, a number of states have reintroduced family responsibility amendments requiring adult children to contribute to nursing home costs prior to application for Medicaid. These amendments are intended to deter wealthy families from "dumping" their parents in nursing homes, a rationale that does not accord with the reality that most families turn to institutionalization only as a last resort. Such public demands for filial responsibility mask social irresponsibility. They label adults, primarily women, as unloving deviants if they institutionalize their relatives, scapegoat them for the escalating long-term care costs, and place the legitimate needs of generations in conflict with one another (Brody, 1985). In addition, such legislation avoids the fundamental policy question of whether and under what conditions the responsibility for long-term care of the elderly ought to remain private.

Financial incentives for family caregivers of the elderly have been debated in Congress since 1965. These debates imply that families need to be induced to perform what they have already been doing for years. In addition, incentives, such as more liberal tax credits and deductions and tax-free stipends to offset home care costs, fail to address nonrational nonmonetary motives for providing care. They also ignore caregivers' preferences for flexible, highly individualized, support services, such as respite and in-home help, rather than for financial aid (Grassi, 1988; Horowitz & Shindelman, 1980; Lewis & Meredith, 1988; Sommers & Shields, 1987; Stone et al., 1986).

Policy makers concerned with cost containment frequently argue that services such as Meals on Wheels and home help supplant what families should naturally be doing. For example, in-home health programs have been criticized as a cost-inefficient way to perform custodial functions that families could assume (Sommers, 1983). In some states, in-home supportive services have been denied to frail elders with an "able and available" spouse (Estes, Newcomer, & Associates, 1983). Some recent state programs to encourage in-home care will pay a nonfamily member as caregiver, but not a relative. Such policies artificially frame formal services as antithetical to informal family supports and overlook the fact that services often strengthen families' caregiving capacities rather than encourage an abdication of care

(Horowitz & Dobrof, 1982; Zimmer & Sainer, 1978). In fact, since only 10% of all caregivers of the elderly utilize formal services, they clearly are not neglecting their care responsibilities (Stone et al., 1986). Alternatively, older people whose caregivers experience greater stress tend to use more community services; this suggests that targeting services to reduce caregiver burden would, in the long run, be more cost-effective than expecting families to manage on their own (Bass & Noelker, 1985).

Education and support programs are a recent policy development oriented to reducing caregiver burden. Yet their cost-effectiveness is often evaluated in terms of whether they prolong the caregiving relationship, not the caregivers' well-being. Policies that rely on caregivers' sacrifice can be considered "cost-effective" only if the emotional, physical, and financial costs incurred by caregivers are omitted from calculations. As noted above, most caregivers will persevere to the breaking point, bound by love or duty to those for whom they care. Under such conditions, cost containment approaches make the public purse the beneficiary of policies, while victimizing caregivers as unpaid servants. Efficiency is a misplaced standard for caregiving, and cost-effectiveness questions are the wrong ones. Instead of asking what is the cheapest way to keep an older person alive, we should be determining the best way to care for them (Sommers & Shields, 1987). Accordingly, we need to question whether and when home-based care is the best alternative and to recognize situations where institutionalization is the better option for both the dependent person and the caregiver. Care *in* the community—with the dependent person supported by informal caring networks *and* community and institutional services as necessary—needs to be differentiated from care *by* the community where the emphasis is on informal family care (Lewis & Meredith, 1988).

Policy Directions

To be able to consider a broader public role in long-term care, it is important to break out of the mindset that caregiving is a private duty. The assumption that family caregivers' welfare should be a central goal of social and health policy, not a means to low cost care, is fundamental to this discussion of policy directions. As noted above, criteria other than efficiency and cost-containment need to be used for developing and evaluating policies to support family caregivers. New criteria, based on compassion as the primary value, include the following: do they share the responsibility for care between public/private domains as well as among family members, regardless of gender; allow families choice about their level and type of caregiving involvement; and provide tangible relief from physically and emotionally draining chores? In sum, do they recognize that the best form of care varies with both the caregiver's and care-recipient's needs and that gender should not be a criterion for determining formal care?

Even though caregivers are not motivated primarily by financial gain, the link between caregiving and economic hardship cannot be ignored. Therefore, monetary compensation for caregiving is an important first strategy, although fraught with the paradox of financially rewarding nonmonetary values (Grassi, 1988). For example, an attendant allowance could help expand caregivers' options to purchase respite services and other concrete supports, even though only a small amount of money would be available per caregiver. To avoid the gender inequities inherent in the allowances given only to unmarried women in some Western European countries, caregiver allowances should be a recognized right for performing a service to society, regardless of the caregiver's marital or occupational status. Otherwise, such allowances will reinforce women's positions as the allegedly "natural" caretakers in the family. Similarly, proposals for earnings sharing of Social Security benefits require careful examination in terms of their potential support for caregivers of dependent populations.

Closely related is the need to examine the word caregiver itself. It implies "caring" and "giving" for free, which leaves the receiver in debt. "Caring" and "giving" define the compassion trap. MacDonald (1988) suggests that the concept of caregiving itself is a trap, because it is an attempt to empower one group by praise through implying self-sacrifice, and disempower the other who is in debt of the "caring" and the "giving." A useful distinction is that caring *about* and caring *for* someone can be separated: caring for can be seen as an obligation, which can be performed by nonfamily members such as attendants as well as divided between the private and public spheres (Aronson, 1986; Jarrett, 1985). If both family and nonfamily care providers are called attendants, this then implies that one person attends to those aspects of living that cannot be accomplished by another because of disability or illness. One gets a service, the other a wage. By paying an attendant, the dependent person preserves autonomy in meeting his or her needs.

Yet the fundamental imbalance of caregiving responsibilities will not be addressed if such services are provided by female volunteers or unskilled minimum-wage women, leaving both unpaid and underpaid women serving dependent populations. Without a major shift in the organization of caregiving services, women with economic resources will confront a bind they have always faced: gaining freedom from caregiving chores at the expense of women with less money. Therefore, attendants should be adequately compensated with both wages and benefits, including vacations and health care, that recognize the importance of their caregiving work. Such organization addresses concerns raised by the Older Women's League and the American Federation of State, County and Municipal Employees in their 1988 report, *Chronic Care Workers: Crisis Among Paid Caregivers of the Elderly*, and could serve, in the long run, to help break the cycle of the feminization of poverty.

Traditional assumptions of caregiving roles also must be challenged through policy changes in the workplace. Specifically, the separate spheres assumption that exonerates the workplace from responsibility for family care must be altered. Business benefits in innumerable ways from family caregiving. Rather than penalizing workers' involvement in family life, businesses could support it through benefit packages available to both men and women that include the options of day care and in-home services for employees' older relatives. The growing number of Employee Assistance Programs could provide counseling and referrals to appropriate services. The Family and Medical Leave Act, legislation currently before Congress, is an important first step in providing caregivers of dependents of any age with an unpaid leave. Yet this Act needs to be extended for longer coverage periods of leave and to include caregiving spouses. A further step would be the development of an insurance system for paid dependent-care leave, perhaps as part of an expanded unemployment insurance scheme.

Workplace modifications are also necessary to enable men and women to share caregiving tasks more equitably and thus to integrate their public and private lives. The work setting could be restructured to better accommodate family responsibilities of both men and women through flex-time, part-time jobs with full benefits, job sharing, and shorter workdays. Such policies and benefits should not only support the social care functions of employees, but finance substitute care, when necessary. A long run strategy would be to make the 30-hour work week the norm, through amendment of the Fair Labor Standards Act. This would require overtime premiums after a 30-hour week or a 6-hour day to assure that both men and women have time for family concerns. The 40-hour work week was based on the wife's economic dependence on the husband. As a long run strategy, shortening the work week is preferable to encouraging flex-time and part-time work, options which are likely to be used more by women than men, thereby perpetuating gender-based inequities and doing nothing toward reclaiming time for families to maintain themselves.

A long-range challenge for social welfare policy and practice is how to mainstream caregiving values as a central force in shaping society. Ultimately, caregiving values must become public values, rather than be divided along economic and gender lines. Traditional values of family responsibility must be given equal footing with marketplace values in shaping the course of a society built around human needs. Accordingly, if unpaid work was established as a legitimate economic category, it would have its own criteria of value and own rewards for both men and women (Scott, 1984; Walker, 1986). Therefore, a long-range solution to the inequity of women bearing the burdens of care is the reintegration of women's and men's private and work lives (Ehrenreich & English, 1979). In other words, a policy goal is not only the integration of women into the public sphere but of men into the private sphere. Such reintegration would enable women to pursue their own marketplace aspirations while achieving an equitable distribution of domestic and interpersonal care. Major societal changes will be required to overcome the normative designation of women as carers and the moral imperative on them to care (Walker, 1985).

In sum, women's full social and political participation in our society is not possible until their economic roles are enhanced. For women to achieve their economic aspirations, not only a substantial increase in their wage-earning capacity is required, but also societal support for the functions generally performed by women on an unpaid basis, in this instance elder care. Key components of such supports are publicly provided, universally available, elder care (through adult day care and respite programs, home help, and meal programs), and, as noted above, a 30-hour work week. As part of a social infrastructure that builds communities and supports family life, a publicly supported national health care system is critical. Housing and neighborhoods could be designed to better meet family needs, through communal facilities that provide meals, meeting places, and elder care.

Critics will contend that such major policy changes are not possible. Yet social intervention on a grand scale occurred in the face of economic crises in the 1930s. Today's crises facing families are also severe, and the social policies that once seemed daring are no longer adequate. Social justice demands that women and men who are caregivers have a choice about whether and how to care for dependent relatives—that they not be victims who are required to make heroic sacrifices in order to keep a relative out of an institution (Callahan, 1988). For those who do choose to assume the social role of providing compassion and care, there must be the public resources to support them (Briggs & Oliver, 1985). Callahan (1988) has argued that even with adequate social support, we are still faced with moral claims that confront caregivers with imperative duties that are oftentimes impossible demands. If we must ask caregivers to make these sacrifices and if they agree, then it becomes essential that we reward and sustain them. Over a decade of research has shown us what family caregivers of the elderly need. The challenge for our society is to redefine its responsibility to the growing number of caregivers and care-recipients so that caregiving work is equitably shared and the autonomy of caregiver and care-recipient ensured. Such a redistribution is essential to move toward a society where dependent elders are the concern of all, and where individuals are able to receive and to give to others the care that they want and need.

References

Aronson, J. (1986). Care of the frail elderly. Whose curse? Whose responsibility? *Canadian Social Work Review, 3*, 45-84.

Bass, D., & Noelker, L. (1985). *The influence of family caregivers on elder's use of in-home services: An expanded conceptual framework.* Presented at the 38th Annual Meeting of the Gerontological Society of America, New Orleans, LA.

Belle, D. (1982). The stress of caring: Women as providers of social support. In L. Goldberger & S. Breznitz (Eds.), *The handbook of stress.* New York: Free Press.

Bernard, J. (1983). The good-provider role: Its rise and fall. In A. Skolnick & J. Skolnick (Eds.), *Family in transition* (4th ed.). Boston: Little, Brown.

Biegel, D., & Naparstek, A. (Eds.). (1982). *Community support systems and mental health: Practice, policy, and research.* New York: Springer.

Birenbaum, A,. & Re, M. A. (1983). Family care providers: Sources of role strain and its management. *Journal of Family Issues, 4*(4), 633-658.

Briar, K., & Ryan, R. (1986). The anti-institution movement and women caregivers. *Affilia, 1*(1), 20-32.

Briggs, A., & Oliver, J. (1985). *Caring: Experiences of looking after disabled relatives.* London: Routledge & Kegan Paul.

Brody, E. (1981). Women in the middle and family help to older people. *The Gerontologist, 21*(5), 471-480.

Brody, E. (1985). Parent care as a normative family stress. *The Gerontologist, 25* (1), 19-30.

Brody, E. M., Johnson, P. T., & Fulcomer, M. C. (1984). What should adult children do for elderly parents? Opinions and preferences of three generations of women. *Journal of Gerontology, 39*(6), 736-747.

Brody, E. M., Kleban, M., Johnson, P., & Hoffman, C. (1984). *Women who help elderly mothers: Do work and parent care compete?* Paper presented at the 37th Annual Scientific Meeting of the Gerontological Society of America, San Antonio, TX.

Callahan, D. (1988). Families as caregivers: The limits of morality. *Archives of Physical Medicine Rehabilitation, 69*, 323-328.

Cantor, M. H. (1983). Strain among caregivers: A study of experience in the United States. *The Gerontologist, 23*(6), 597-607.

Chodorow, N. (1978). *The reproduction of mothering: Psychoanalysis and the sociology of gender.* Berkeley, CA: University of California Press.

Chodorow, N., & Contratto, S. (1982). The fantasy of the perfect mother. In B. Thorne & M. Yalom (Eds.), *Rethinking the family: Some feminist questions.* New York: Longman.

Cott, N. (1977). *The bonds of womanhood: Woman's sphere in New England, 1780-1835*. New Haven, CT: Yale University Press.

Daatland, S., & Sundstrom, G. (1985). *Gammd i Norden*. Stockholm, Sweden.

Darling, R. B. (1979). *Families against society*. Beverly Hills, CA: Sage.

Ehrenreich, B. (1983). *The hearts of men: American dreams and the flight from commitment*. Garden City, NY: Doubleday.

Ehrenreich, B., and English, D. (1979). *For her own good: 150 years of the experts' advice to women*. Garden City, NY: Anchor Press.

Estes, C. L., Newcomer, R. J., and Associates. (1983). *Fiscal austerity and aging: Shifting government responsibility for the elderly*. Newbury Park, CA: Sage.

Fengler, A., & Goodrich, N. (1979). Wives of elderly disabled men: The hidden patients. *The Gerontologist, 12*(2), 175-183.

Finch, J., & Groves, D. (1983). *A labour of love: Women, work and caring*. London: Routledge & Kegan Paul.

Fischer, C. S. (1982). *To dwell among friends: Personal networks in town/city*. Chicago: University of Chicago Press.

Gallagher, D., Lovett, S., & Zeiss, A. (1988). Interventions with caregivers of frail older persons. In M. Ory & K. Bond (Eds.), *Aging and health care: Social science and policy perspectives*. New York: Tavistock.

George, L. K., and Gwyther, L. P. (1986). Caregiver well-being: A multidimensional examination of family caregivers of demented adults. *The Gerontologist, 26* (2), 253-259.

Gilligan, C. (1982). *In a different voice: Psychological theory and women's development*. Cambridge, MA: Harvard University Press.

Graham, H. (1983). Caring: A labor of love. In J. Finch & D. Groves, *A labour of love: Women, work and caring* (pp. 13-30). London: Routledge & Kegan Paul.

Grassi, L. (1988). The frail elderly and long-term care administration. *Caring, 7* (3), 24-30.

Guberman, N. (1986). Who's at home to pick up the pieces? *Canadian Social Work Review*. pp. 219-227.

Guberman, N. (1988). The family, women, and caring: Who cares for the carers? *New Feminist Research, 17*(2), 37-41.

Haddow, C. McClain. (1985). *Growing old in America*. ABC News. Close-up Show #126, December 28.

Haley, W. E., Levine, E. C., Brown, S. L., Berry, J. W., & Hughes, G. H. (1987). Psychological, social and health consequences of caring for a relative with senile dementia. *Journal of the American Geriatrics Society, 35*, 405-411.

Hartman, H. (1988). Achieving economic equity for women. In M. Raskin & C. Hartman (Eds.), *Winning America: Ideas and leadership for the 1990s* (pp. 95-105). Boston: South End Press and the Institute for Policy Studies.

Hooyman, N. R., & Ryan, R. (1987). Women as caregivers of the elderly: Catch-22 dilemmas. In J. Figueira-McDonough and R. Sarri (Eds.), *The trapped woman* (pp. 143-171). Newbury Park, CA: Sage.

Horowitz, A., & Dobrof, R. (1982). *The role of families in providing long-term care to the frail and chronically ill elderly living in the community*. [Final Report to the Health Care Financing Administration, U.S. Department of Health and Human Resources], pp. 132-137.

Horowitz, A., & Shindelman, L. (1980). *Social and economic incentives for family caregivers*. Paper presented at the 33rd Annual Scientific Meeting of the Gerontological Society of America, San Diego, CA.

Jarrett, W. H. (1985). Caregiving within kinship systems: Is affection really necessary? *The Gerontologist, 25*(6), 5-10.

Johnson, C., & Catalano, D. (1983). A longitudinal study of family supports to impaired elderly. *The Gerontologist, 23*(6), 612-618.

Kane, R. A. (1985). Long-term care status quo untenable? What is more ideal for nation's elderly? *Perspectives in Aging, 14*, 23-26.

Lagergren, M. (1984). *Time to care*. Elmsford, NY: Pergamon.

Lang, A. M., & Brody, E. M. (1983). Characteristics of middle-aged daughters and help to their elderly mothers. *Journal of Marriage and the Family, 45*, 193.

Lewis, J., & Meredith, B. (1988). *Daughters who care: Daughters caring for mothers at home*. London: Routledge & Kegan Paul.

Long-term care: A woman's issue. (1987). *Caring, 6*(10), 67-75.

Lyons, N. (1983). Two perspectives on self, relationship & morality. *Harvard Educational Review, 53*, 125-145.

MacDonald, B. (1988). Presentation at Working Conference on Older Women, University of Utah, Salt Lake City, UT.

Minkler, M., & Stone, R. (1985). The feminization of poverty and older women. *The Gerontologist*, 351-358.

Moroney, R. (1980). *Families, social services, and social policy: The issue of shared responsibility*. Rockville, MD: National Institute of Mental Health.

Newman, S. J. (1980). *Government policy and the relationship between adult children and their aging parents: Filial support, Medicare and Medicaid* (pp. 10-19). Institute for Social Research, Ann Arbor, MI. Unpublished manuscript.

Nygard, L. (1982). *Omsorgsressursow has naere Parorende*. National Institute for Sociology, Report 2, Trondheim, Norway.

Older Women's League. (1986). *Report on the status of midlife and older women*. Washington, DC: Author.

Older Women's League & American Federation of State, County & Municipal Employees. (1988). *Chronic care workers: Crisis among paid caregivers of the elderly*. Washington, DC: Author.

Pearson, J., & Roberto, K. (1985). Use of informal and formal support networks by rural elderly poor. *The Gerontologist, 25*(6), 624-631.

Perry, M. (1987). New bill proposed for long-term home care. *Aging Connection, 8*(6), 1.

Pilisuk, M., & Park, S. H. (1988). Caregiving: Where families need help. *Social Work, 33*(5), 436-442.

Polansky, E. (1985). *A feminist analysis of hospital discharge planning: Women as caregivers of disabled family members*. Presented at the Women's Symposium, the Annual Program Meeting of the Council on Social Work Education, Washington, DC.

Robinson, B., & Thurnher, M. (1979). Taking care of aged parents: A family cycle transition. *The Gerontologist, 19*(6), 586-593.

Rossi, A. (1985). Gender and parenthood. In A. Rossi (Ed.), *Gender and the life course*. Hawthorne, NY: Aldine.

Scott, H. (1984). *Working your way to the bottom: The feminization of poverty*. London: Pandora Press.

Shapiro, J. (1983). Family reactions and coping strategies in response to the physically ill or handicapped child: A review. *Journal of Social and Behavioral Sciences* 913-931.

Sommers, T. (1983). Cost of care: What do we do with grandmother? *Gray Panther Network*. National Office of Gray Panthers, 311 South Juniper St, PA 19107.

Sommers, T., & Shields, L. (1987). *Women take care*. Gainsville, FL: Triad.

Steinitz, L. (1981). *Informal supports in long-term care: Implications and policy options*. Presented to the National Conference on Social Welfare.

Stober, M. H. (1982). Market work, housework and child care: Burying archaic tenets, building new arrangements. In P. W. Berman and E. R. Ramey (Eds.), *Women: A developmental perspective* (pp. 207-219). Bethesda, MA: National Institute of Health.

Stoller, E. P. (1983). Parental caring of adult children. *Journal of Marriage and the Family, 45*, 851-858.

Stone, R., Cafferata, G., & Sangle, J. (1986). *Caregivers of the frail elderly: A national profile*. Washington, DC: National Center for Health Services Research.

Sundstrom, G. (1983). *Caring for the aged in the welfare states*. Stockholm, Sweden.

Teresi, J. A., Toner, J. A., Bennett, R. G., & Wilder, D. E. (1980). *Factors related to family attitudes toward institutionalizing older relatives*. Paper presented at the 33rd Annual Scientific Meeting of the Gerontological Society, San Diego, CA .

Vanek, J. (1983). Household work, wage work, and sexual equality. In A. Skolnick and J. Skolnick (Eds.), *Family in transition* (4th ed.). Boston: Little, Brown.

Waerness, K. (1978). The invisible welfare state: Women's work at home. *Acta Sociologica, 19*, 193-206.

Waerness, K. (1983). *Caring as women's work in the welfare state*. Bergen, Norway: University of Bergen. Unpublished manuscript.

Waerness, K. (1985). *Informal and formal care in old age—what is wrong with the new ideology of community care in the Scandinavian welfare state today?* Presented at the conference on Gender Divisions and Policies for Community Care, University of Kent at Canterbury, England.

Walker, A. (1985). From welfare state to caring society? The promise of informal support networks. In J. Jonker, R. Leaper, & J. Yoder (Eds.), *Support networks in a caring community* (pp. 41-49). Lancaster, England: Martins Nijhoff.

Walker, A. (1986). Community care: Fact and fantasy. In A. Walker, P. Ekblom, & N. Deakin (Eds.), *The debate about community: Papers from a seminar on community in social policy*. London: PSI.

Wethington, E., McLeod, J., & Kessler, R. (1987). The importance of life events for explaining sex differences in psychological distress. In R. Barnett, L. Biener, & G. Baruch (Eds.), *Gender and stress* (pp. 144-159). New York: Free Press.

Wood, J. B., & Estes, C. I. (1986-1987). Effects of health care cost containment policies. *Generations, 11* (29), 28-33.

Wright, F. (1983). Single careers: Employment, housework, and caring. In J. Finch & D. Groves (Eds.), *A labour of love: Women, work, and caring* (pp.89-105). London: Routledge & Kegan Paul.

Zarit, S. H., Reever, K. E., & Bach-Peterson, J. (1980). Relatives of the impaired elderly: Correlates of feelings of burden. *The Gerontologist, 20*(6), 649-655.

Zimmer, A., & Sainer, J. (1978). Strengthening the family as an informal support for their aged: Implication for social policy and planning. Paper presented at the 31st Annual Meeting of the Gerontological Society, Dallas, Texas, November.

11

Public Opinion and Long-Term Care Policy

NANCY GILLILAND
LINDA HAVIR

In the summer of 1988, the United States Congress passed what is usually referred to as the "Catastrophic Coverage Act." This legislation, which was subsequently repealed, protected Medicare beneficiaries against the cost of expensive medical procedures or unusually long hospitalizations. At about the same time, a second bill, which would have provided home care benefits, was rejected when the House refused it floor consideration.

It was our impression that media discussion of these bills prior to congressional action almost always contained references to opinion poll results showing overwhelming public support for them. This unusual emphasis on public opinion aroused our interest in the relationship between public preferences and public policy formulation, generally, and specifically, with respect to long-term care for elderly people.

We recognize, of course, that public opinion is only one of many factors that influence social policy choices. Economic conditions, charismatic leadership in or outside government, and powerful interest groups are prominent among these. We chose to focus on just one factor, public opinion, to see if there is a pattern of consistency between public opinion, as expressed

AUTHORS' NOTE

The authors thank Polly Fassinger, Linda Johnson, and Cameron Young for their helpful comments.

242

in polls, and policies and legislation at the federal level. We were particularly interested in examining opinions about the extent to which government was expected to have major financial responsibility for the long-term care of elderly people.

Survey questions typically frame this issue as a choice between public (government) or private (individual or family) responsibility. What we found by examining data from national public opinion polls was that in the last 10 years the preponderance of public opinion has fallen on the public responsibility side. That is, the majority of respondents in opinion polls express the view that financial responsibility for long-term care of elderly people should fall primarily on government. Given this public preference, we were interested in knowing if long-term care policy has moved in the direction of greater public responsibility. Passage of the catastrophic coverage bill expanding Medicare benefits would seem to suggest that it has.

We looked first at the literature on the influence of public opinion on policy formulation in general, and then at the case of long-term care. We suggest that the assessment of whether or not long-term care policy has followed public opinion depends on definitions of public responsibility. When the public states a preference for more "public" responsibility, what does that mean? We suggest that when benefits are funded by the beneficiaries themselves and/or a regressive tax, it does not constitute genuine public responsibility.

Impact of Public Opinion on Policy

To what extent has public opinion influenced policy in the past? The question of government responsiveness to citizens' preferences has long been a central issue for political scientists and theorists of democracy. In the words of Key (1961, p.7), "Unless mass views have some place in the shaping of policy, all the talk about democracy is nonsense." George Gallup, at the outset of his career in the 1930s, envisioned his polls as improving the machinery of democracy by allowing citizens to make their wishes known to government and also by countering the effects of pressure and lobbyist groups (Sussman, 1988). Public opinion polls are an important mechanism for assessing citizen views on various issues since referenda and elections are expensive and relatively rare. Opinion polling also helps to reduce a sense of alienation from government (Webb & Hatry, 1973).

Because opinions from representative samples of the public reflect concerns and priorities, it is important to assess the impact of this opinion on policy. A review of empirical studies of government responsiveness to public opinion indicates that public preferences do shape policy. Wright, Erikson, and McIver (1987) found that states with the most liberal electorates enacted the most liberal policies (and vice versa). They concluded that: "Across an impressive range of policies, public opinion counts, and not just a little." (Wright, Erikson, & McIver, 1987, p.999)

More detailed studies of specific issues by Monroe (1979) and Page and Shapiro (1983) also report significant correspondence between public opinion and policy. Page and Shapiro (1983) studied changes in public opinion as measured by a series of polls that repeated the same question. When changes occurred, they ascertained whether policy change followed. They found that congruence between national opinion and policy was greater in the 1970s than in the 1950s and 1960s. They attributed this to more educated and knowledgable respondents and better quality data, however, rather than to more responsive government. Other variables associated with greater congruence between change in opinion and change in policy included salience of the issue (number of times the question was repeated in polls and number of "Don't know" and "No opinion" answers were measures of salience), magnitude and stability of the change in public opinion, and nature of the issue. For example, they found that "moral" issues, such as divorce, abortion, and capital punishment, which tend to be debated at the state level, showed higher levels of congruence between opinion change and policy.

With respect to magnitude of opinion change, these authors pointed out that federal legislation (as opposed to state legislation or executive and judicial policy making) requires a larger change in opinion and one of longer duration than other levels of policy because "new congressional legislation is hard to get" (Page & Shapiro, 1983, p.183). Similarly, Monroe (1979) suggested that a key factor in preventing an even higher level of correspondence between opinion and policy is the failure of the legislative branch of federal government, in particular, to act quickly on proposals for change.

Once a correspondence between opinion and policy is found, there still remains the question of whether it is a causal relationship and, if so, the direction of effect. Page and Shapiro (1983) concluded, based primarily on time sequences, that the main direction of effect is from opinion to policy. Even so, these authors urge caution in jumping to conclusions about democratic responsiveness. Policy might be changed, but not as far as opinion dictates, for example.

All of these possibilities may apply in the case of government responsibility for long-term care. Our general conclusion from these findings, however, is that if public opinion has been strong, stable, and relatively unambiguous in its support for tax-supported long-term care (as opposed to individual or family responsibility), we can expect public policy to move in that direction.

We turn now to the case of long-term care to see whether it is an exception to the (statistical) rule of congruence between opinion and policy.

Public Opinion on Long-Term Care: Public or Private Responsibility?

Compared with recipients of Aid to Families with Dependent Children (AFDC) and other groups, the elderly are generally seen by the public as more deserving of government support. Cook (1979), for example, found the Chicago area public more willing to have their tax money support social services for poor and disabled elderly people than for any other group.

National polls have also reflected widespread support for public programs for elderly people. In a 1981 Roper poll, 69% of respondents expressed the opinion that spending on social services for older people was too low, while only 5% thought it was too high (Roper Center for Public Opinion, 1981). As early as 1983, 66% thought the Reagan administration was treating elderly people unfairly (Gallup Report, 1983). In a 1984 Gallup poll, 88% of respondents favored maintaining the cost of living increases in Social Security benefits (Gallup Report, 1984). During the 1983–87 period, the vast majority (83–88%) of Gallup's respondents disapproved of "cuts in entitlement programs such as Social Security, Medicare and the like to reduce the deficit" (Gallup Report, 1987). All of these findings reflect willingness to use tax funds to finance programs for elderly people and thus can be interpreted as support for government, as opposed to private, responsibility. In an explicit choice between government and family responsibility for care of the elderly, a 1981 Harris poll showed 54% favoring government responsibility (Harris & Associates, 1981).

The clearest evidence of public support for government responsibility appears in two polls done expressly to assess public support for the catastrophic coverage and home care bills. The polls were conducted by R L Associates (1987) for the American Association of Retired Persons/Villers Foundation and by Louis Harris and Associates (cited in Staff, 1988) for release by Congressman Claude Pepper (D-Florida). The two major findings in both polls were: (a) strong support for government responsibility for financing long-term care of the elderly; and (b) large numbers of respondents with firsthand experience with need for long-term care by a family member or friend (50% in the R L Associates poll; 37% in Harris). R L Associates reported that half the respondents anticipated the need for long-term care in their family in the next five years.

In the poll by R L Associates (1987), about 80% of respondents stated that long-term care is a major financial concern for families and that nursing home costs would be "impossible to pay" or would constitute "a major sacrifice" for them. This public perception was confirmed by a recent Brookings Institution report which concluded that private insurance and personal savings are not likely to provide enough protection for the majority of those who need long-term care. The report estimated that 26–45% of Americans will be able to afford long-term care insurance by the year 2020 and that this coverage will account for only 7–12% of the total nursing home expenses (Pressman, 1988).

Having accurately perceived that private solutions to the problem of paying for long-term care may not be feasible, respondents to a number of polls went on to express their willingness to help pay for long-term care by means of taxes. About 71% in the R L Associates poll (1987) did so. Hamilton (Long-Term Care, 1988) found that 73% of a national sample of 2,000 respondents over age 45 chose long-term care over 10 other issues for "increased government spending." About 61% preferred to finance it through a social insurance program such as Social Security, rather than by private financing with government funding only for the poor. More than two thirds (68%) were willing to pay for long-term care through higher taxes of $10–$60 a month, depending on their income (Long-Term Care, 1988).

In sum, in the case of long-term care, opinion poll results show that the issue is salient and that opinion favoring government responsibility for financing it has been strong and stable for approximately the past decade. We have also noted passage of the Catastrophic Loss Prevention Act in 1988 and congressional discussion of home care legislation. Do we conclude from all this that long-term care policy is consistent (or increasingly consistent) with public preferences? To answer that question, we turn now to long-term care policy.

Public Policy on Long-Term Care: Public or Private Responsibility?

Public support for the idea that long-term health care needs of the elderly should be met primarily by the government is not new. The view that old age, with its problems of frailty and disability, is not just a private trouble to be dealt with individually by the elderly and their families can be traced back to the New Deal. Creation of the Medicare and Medicaid programs in 1965 reaffirmed this notion; most accounts of their enactment describe them as a response to public pressure for health care benefits. Medicare benefits were limited to elderly people, however, as a political compromise. Opposition to national health insurance (viewed by many people as "socialized medicine") was offset by public sympathy for the elderly and resulted in this compromise legislation. Though not without benefit to elderly people, Medicare was not designed with their unique health care needs in mind (Achenbaum, 1983). A major omission was provision for long-term care.

As a response to public demand for government responsibility for health care, Medicare and Medicaid fell far short of ideal. In fact, Medicaid benefits, a large portion of which go toward nursing home care for the elderly, were curtailed early in the life of the program as costs exceeded projections. Today, less than half of those below the poverty level are eligible for Medicaid (Oberg & Polich, 1988), and Medicare deductibles and premiums have increased substantially.

During the early 1980s a philosophy of cost containment by means of benefit cuts was predominant. The cuts were overt, such as more restrictive eligibility for Medicaid, and covert, such as hospital stays shortened by Diagnosis Related Groups which require families to provide care previously given by hospitals. In both cases, "privatization" occurred, shifting responsibility from public to private sources.

In contrast to the benefit cuts of the early 1980s, 1988 produced a major expansion of Medicare: the Medicare Catastrophic Loss Prevention Act. This was an apparent reversal of long-term care policy in the direction of public opinion. But while the Catastrophic Loss Prevention Act began to address some of the costs related to long-term care, it focused mainly on expenses stemming from acute illnesses. If it had been fully implemented on January 1, 1993, the maximum out-of-pocket costs a beneficiary would have paid was about $3,000, plus a 20% copayment for drug costs in excess of the deductible, and any excess charges from physicians who do not accept assignment (Advocates Senior Alert Process, 1988, November).

The measure failed to address the greatest sources of catastrophic costs for older people—extended nursing home stays and home care. The average cost of nursing home care is $25,000 a year. More than half of all nursing home costs are borne by families or individuals and 3% by private insurance and Medicare (Deets, 1988). The remainder is paid by Medicaid, which provides benefits to lower income people and to those who must "spend down" their income and assets in order to qualify for coverage.

Despite the expanded benefits, this bill was not a clear instance of increasing government responsibility. As its proponents argued early on, it was a "revenue neutral" bill. That is, it would have been paid for primarily by Medicare recipients themselves. For all covered by Medicare Part B, there would have been an increase of about $4 in the monthly premium. This flat premium of $48 per year in 1989 would have covered about 40% of the cost of the new benefits; the other 60% would have been collected from bene-iaries with higher incomes—about 30% of Medicare enrollees (Advocates Senior Alert Process, 1988, November).

The only way in which this bill represented a true shift toward public re-sponsibility was in its Medicare "buy-in" provision and its protection against the impoverishment of a noninstitutionalized spouse, provisions that were not repealed. In the "buy-in" provision, state Medicaid programs will pay Medicare premiums, deductibles, and copayments for beneficiaries whose incomes fall below the poverty level. The "spousal impoverishment" provi-sion allows the spouse of a Medicaid-covered nursing home resident to retain more income and assets than is currently permitted. Both provisions will be financed by state and federal general funds.

We believe that although policy makers seemed to be responding to public expectations that government take more financial responsibility for long-term care, it was only an appearance. When long-term care is financed only by Medicare beneficiaries and Social Security, a regressive payroll tax, it is not true public responsibility.

How, then, can we explain this lack of congruence between opinion and policy? Why are policy makers reluctant to make long-term care a responsi-bility of the entire society through general fund financing? We suggest two ways of making sense of this. First, the reluctance is consistent with political economy theory (Olson, 1982). This theory suggests that the state has the contradictory role of legitimizing the social and economic order (which re-quires social spending to cushion some of the effects of a capitalist economy) while at the same time limiting social spending so as to conserve tax funds to be used to enhance accumulation of private profit (Estes, Gerard, Jones, & Swan, 1984).

Reluctance of policy makers to make long-term care a public responsibil-ity can also be understood as resulting from misconceptions about the role of families (frequently called the myth of family abandonment), and about the extent to which elderly people are in need. Both of these—political economy theory and the misconceptions about older people and their family relation-ships—will be discussed in the next two sections. We turn to the latter first.

Myth-Based Public Policy

Policy makers and the general public both subscribe, to some extent, to the notion that families are alienated from and abandon their elderly mem-bers to the care of the state. In the face of considerable evidence to the con-trary, the belief persists that adult children do not care for elderly parents as they did in the past. For example, a 1981 Roper survey found more than 60% of respondents agreeing that families are less willing to care for their elderly parents than they were 25 years ago (Roper Center for Public Opinion, 1981). This perception that family caregiving is on the decline in the United States is shared by policy makers, who express the fear that publicly sponsored programs will begin to supplant family care, adding to the already exorbitant cost of long-term care for the elderly (U.S. House of Representatives, 1987). According to Kelman and Thomas (1987), this "substitution effect" was erroneously inferred from two cross-sectional studies with small unrepresentative samples. The apparent substitution of formal for informal services was an artifact of the research method and did not appear in more careful longitudinal studies.

Nevertheless, the idea was used by the Health Care Financing Administration (HCFA) in its efforts at cost containment. In 1983, for example, HCFA instructed state governments that they could require adult children to contribute to the cost of care for parents whose nursing home care was being paid by Medicaid (Gilliland, 1986). In this way, as Brody (1985) has pointed out, the myth of family neglect has been used against families in the interest of cost containment. It is used despite the fact that 80% of the care of disabled elderly people living outside institutions comes from family members (Day, 1985).

The public has other misconceptions about older people as well. One that may be pertinent to the opinion–policy link is the belief that most older people are in poverty. "The majority of older people have incomes below the poverty level" is one of the most frequently missed items in Palmore's Facts on Aging Quiz (Palmore, 1980). The Harris polls of 1975 and 1981 for the National Council on Aging (Harris & Associates, 1975, 1981) also indicate a public perception of poverty among the elderly. The Villers Foundation in their 1987 report, *On the Other Side of Easy Street,* argued, however, that this stereotype of older people as poor has changed to one that sees them all as well off. Despite its fallacies, which the report documents well, this new stereotype has raised the issue of intergenerational inequity and conflict. The media compare poverty levels and benefits of older people with those of children, presenting the comparison in such a way that it appears to the public that whatever benefits are received by the elderly would otherwise go to children (Longman, 1986; Preston, 1984).

A national organization, Americans for Generational Equity (AGE), was formed recently, ostensibly to ensure "equity" for people of all ages. Public statements by staff members, however, suggest that its real intent is to protect the interests of young people and children from the greedy elderly

(Longman, 1985). According to the chairperson of the National Council on the Aging, AGE has received strong support from corporations (Walker, 1988). A counterorganization, Generations United, was founded by the Children's Welfare League of America and the National Council on Aging to oppose the pitting of children and elderly people against each other. The Gerontological Society of America also acted to refute the notion of intergenerational inequity by sponsoring the publication of *Ties That Bind: The Interdependence of Generations* (Kingson, Hirshorn, & Cornman, 1986).

As these myths persist, and headlines focus on negative family relations, politicians' reservations about the extent of responsibility the government should assume in caring for the elderly appear justified. Policy makers' often expressed fear is that families will "come out of the woodwork" to demand services if they were made available (Eustis, Greenberg, & Patton, 1984). The way to control this, from their perspective, is to limit benefits and services.

The Political Economy of Long-Term Care

Political economy theory in gerontology provides a way of making sense of long-term care policy. According to this theory, there is always tension between democracy and capitalism, with elites attempting to curtail social spending which they see as limiting the resources available to them, that is, resources that could otherwise be used for tax abatements, tax reductions, and the like. That much of social spending is financed by the working class through a regressive payroll tax is no accident, according to political economists (Olson, 1982).

Political economy theory leads us to suggest that the *appearance* of compliance with public preference for government responsibility fulfills the legitimizing function of the state. That is, it gives the appearance that the best interests of elderly people are being protected, thus preventing a major challenge to the existing distribution of wealth and power. At the same time, because social spending (for long-term care) is limited, it will not interfere with the most important function of the state for elites, that is, fostering the growth of profit and concentration of wealth.

Prospects for Public Responsibility

The issue of an equitable distribution of the burden of increased costs of long-term care in society is typically not posed in public opinion questions.

When respondents ask for increased federal spending for long-term care, and even express willingness to pay more in taxes themselves, they probably do not differentiate between progressive and regressive taxes to finance the spending. The popularity of Social Security (or perhaps the fact that it is less visible than the income tax) seems to obscure the fact that it is a regressive tax.

As Obler (1979) pointed out, the public generally is not concerned about income or wealth redistribution. That is, whether a tax is regressive or not has little salience to most people. According to Obler, people's attitudes toward a tax are determined more by how much it extracts from their incomes than by how much they pay relative to what other people pay.

Benefits provided in the home care bill that failed to pass in the summer of 1988 were to be financed by extending the Medicare payroll tax to workers who earn more than $45,000 and their employers. This constitutes a larger step toward genuine public responsibility than did the Catastrophic Loss Protection Act; however, the public which was to be responsible represents a very small proportion of the general public. Only about 5% of wage earners earn more than $45,000 (Advocates Senior Alert Process, 1988, March). This move toward progressiveness within a regressive tax may sensitize the public to the issue of what "public responsibility" means. That is, discussion of this bill may raise public consciousness that there is something unfair about the fact that they pay Social Security and Medicare payroll taxes on their entire income, whereas high earners and those whose livelihood comes from investments rather than wages do not.

The Long-Term Home Care bill sponsored by Representative Claude Pepper (D-Florida) and others was rejected in the House, but other similar bills have been proposed. Senator George Mitchell (D-Maine), for example, has proposed a bill which includes both home care and some coverage of nursing home care, with possible participation by private insurance companies to cover the first two years of nursing home care. Funding for this bill would combine raising the $45,000 cap on the Medicare tax and private long-term care insurance ("Kennedy Asks," 1988). Senator Edward Kennedy's (D-Mass) Lifecare proposal likewise includes both home and institutional care. His bill would be funded by a combination of raising the cap on Medicare payroll taxes to incomes of $75,000 and premiums paid by participants ("Kennedy Asks," 1988).

Whatever proposal becomes law, it appears unlikely that it will be financed by the income-tax supported general fund. Failing that, we would argue, policy will still not have responded to the call for public responsibility. To do so would require that the whole society—not just workers and elderly beneficiaries—pay for long-term care.

References

Achenbaum, W.A. (1983). *Shades of gray: Old age, American values, and federal policies since 1920*. Boston: Little, Brown.

Advocates Senior Alert Proccess (1988, March). *The Pepper long-term home care bill*. Washington, DC: Author.

Advocates Senior Alert Process. (1988, November). *Common questions about the Medicare Catastrophic Protection Act*. Washington, DC: Author.

Brody, E.M. (1985). Parent care as a normative family stress. *The Gerontologist, 25*, 19-29.

Cook, F.L. (1979). The disabled and the poor elderly: Preferred groups for public support? *The Gerontologist, 19*, 344-353.

Day, A.T. (1985). Who cares? Demographic trends challenge family care for the elderly. *Population trends and public policy*, Number 9. Washington, DC: Population References Bureau.

Deets, H.B. (1988, July–August). Executive director's report. *AARP News Bulletin, 3*.

Estes, C.L., Gerard, L.E., Jones, J.S., & Swan, J.H. (1984). *Political economy, health, and aging*. Boston: Little, Brown.

Eustis, N., Greenberg, J., & Patton, S. (1984). *Long-term care for older persons: A policy perspective*. Monterey, CA: Brooks/Cole.

Gallup Report. (1983, May, Number 212). p. 14.

Gallup Report. (1984, October, Number 229). p. 28.

Gallup Report. (1987, August, Number 263). pp. 25-27.

Gilliland, N. (1986). Mandating family responsibility for elderly members: costs and benefits. *Journal of Applied Gerontology, 5*, 26-36.

Harris, L., & Associates. (1975). *The myth and reality of aging in America*. Washington, DC: National Council on the Aging.

Harris, L., & Associates. (1981). *Aging in the eighties: America in transition*. Washington, DC: National Council on the Aging.

Kelman, H.R., & Thomas, C. (1987, August 17-21). *Family care and social policy*. Paper presented at American Sociological Association annual meeting, Chicago, IL.

Kennedy asks employers to fund long-term care. (1988, April 30.) *Medical benefits: The Medical Economic Digest, 5*, 2-3.

Key, V.O., Jr. (1961). *Public opinion and American democracy*. New York: Alfred A. Knopf.

Kingson, E.R., Hirshorn, B.A., & Cornman, J.M. (1986). *Ties that bind: The interdependence of generations*. Washington, DC: Seven Locks Press.

Longman, P. (1985, June). Justice between generations. *The Atlantic Monthly*, pp. 73-81.

Longman, P. (1986). Age wars: The coming battle between young and old. *Futurist, 20*, 8-11.

Long-Term Care '88: A National Campaign. (1988). *Public opinion on long-term care* (pp. 2-4). Washington, DC: Author.

Monroe, A. (1979). Consistency between public preferences and national policy decisions. *American Politics Quarterly, 7*, 3-19.

Oberg, C.N., & Polich, C.L. (1988). Medicaid: Entering the third decade. *Health Affairs, 7*, 83-96.

Obler, J. (1979). The odd compartmentalization: Public opinion, aggregate data, and policy analysis. *Policy Studies Journal, 7*, 524-540.

Olson, L.K. (1982). *The political economy of aging*. New York: Columbia University Press.

Page, B.I., & Shapiro, R.Y. (1983). Effects of public opinion on policy. *American Political Science Review, 77*, 175-190.

Palmore, E. (1980). The facts on aging quiz: Part II. *The Gerontologist, 21*, 431-437.

Pressman, S. (1988, May). The long-term care debate. *AARP News Bulletin*, pp. 14-15.

Preston, S. H. (1984). Children and the elderly in the United States. *Scientific American, 251*, 44-49.

R L Associates. (1987, October). *The American public views long-term care: A survey conducted for the American Association of Retired Persons and the Villers Foundation.*

Roper Center for Public Opinion. (1981). *Research for the American Enterprise Institute*, November 14-21.

Staff. (1988) Majorities favor passage of long-term health care legislation. *Medical Benefits: The Medical-Economic Digest*, (April 30, p. 1).

Sussman, B. (1988). *What Americans really think and why our politicians pay no attention.* Westminister, MD: Pantheon.

U.S. House of Representatives Subcommittee on Human Services of the Select Committee on Aging. (1987). *Exploding the myths: Caregiving in America* (Comm. Pub. No. 99-611). Washington, DC: U.S. Government Printing Office.

Villers Foundation. (1987). *On the other side of easy street: Myths and facts about the economics of old age.* Washington, DC: Author.

Walker, E. (1988, December 2). *Is aging safe while Congress is in session?* Presentation at the "Graying" of Society: Impacts on Families Today and in the Future Conference, sponsored by Minnesota Council on Family Relations, Minneapolis, MN.

Webb, K., & Hatry, H.P. (1973). *Obtaining citizen feedback: The application of citizen surveys to local governments.* Washington, DC: Urban Institute.

Wright, G.C., Erikson, R.S., & McIver, J.P. (1987). Public opinion and policy liberalism in the American states. *American Journal of Political Science 31*, 980-1001.

12

Caregiving for the Elderly in Sweden

Program Challenges and Policy Initiatives

MERL C. HOKENSTAD
LENNARTH JOHANSSON

Overview

Elderly care policy in Sweden has for a number of years emphasized community and home-based services designed to keep older people out of institutions. It has provided for the development of a comprehensive formal service system, operated primarily by local government. Coupled with a generous and well-funded public pension program, this system has had considerable success both in helping the elderly to manage at home, and in beginning to reduce nursing home occupancy rates in that country. Recent policy initiatives are focusing even more sharply on elderly care outside of institutions.

New policy proposals reflect a recent rediscovered interest in family caregiving in the country which exemplifies a welfare state. Recent Swedish research has shown that the majority of elderly care in that country is provided by families, as is true in the United States and other nations. In spite of the fact that 82% of Swedish women 16–64 years of age are in the labor market, informal caregivers provide about twice as much care as the well-developed home and community care services provide as a result of public policy. Renewed attention to family caregiving has led to a policy debate about the interaction between informal and formal care, and to policy initiatives designed to better support caregivers in Sweden.

Debate about the relationship between formal and informal care has a different point of departure in Sweden than in the United States. The accepted policy position is that publicly provided care is a citizen's right, and should be available to any individual or family who needs it. The decision regarding the mix of informal and formal care is a choice which rests with the family. In fact, the issue of care substitution is framed very differently in Sweden. There, the discussion is centered around the question of how much formal care is necessary so that no family is forced to substitute informal care for formal care. Families are not statutorily required to take care of the elderly, but the government does have this obligation.

Still, there is recognition that many families prefer informal care, or at least a combination of informal and formal care. Thus, the recent policy debate has centered on how formal care can be used to complement and reinforce family care. The results of recent research indicate that even within this system there is considerable caregiver burden. There is also recognition that better support for informal caregivers will decrease the amount of additional public resources which must go into the formal caregiving system. Thus, while substitution of care is approached from a different point of view as a policy issue in Sweden, economic and budgetary concerns certainly play a role in the policy debate.

Recognition of the need to better support family caregivers, and to make the formal system more complementary with the informal system, has led to several policy initiatives. These detail the provision of more economic assistance and better-focused service support for caregiving families. The most innovative of these initiatives is the incorporation of a care leave policy into the Swedish Social Insurance System. Swedish family caregivers will now be able to take up to 30 days of paid leave from their employment to provide special care for an elderly parent or spouse. Increased emphasis is also being given to the provision of caregiving salaries when caregiving is a regular, part-time, or full-time job. Although this is not a new form of support, it will now include the possibility for the caregiver to be retrained by the employer if she or he wishes to reenter the labor market.

In the area of service support, proposed policy would require more outreach in order to identify family caregivers in need of assistance and better targeting of home help services to reinforce caregivers. Thus, the substantial home care program of the municipalities would be better coordinated with informal caregiving. This emphasis, coupled with the increased economic assistance, is designed to strengthen interaction between the two caregiving systems.

This chapter provides a more detailed discussion about research findings and policy initiatives pertaining to care of the elderly in Sweden. As a background for this discussion, it first presents a brief review of policies and programs for older people in Sweden.

Policy Foundations of Elderly Care

Caregiving in Sweden must be viewed in the context of overall Swedish social policy. Sweden is considered the model welfare state. Its income support and social service programs are providing cradle to grave security for the Swedish people. Public policy is the basis for the funding and provision of these programs. It has produced a real safety net which has substantially eliminated poverty, and reduced the incidents of associated health and human problems. While policy has not solved all of the social problems in that country, it has prevented or alleviated many associated with economic hardship and social neglect (Hokenstad, 1983, 1989).

Social benefit programs for the elderly are a cornerstone of the Swedish welfare state. A basic pension is awarded to all citizens at age 65, regardless of prior employment. This demogrant includes a full widow's pension identical to the pension of an older person living alone, and a children's supplement to any pensioner who has children under 16 years of age living at home. A supplemental disability allowance and a wife's supplement are other payments under this basic pension plan.

Pension income beyond that of the basic pension is provided by a social insurance program based on employment. The National Supplementary Pension (ATP) provides benefits on the basis of the number of years employed and the average income for the best 15 years. Widows' and childrens' pensions also are available under ATP. A system of partial pensions enables persons between the ages of 60 and 65 years to shorten their working hours gradually. Pension increments to augment the basic pension are available if the pensioner is entitled to little, or no, supplemental pension.

These pension programs, coupled with national health insurance, which covers medical care and provides cash benefits in case of illness, have produced an income floor which prevents the elderly from falling into poverty. A full supplement pension comes to 60% of the average income earned in prior years. The total income replacement rate for an aged couple in Sweden is 83% (Nusberg, 1984). Income support programs directly impact on the ability of the elderly to live independently, and Swedish social policy provides benefits which allow the great majority of the elderly self-sufficient living (Hokenstad, 1988, 1989).

Social service policy designed to enable older people to manage in their own homes and remain out of institutions has been given increased attention in Sweden, as in the United States and other industrialized countries. Sweden's community and home-based care system is well developed and offers an important complement to the income support systems. A comprehensive system of open care for the elderly continues to receive attention in social policy. Currently proposed legislation has the strengthening of municipally based health care and social services as a major objective. The emphasis is on services which will promote the most independent living situation possible.

Service Provisions for the Elderly in Sweden

Swedish principles of service provision for the elderly are well articulated in the social legislation of the 1980s. Both the Social Services Act (1982) and the Health Care Act (1983) include the following principles: (a) normalization—old people should be given an opportunity to live in as normal a setting as possible; (b) influence and participation—old people should have an opportunity to participate in society as a whole; (c) self determination—old people should have involvement and options in life decisions. These commitments provide the foundation of the formal system for elderly care in Sweden.

Personal social services, along with pensions and health care, are considered entitlements, and the legislation mandates that services be universally available. Publicly funded social supports are provided by the municipality for all residents on the basis of need regardless of economic means. This includes a number of services for the elderly, such as help in the home (personal care and health care), meals on wheels, and special transportation. Local governments can organize social service programs in accordance with their own structures and local needs, but they are responsible for offering a number of services mandated by the law (Nasenius, 1981).

Programs in old-age care provided by the Swedish kommunerna (municipalities) include housing, community-based service centers, recreational activities, and home-based services such as home helps and hot meals. The comprehensive and universal characteristics of the service system help make it effective in promoting independence, participation, and normalcy of living condition for the Swedish elders. Along with the pension system, it has been a major factor in enabling older people to manage at home, thus remaining independent for longer periods of time. In particular, the highly developed and readily accessible home help services have postponed the necessity of nursing home care for a sizeable number of the frail elderly in Sweden (Hokenstad, 1989).

A decrease in the proportion of Swedish older people using institutional care has occurred, beginning in the middle 1970s. Between 1975 and 1985 the proportion of the elderly found in institutions decreased by 16%. According to Sundstrom and Berg (1988), there were 15% fewer long-term care beds in use in 1985 than ten years earlier. Clearly, a trend of deinstitutionalization of the elderly occurred during this period of time.

There also has been somewhat less of a reliance on informal care in recent years. Sundstrom (1983) concludes that increasing independence of the elderly as the result of readily available health care and social services has meant less need for family care in activities of daily living. However, he also reports that family bonds between the elderly and their adult children remain strong. Self-sufficient older people maintain close social and emotional ties with their families and are neither isolated nor lonely. In fact, financial and physical independence may well strengthen social and emotional ties according to the findings of this study.

Swedish Caregiving for the Elderly

Demographic Change and the Informal Support System

While care for the elderly has traditionally been one of the cornerstones of the Swedish welfare society, it recently has become a more arduous and challenging ambition. The prime reasons are the demographic changes within the elderly population, as shown in Table 12.1.

Out of Sweden's 8.4 million inhabitants, almost 1.5 million (17.4%) are pensioners, that is, aged 65 years or older. Few other countries have such a large proportion of elderly people in the population, and Sweden's average life expectancy is among the highest in the world, 80.2 years for women and 74.2 for men. The total proportion of elderly in the population will not change dramatically in the coming decades, but within the elderly group, considerable changes will occur. The old old group (80+) will grow 40% from 1985 to the year 2000. Furthermore, the number of single persons in this group is expected to increase by 35%. They also will have fewer children of their own to support them. Altogether, these trends impose a heavy burden on caregivers and society.

Another demographic change that will have consequences for caregiving is the shrinking household. In 1980, the small household share (one or two persons) was nearly 70% of all households, compared with roughly 50% in

Table 12.1   Population Growth Among the Elderly 1985–2010

Age	1985	1990	2000	2010
65–69	442,691	441,300	369,500	523,800
70–74	389,642	393,500	352,200	363,600
75–79	308,575	318,500	326,700	275,600
80–84	190,798	220,200	238,700	215,400
85–89	89,195	108,900	135,500	141,200
90–94	27,693	35,400	52,200	58,200
95 +	5,517	7,400	12,000	15,400
Total 65 +	1,454,111	1,525,200	1,486,800	1,593,200
80 +	313,203	371,900	438,400	430,200
Tot. pop.	8,358,139	8,432,200	8,538,700	8,513,500
65 +	17.4%	18.1%	17.4%	18.7%
80 +	3.7%	4.4%	5.1%	5.1%

Source: Statistics Sweden (1986a).

1960. Among the elderly households (households with at least one member age 65 or older), the proportion of one-person households increased from 30% in 1965 to 47% in 1980. Today, only 4% of the elderly live with their children as compared with 16% in 1954 (Daatland & Sundstrom, 1985).

These demographic trends, along with migration, urbanization, and broken families, put limits on the informal support system. Yet, there is continued evidence of ties between the elderly and their adult children. Data from surveys show that the contacts between the generations have not declined in recent decades. Johansson (1981) indicated that the proportion of Swedish elderly having regular contacts with kin actually increased slightly from 87.6% in 1968 to 90.6% in 1981. These quantitative data say nothing about the extent of informal support, but indicate an intact social network which can serve as the basis for caregiving.

As in other countries, it is largely women who preserve the social links, and function as the prime caregiver in the family. At the same time, there is an increasing proportion of women entering the labor market. Today, almost as many women as men are in gainful employment. Between 1963 and 1985 the percentage of women aged 16–64 who were employed grew from 54% to 82% (Statistics Sweden, 1986b). Therefore, many women carry expectations linked to a triple role as caretaker, worker, and mother. This creates a considerable stress for the women and their families.

Caregiving in Sweden: A Review of the Research

Research studies and policy debates concerning care of the elderly in Sweden have been largely focused on the formal care system for a number of reasons. Public policies and programs providing health and social services, as well as pensions and other forms of social insurance, are highly developed. The high percentage of women in the labor market presupposes a formal system of care for the elderly. There is no statutory requirement for children to provide care for the elderly. Thus, little public interest has been given to the role of the family and the informal care system until recently.

Today, however, there is growing interest in family caregiving. A policy focus on home-based care has stimulated this interest. Also, initial research has confirmed the importance of informal help. There is a growing body of information about caregiving resulting from recent studies, even though data are still limited and considerably more knowledge is needed for a complete picture.

The first important study to consider the role of informal caregiving among elderly was done in 1979 by the Secretariat for Future Studies (Lagergren, Lundh, Orkan, & Sanne, 1984). On the basis of interview data from a representative sample of 990, it was found that the elderly received almost three times as much informal as formal help (counted in number of hours). These data were not correlated to any data on assessed needs, but they at least gave an idea of the quantity of informal caregiving.

Analysis of data from a more recent nationwide cross-sectional study of 4,000 noninstitutionalized elderly (65 to 84 years of age) confirmed the scope of informal care (Johansson, 1985). Projected to a total population of 1,280,000, approximately 200,000 needed help with cooking and shopping. Seventy-seven percent of those needing help actually received it. Seventeen percent of this group had help from both the informal and the formal system. The remaining 60% were evenly divided between those receiving informal care (30%) and formal care (30%).

This study also examined care provided for persons needing help with dressing and/or personal hygiene. In this group, approximately 36,000 (83%) received some help. Informal care was received by more than two times those receiving formal care. Five percent of this group reported unsatisfied needs. Of the 17% not getting help, only 2% indicated need.

The same study provided comparisons between different geographic areas in Sweden, and between towns and rural regions, giving the same results about the amount of informal and formal care. Informal care is given more often in rural areas, but the differences between regions are very small.

Comparisons by sex show one definitive difference: men receive more help from the informal system than women. Other comparisons indicate that those living alone obtain more help from the formal system, as might be expected. These general findings about the scope of informal care have been confirmed in another study by Sundstrom (1984).

A more detailed and localized study of family caregiving was recently carried out in Tierp, a rural municipality with about 20,000 inhabitants (Wernberg, 1989). During the fall of 1986, all 2,000 persons 75 years and older were surveyed in different ways (questionnaires, interviews, register studies) regarding health status, activities of daily living, social contacts, living conditions, and so forth. The major purpose of the study was to complete the register data with information on the need for service and the amount and type of informal care given. District nurses interviewed and assessed a sample of noninstitutionalized elderly aged 75 to 84 years and all residents over 85 years of age.

The results showed that the elderly living in their own homes were rather independent. Those who needed help, needed to be assisted primarily with chores, bathing, showering, and walking outdoors. A comparison of formal and informal support given to these elderly documented the fact that most of the care was given by families. Family caregivers functioned as prime caregivers in 75% of all cases. All those persons who were totally dependent on another person for their daily living were cared for by family members. Other local studies have repeatedly confirmed these findings (Pikwer, 1986; Ribacke & Olsson, 1986).

As part of the Tierp research, case studies were conducted with a sample of family caregivers (Johansson, 1987). A group of 39 family caregivers (primarily spouses and daughters) were selected for in-depth interviews. In the cases selected, the elderly would probably have had to move to an institution if intensive family caregiving were not available.

Results of this study revealed that caregiving for a dependent family member was clearly connected to propinquity with the person in need of help (also confirmed by Sundstrom & Cronholm, 1988). Families were strongly committed to caregiving, but at the same time they wanted to share the helping role with the society and its formal caregiving system. Family caregivers needed support, but often were poorly informed about available services. An urgent need for psychological support, counseling, and help in coping with everyday caregiving problems was particularly evident from the interviews.

Another study of family caregivers in two different municipalities found that they often experienced caregiving as a heavy burden (Berg & Holmgren,

1984). Almost 60% of the respondents said they had to curtail social contacts due to the caregiving task. Fifty-five percent experienced mental strain and 40% found themselves "tied to" the care situation.

Other Swedish studies also have revealed that family caregiving is often connected to personal sacrifice and emotional strain. Caring for an older relative suffering from dementia compounds the caregiver's task. Data from several studies document different problems. Adolfsson et al. (1981) reported on psychosomatic illness among caregivers. Tornefelt and Johansson (1988) found emotional strain, and Winquist (1984) found symptoms of depression, anxiety, and remose. Informal care of the demented by family members is one of the most important areas where additional research is considered necessary.

In summarizing available information about elderly care, one can conclude that Swedish families do care for their elderly, and the informal support system is the foundation for the entire elderly care system. The formal support system has a complementary role in care for the elderly and not vice versa. Important tasks for the future should be to provide support for family caregivers and to develop coordination between informal and formal care. There are policies and programs for caregiver support, but adequate linkage between the two systems continues to offer a challenge.

Formal Supports for Caregivers

The integration of formal and informal family care of the elderly presents a mixed picture in Swedish society. Public policy provides the mandate for economic supports, including both cash subsidies for caregiving and salaries for family caregivers. However, the home- and community-based services in the formal care system, which are considered to be the foundation support for helping the elderly to manage at home and maintain their independence, are less clearly linked to informal caregiving. The relationship between them and caregiving by the family still has to be fully defined in public policy. There is the potential for a comprehensive and coordinated approach to care of the elderly in Sweden, but the strategy for accomplishing this goal has yet to be totally realized.

Direct cash payments by local government are available if a permanent need for in-home care is established. The payment goes to the older person and is used as compensation for the cost of care to the family. The level of economic support is based on the assessed need for care and the number of hours of help needed by the elderly person. Certification of need is most often done by a district nurse with a doctor's approval. An economic means test is not required. The subsidies may come from either the county or the municipality, but the latter is now assuming primary responsibility for this type of support. Cash allowances are financed through local income taxes. They are not subject to taxation.

About 20,000 Swedish families are receiving cash allowances for caregiving. Many more are entitled to this type of support but, for various reasons, they do not claim it. One explanation is lack of knowledge about the availability of the cash allowances. Another is the use of differing eligibility criteria in different parts of the country (this is also a program of local government). There are also families that, for ideological reasons, do not want to depend on this type of public support. Still, the home care allowance is an important form of support for many Swedish families.

When the elderly person needs more constant care and attention, a family member can be employed by the municipality or the county as a paid caregiver. As a rule, this arrangement is possible when there is a need for 20 hours or more of care per week. To be employed as a caregiver for one's own family means giving up other jobs unless it is possible to combine part-time caregiving with other part-time work. The salary is equivalent to that of a homemaker or nurse's aid. This type of work does provide fringe benefits, for example, vacation, health insurance, and so forth, and the salary is taxable. According to recent data, about 9,000 persons in Sweden are now employed as family caregivers for their own family.

Under current social policy, these programs of economic subsidies and family caregiver employment are viewed as supplemental to the personal social services which are provided as part of the formal support system. As previously indicated, publicly funded and provided services such as home help, home nursing, day care, respite care, meals on wheels, and special transportation are available to all of the elderly regardless of economic circumstances. At the present time, 19% of the older people in Sweden (280,000 persons) receive home help in various forms. On the average, each person over 65 years of age receives about five hours of help per week. Some individuals (usually over 80 years of age) receive 20–30 weekly hours of help. Home help fees are moderate and seldom constitute any obstacle to care. There also are about 50,000 persons who receive home nursing (many of these also receive home help) on a fairly regular basis. Home nursing is usually free of charge. In addition, day care and respite care services are available in most Swedish municipalities.

Nongovernmental policies and programs also have provided some support for caregivers. Fringe benefit policies often include employment leaves for family members in the case of acute illness, or terminal care situations requiring special support for an elderly relative. The length of leave time available ranges from 3 to 10 days, and has been determined by local negotiations between the unions and the employers. As we shall see, new legislative mandates cover such leaves through the social insurances system.

Voluntary organizations play a small, but significant, role in elderly care. These are primarily church related organizations, but they also include the Red Cross and other nonsectarian groups. They provide social contact activities such as friendly visiting and escort services and, occasionally, volunteer housekeeping or chore services. Pensioner organizations, which include 30% of retired people, also perform some services, but their main role is to function as an advocacy group for the elderly.

In recent years, voluntary organizations have become more involved in service activities for older people. They function as a "gap-filler" in the formal system and provide indirect help to informal caregivers. There is no accurate data about the extent of their activities. Although helpful in some situations, they clearly play a minor role in the formal care system.

Caregiving Issues and Policy Initiatives

Informal and Formal Support:
Issues of Citizen Preferences and
Role Complementarity

There are two major issues facing Swedish society today in the development of policies and programs for the support of caregivers. The first is how to support and strengthen informal caregiving without detracting from the importance or support of the formal service system. The issue is different from that expressed in policy deliberations in the United States. In Sweden, there is no concern that too much formal care will substitute for informal care. Rather, the concern is to maintain the commitment to the policy that older people and their families should have a choice between adequate support for informal care and sufficient formal services based on preference. Of course, the choice might often be a combination of the two types of care. Swedish policy, thus, is focused on providing the best possible package of formal care and informal care supports.

Few Swedish studies have focused on the question of whether the elderly prefer informal support or formal support. Some limited information about attitudes towards help is available. It suggests that many Swedish elders consider it unreasonable to put too heavy a care burden on their children. The general preference is towards formal care, but the evidence is mixed and there is some indication of differing attitudes among different age cohorts. Andersson (1986) studied a group of elderly widows living on their own and found that they preferred help from the formal system. However, 60% of the respondents in this study were already receiving home help services and the entire sample was on the waiting list for residential care. Thus, it is not possible to generalize the findings from this research. Tornstam (1984) examined the preferences of a representative sample of persons 15–75 years of age. He found that younger persons (under 40) were in favor of informal care and those over 40 preferred formal services. This difference in attitudes might be explained by concluding that younger cohorts feel an obligation to provide care for their parents while older Swedes prefer not to be dependent on their children. Thus, there is a shift in preference based on the life-cycle stage and dependency position of the respondent.

Attitudes of the elderly in favor of formal support are consistent with general beliefs among the Swedish people that public support is a citizen's right. This includes positive attitudes toward a comprehensive income support system with public pensions as a cornerstone. It also includes commitment to comprehensive health care and social services for all citizens and, in particular, the older members of the society. The commitment is reflected in the continually developing and expanding formal care system. While the emphasis in formal care is moving from institutional care to community and home-based care, there is little questioning of publicly financed and professionally provided services as the foundation of the elderly care system. Formal support, it is believed, should be available for any Swedish citizen who needs it.

At the same time, there is growing recognition of the need for better support of the informal care system which has always been, and continues to be, the focus of care for a large percentage of the Swedish elderly. This is reflected in policies providing financial support for informal caregivers. These policies signify recognition of caregiving realities. They are the result of a growing concern that if caregivers are not supported by elderly care programs, there will be less motivation for families to take on caring tasks in the future. In addition, they give recognition to the financial limitations faced by any society in providing comprehensive formal caregiving services.

A second caregiving issue being considered in Sweden today is the development of policies and programs which enhance complementary roles for formal and informal caregivers. With a comprehensive and well-developed formal support system, Sweden starts from a different point than many other nations, including the United States. The issue is not the adequacy of the formal support system, but rather the interaction between this system and family caregiving. The strong public system has not always given recognition and reinforcement to the informal care being provided by Swedish families. There has been a lack of attention to the burdens and needs of family caregivers in program development. There has also been inadequate coordination between the home help services and family caregiving. Thus, the policy issue becomes how to use formal care more effectively so it is complementary to, and coordinated with, family caregiving.

Swedish Policy Initiatives in Elderly Care

Social policy authorizing major new initiatives in elderly care is currently being considered by the Swedish Parliament. A June, 1988 government proposal entitled *Care of the Elderly in the 90s* focuses on the goal of replacing institutional care with less costly care alternatives. It also gives special attention to the support of informal caregiving. For the first time in Swedish elderly care policy, the importance of informal caregiving is stressed and the support of family caregivers is highlighted. The new initiatives are based on the work of the Elderly Care Committee, a citizen's commission appointed by the government. The legislation is regarded as a milestone in the development of care policy in Sweden.

One important initiative in the new policy is the designation of municipal government as the principal agency responsible for care of the elderly. Local nursing homes as well as home nursing care will now be the responsibility of the kommunerna, rather than different levels of government. There will be shifts in funding patterns to support this initiative. While the details of the process are still being worked out, this change will encourage expansion of home care and decreased use of institutional care.

Objectives of the new policy include allowing older people to live in noninstitutional settings as long as possible. No one should be required to move to institutional care because of poor housing or inadequate available care. Thus, the legislation has provisions to improve housing, as well as increase home- and community-based care for the elderly. If the present housing situation cannot be improved, alternative housing of a higher standard should be available. The policy calls for the development of assisted living arrangements when appropriate. All housing for the elderly will be developed to maximize choice and to support independent living.

The policy calls for decreased institutional care, both through the expansion of home care and by the elimination of some nursing home beds. Nursing homes may be either closed down or converted to noninstitutional forms of care. While the exact number of institutions to be closed is not specified, the goal is the substitution of home care for institutional care rather than merely adding home care resources. The new reimbursement system will encourage this care substitution plan, resulting in an absolute decrease in the number of elderly being cared for within institutional settings.

Caregiver Support Policy

Informal caregiving is included as an integral part of the new elderly care policy. Attention is given to the significant role that family caregiving plays in Swedish society and the need to support informal caregivers through both income subsidies and formal services. The emphasis on the informal system is a new development. At the same time, informal care is envisioned as complementary to, rather than a replacement for, formal care. The emphasis is still on adequate formal support to keep the elderly independent and to meet their service needs. If a family by choice wishes to care for its elderly members, there should be societal support for this effort. If not, the formal system should be sufficient to give the necessary support.

Under the proposed legislation, there is an expectation that the home- and community-based services provided by local government will be delivered strategically to support caregivers in addition to the elderly themselves. For example, day care and respite care services should be guaranteed for support of every caregiver. Home nursing and homemaker services are to be organized in such a way that they complement the informal support provided by families. The key element is service planning and delivery which recognizes and reinforces the informal caregiving being provided. The emphasis is clearly on complementary forms of care.

In order to accomplish this objective, local governments are to be responsible for case finding related to caregivers as well as care-recipients. Health care and social service agencies will be expected to identify caregivers and to inform them of their rights and the services available. Thus, caregivers are to be included in the care planning process. Case finding and case planning are the major mechanisms by which the informal and formal care systems are to be better coordinated as part of the strategy to keep the elderly out of institutions.

The employment of family members as caregivers is also extended under the policy initiatives. In situations involving major and extended care of the elderly, there will be increased funding to provide salaries for informal caregivers. Formal support will still be available to complement the salaried caregivers, but they will assume the primary caregiving role. Also, local government will be responsible for helping salaried caregivers return to the labor market at such time as the paid caregiving is completed. This will include job training, placement, and other labor market services. An additional policy initiative has been enacted by Parliament and will come into force on July 1, 1989. It gives family caregivers the statutory right to a paid leave from work of up to 30 days to care for an elderly family member. This leave can be used for terminal care and for acute care situations. The caregiver will be reimbursed from the social insurance system for his or her total salary during the caregiving leave. A written application, supplemented with a doctor's statement of the need for care, is necessary to receive this type of caregiver support. Also, the elderly person receiving care must consent to the arrangement. This policy gives the temporary care of elderly family members the same recognition in Swedish social policy that is now given to the temporary care of ill children by working parents. It marks a major step forward in the support of informal caregivers.

The remaining caregiver support policies, along with other policy initiatives, are still being debated by Parliament. As government proposals, they are likely to be approved in the next year and most likely will be implemented in January, 1992. To work out all of the details involved in implementing the proposed policy, the Swedish government has appointed a special delegation to develop a reimbursement scheme which will support the new services provided by local government.

The initiatives outlined in this legislation are mainly designed to accelerate the deinstitutionalization of elderly care in Sweden. In order to accomplish this objective, more responsibility for caregiving is transferred to the local community level. At the same time, an important outcome of the policy is official recognition of the importance of informal caregiving. While this is a major step forward, it is only a first step. Support services for informal caregivers must still be developed and fully incorporated into the caregiving system. Methods of cooperation between informal and formal care must be tested and refined. Nevertheless, a new direction in elderly care is being charted and it includes emphasis on the complementary roles of the informal and formal caregiving systems.

References

Adolfsson, R., Kajsajuntti, G., Larsson, N., Myrstener, A., Nystrom, L., Olofsson, B., Sandman, P.O., & Winberg, J. (1981). Anhorigas synpunker pa omhandertagandet av aldersdementa. *Lakartidningen, 28-29,* 2519-2521.

Andersson, L. (1986). Onskemal om informell och formell hjalp och vard. *Socialmedicinsk tidskrift, 63*, 225-233.

Berg, S., & Holmgren, A.L. (1984). *Sjukvard i hemmet*. En studie bland patienter anhoriga och personal. Jonkoping: Institutet for Gerontologi (56).

Daatland, S.O., & Sundstrom, G. (1985). *Gammal i Norden. Boende, omsorg och service 1965-1982*. Oslo: Norsk Gerontologisk Institutt/Stockholm: Socialhogskolan.

Governmental proposal (1987/1988: 176). Aldreomsorgen infor 90-talet. Stockholm.

Hokenstad, M.C. (1983). Social policy and the quality of life in America. In L. S. Swack (Ed.), *Quest for a Caring Society* (pp. 1-12). Cleveland: Case Western Reserve University.

Hokenstad, M.C. (1988). Cross national trends and issues in social service provision and social work practice for the elderly. In M.C. Hokenstad & K. Kendall (Eds.), *Gerontological social work: International perspectives*. New York: The Hayworth Press.

Hokenstad, M.C. (1989). Social welfare policy in Sweden. In J.P. De Sario (Ed.), *International Public Policy Sourcebook: Volume 1*. Westport, CT: Greenwood Press.

Johansson, L. (1981). Valfardsforandringar vid sidan av inkomster 1968, 1974, 1981. Stockholm: Institutet for Social Forskning.

Johansson, L. (1985). Informell kontra offentlig aldreomsorg-nagra data fran ULF-studien 1980/81. Goteborg: Nordiska halsovardshogskolan.

Johansson, L. (1987). Om inte anhoriga stallde upp. Uppsala: Enheten for forskning inom primarvard och socialtjanst.

Lagergren, M., Lundh, L., Orkan, M., & Sanne, C. (1984). *Time to care*. New York: Pergamon.

Nasenius, J. (1981). *New Swedish social services legislation*. Stockholm: The Swedish Institute.

Nusberg, C. (1984). *Innovative aging programs abroad: Implications for the United States*. Westport, CT: Greenwood Press.

Pikwer, P. (1986). Aldres beroende av anhorigvard. Lund: Sociologiska institutionen (25).

Ribacke, M., & Olsson, B. (1986). Halsotillstand och levnadsvillkor bland hemmaboende aldre i Hofors. Hofors: Utvecklingsenheten (26).

Statistics Sweden (1986a). Den framtida befolkningen. Stockholm.

Statistics Sweden (1986b). Ett tidsperspektiv pa mans och kvinnors arbete. Stockholm: Valfardsbulletinen (2).

Sundstrom, G. (1983). *Caring for the aged in welfare society*. Stockhom: Liber.

Sundstrom, G. (1984). De gamla, deras anhoriga och hemtjansten. Stockholm: Socialhogskolan (22).

Sundstrom, G., & Berg, S. (1988). Vad har egentligen hant inom aldreomsorgen? Har vard i hemmet ersatt institutionsvard? Erfarenheter 1965-1985. Jonkoping: Institutet for Gerontologi (69).

Sundstrom, G., & Cronholm, I. (1988). *Hemtjansten: De aldsta vardtagarna och omsorgsapparaten*. Jonkoping: Institutet for Gerontologi (68).

Tornefelt, E., & Johansson, L. (1988). Anhoriga till senildementa i dagsjukvarden blir ofta helt utarbetade. *Larkartidningen, 4*, 207-208.

Tornstam, L. (1984). Sociala attityder till aldre. Uppsala: Sociologiska institutionen (19).

Wernberg, K. (1989). Aldre hemmaboendes behov av service och vard. Uppsala: Enheten for forskning inom primvarvard och socialtjanst.

Winquist, M. (1984). SOS-syndromet: sorg, oro och samvetsforebraelser hos anhoriga till personer med aldersdement beteende. Uppsala: Sociologiska institutionen (24).

13

Family Caregivers and the Elderly in China

CHARLOTTE IKELS

Decreases in mortality and birthrates have been contributing to a rapid "aging" of the Chinese population. In 1985, 87 million people, 8.25% of the population, were aged 60 or older. According to Wei (1987), by 1995 the number of elderly will climb to 120 million and, if the One Child Family policy remains in effect, will constitute 10% of the total population. The question of how to assure a secure old age to so many people is one to which Chinese policymakers are directing serious attention. Nevertheless, when foreigners interested in the elderly visit China, they are usually told by confident officials that in China—in presumed contrast to the United States—the family is the guarantor of a secure old age. According to Zeng (1983):

> The extended family, or household, is the basic unit in Chinese society. The obligations of sons and daughters to take care of their elderly parents is part of the Chinese tradition. Old people thus continue to enjoy a family life and also do their part in helping with the grandchildren and household chores (p. 2).

In New China, this tradition of filial obligation has been written into the Constitution.

The traditional (pre-1949) Chinese family is further described as one in which the elderly patriarch retained great power and authority and lived surrounded by several generations of dutiful descendants (e.g., Hsu, 1953). Under the Communist government, family reforms have been aimed at reducing these perceived power inequities between the generations and between the sexes. Parents, for example, can no longer compel their children to marry the partners selected for them, and women now have the right to initiate divorce and to remarry when widowed regardless of what their in-laws think. During political campaigns in the 1950s and 1960s, young people were sometimes advised to "draw a clear line" separating themselves from politically stigmatized parents, but the Communist government quickly made clear that this slogan could not be employed by the masses to shirk filial obligations (Chen & Chen, 1959).

As Ikels (1975, 1983) points out, the realities behind the traditional family stereotype are difficult to know, but it has influenced and continues to influence policymakers charged with developing services for Chinese elderly. The assumption that Chinese elderly do not have any special problems so long as they have their families has meant a genuine reluctance to expand services and programs to them lest such expansion threaten state budgets and prompt families to abdicate their responsibilities—arguments hardly unique to Chinese planners. Consequently, most special services for the elderly are aimed at those without families to support them.

Nevertheless, decisions in several policy arenas, such as migration, employment, and housing, have indirectly served the state's interests in promoting family solidarity and the availability of family caregivers. In the remainder of this chapter, I will examine these policies and their impact on family caregiving potential during two different periods: (a) the commune period extending from the late 1950s to the early 1980s; and (b) the reform period which immediately followed it and continues to the present. While this examination will not make possible an objective assessment of the importance of such values as filial piety in accounting for high rates of coresidence and intergenerational cooperation, it will demonstrate that these values not only do not operate in a vacuum but, in fact, are given firm structural support by the state.

The Commune Period

Rural Policies: Migration, Employment, and Health Care

In discussing the situation of the elderly in China, it is critical to distinguish between the elderly living in rural areas and those living in urban areas. Essentially, the responsibility for family care is (and has been) much greater in the countryside than in the cities because of the general absence of pensions in the countryside. While the commune system operated, rural villages were divided into production brigades (an entire village might have constituted a single brigade) and production teams. Land was owned collectively by the teams, and village residents were automatically assigned to work on the production team to which their segment of the village belonged. A small amount of team land, usually between 5% and 15%, was available for allocation to individual households for their own use. These so-called private plots were used by the households to produce vegetables for personal consumption or for the market.

Young people had almost no way of leaving the village for employment elsewhere. In the mid-1950s, the Chinese government had implemented a household registration system to control population movement, particularly from rural to urban areas. One's rights to housing, rationed goods, and employment were all affected by the nature of one's household registration. Villagers were expected to work on the team until aged 60 when they could retire to perform household tasks or to work on their private plots. Except in the case of a very few wealthy brigades, retirement was not accompanied by a pension. Older people were totally dependent on the income brought in by other members of the household or on that earned by their own efforts on the private plots. In fact, under certain circumstances, income from work on private plots could exceed income from work for the team, so retirement did not necessarily mean a decline in household income (Davis-Friedmann, 1983). On the other hand, if the older person became ill or disabled, he or she could earn nothing.

Only those elderly with no family members were eligible for the rural welfare system known as the Five Guarantees (this program is not exclusive to the elderly, but they are, by far, the primary beneficiaries). Under the provisions of this program, which is still supposed to be in operation in the countryside, recipients are assured a certain standard of food, shelter, clothing, and medical care, as well as a funeral. According to Chow (1988, p.30), in 1985 nearly 3 million people out of a population of more than a billion were assisted under this program.

During the commune period most, but by no means all, production brigades operated a medical insurance system. Each household was assessed an annual per capita contribution, and its members were entitled to visit the lowest level medical practitioner, normally the so-called "barefoot doctor" who, on a part-time basis, operated the village health station. Except in emergencies, referral from the lowest level to the next higher level was essential to be eligible for reimbursement (though many brigades did not in fact reimburse care obtained at higher levels).

To summarize, during the commune period, the typical older rural resident had normally worked for a production team for many years and retired without a pension. The household registration system and the presence of a ban on migration guaranteed the availability of descendants, especially of male descendants, to provide care to the elderly. Since rural Chinese continue to follow the practice of village exogamy, with sons remaining in their natal villages and daughters being sent to marry into other villages, the birth of sons is considered critical for support in old age. This desire for sons is so great that the Chinese government has had to back off from rigorous enforcement of the One Child Family policy in the countryside.

Urban Policies: Employment, Housing, and Health Care

The elderly in the urban areas have had (and continue to have) access to a wider range of benefits and services than those in rural areas. First of all, since the mid-1970s they are increasingly likely to be receiving pensions. As Davis-Friedmann (1985) points out, the cohort currently in its 60s is benefitting from the maturation of the pension programs established under the Labor Insurance Regulations in the early 1950s. More and more urban dwellers have worked enough years to qualify for full pension benefits when they retire, and they are increasingly likely to retire from state sector enterprises, which offer more extensive benefits than the collective and private sectors. Depending upon their years of service, and whether and when they had participated in revolutionary work prior to the establishment of the People's Republic of China, retirees were eligible for from 60 to 100% of their last wages. Since wages were seniority based, these regulations frequently had the effect of maintaining the older person's economic predominance in the household. Furthermore, the Communist government has long supported on ideological grounds the right of women to work; and since the 1950s, nearly all urban women coming of age have been in the labor force full time. When they retire, they have pensions in their own right and not as dependents of their spouses.

Furthermore, the age of retirement has been set so low[1] that Chinese women are less likely than their counterparts in the West to have to choose between employment and caregiving. In the urban areas then, newly retired workers are increasingly viewed as a double benefit: they continue to bring money into their households and simultaneously become available to carry out many routine daily tasks, including the provision of care to family dependents.

Young people in the cities, just as young people in the countryside, were also restricted in terms of migration and employment opportunities. Individuals fortunate enough to attend colleges or universities (a tiny percentage of the school-aged population) were assigned to jobs anywhere in the nation, while those graduating from middle schools were generally assigned jobs within their own urban district. Generally, these jobs were considered lifetime assignments. Job transfers, particularly of higher level officials or party members, were transacted on behalf of the workplace or the party and seldom on behalf of the individual.

Nevertheless, the Chinese government was sensitive to the consequences to parents of having all children assigned far away, and modified policies to prevent parents from being left alone. During the decade of the Cultural Revolution (1966–1976), for example, more than 15 million urban school leavers were relocated ("sent down") to the countryside. An only child or, in the case of families with several children, the last child at home was generally exempted from this policy. After 1978, when many of these sent-down youth were anxiously seeking ways to return to the cities and find employment, the Chinese government authorized the expansion of the *dingti* or substitution policy, whereby a child was allowed to join the parental workplace upon the parent's retirement. Similarly, should a parent's health fail and no child be in the area, the parent's workunit might contact the child's unit and attempt to arrange the child's transfer back to the home area. Thus, nearly all urban parents have a child living in their immediate area, and most have adult children living in their own household.

In the urban areas, the workplace (or "unit") has the primary responsibility of providing housing for its workers. When a unit has no housing of its own, its workers are dependent upon the municipal housing bureau to make assignments. Although some urban residents own their own apartments (and almost all rural residents own their dwellings), there is no real private market in housing. Because of a virtual ban on housing construction during the decade of the Cultural Revolution, residents of older cities, such as Shanghai and Canton, faced a tremendous housing shortage which has only recently begun to be alleviated. One consequence of this has been the inability of newly married couples to acquire independent housing and their consequent doubling up with their parents. Furthermore, children of high-ranking officials often cannot hope to qualify for housing equivalent to what their own parents have, so that even when housing might be available, such children may prefer to remain with their parents.

In any case, coresidence obviously facilitates the delivery of care by the family; and the majority of the elderly continue to live in vertically extended families. According to Hareven (1987), a 1984 study in urban Tianjin found that only 6% of the elderly lived alone while 16.7% lived with a spouse only. Nearly all the rest (71%), whether married or widowed, lived with at least one child, while the remaining 6% lived with grandchildren. In a study of the population over 70 in one Canton neighborhood, Ikels (1988) reports that only 11% of the elderly lived alone while 6% lived with a spouse only. A majority of 71% lived with at least one child, while 12% lived with other relatives, usually grandchildren but also nieces and nephews.

A high rate of coresidence of parents and adult children is frequently interpreted as a measure of familial solidarity. As Zeng (1983) has pointed out, coresidence also means that the older generation can contribute to the efficient running of the household. This contribution is especially appreciated by the younger generation, given that both partners are normally employed full time. Nevertheless, the idea that coresidence is the preferred living arrangement of the Chinese has been challenged by surveys which found, for example, that 55% of the elderly in a rural study (Jia, 1988) would prefer to live separately from their children and that nearly 90% of young people in an urban study (Zeng, 1983) hoped to establish their own nuclear families. The Five City Family Study (Hareven, 1987) also found that about half the elderly expressed a preference for living separately, although—presumably reflecting their own needs—the older the elderly person, the more likely he or she was to express a preference for coresidence.

To summarize, during the commune period and even into the present, the typical retired urban worker has been a leading beneficiary of state policy. Restrictions on migration and employment have promoted the proximity of descendants, while the acute shortage of housing has meant the doubling up of families and the persistence of three-generation households, however inconvenient or conflictual such arrangements may actually be. Similarly, early ages for eligibility for retirement result in a pool of middle-aged women who can provide care. The fact that the majority of the newly retired elderly have substantial pensions and health coverage means that they are unlikely to be perceived as economic liabilities, but rather as major contributors to the household economy. Since about 1980, however, major policy changes in the economic domain have begun to undermine these structural supports to family caregiving.

The Reform Period

Rural Reforms: Employment and Health Care

In late 1978, the Communist Party authorized the first of a series of major reforms of the national economy that eventually resulted in the disappearance of the commune system. Over the next few years, brigades and teams lost most of their authority with the implementation of the "household responsibility system." Under this system, team land was redistributed to individual households, which then signed production contracts with the village authorities to supply the state with a specified grain quota. Any surplus production could be disposed of as the household saw fit.

Because rural underemployment was seen as a major problem, the government sought to move a substantial proportion of the labor force out of agriculture and into other lines of economic activity. Villages (former brigades) and individuals were encouraged to start factories and businesses. The reinvigoration of small towns in the countryside was declared a development priority (Fei et al., 1986). Young people, in particular, have taken advantage of these new opportunities and frequently leave the older people to meet the household's grain quota while they move "temporarily" into the towns.

Not all rural areas have the potential to develop industrial or commercial centers; and for such areas, an alternative solution to underemployment is to export labor. Currently, millions of young men are organized into construction crews in their home areas and sent out to find work all over China. Young women, on the other hand, are recruited from relatively impoverished provinces such as Anhui to fill domestic service positions in Beijing and other large cities. Itinerant peddlers from Sichuan can be found in Tibet, and scores of young people from Zhejiang repair shoes along the streets of Canton. All of these workers continue to hold rural registration; and their tenure, whether in nearby towns or distant provinces, is entirely dependent upon their employment circumstances. Housing (or temporary dwellings in the case of construction workers) is provided by the employer; but since most of the workers are assumed to be temporaries, they are not usually eligible for pensions or medical coverage. When their jobs are terminated, they must immediately find new ones or risk being sent back to their home communities by public security officials.

This loosening of employment opportunities for rural youth is already having an impact on their families. First, much of the increase in household wealth has gone into the construction of housing, particularly for newly married couples. More families are now able to afford to live separately if that is their wish. Second, in many areas the older people now find themselves single-handedly responsible for meeting the household's contracted grain quota. As they age, they increasingly wonder how they are going to be able to manage this laborious work. Third, younger people working outside of agriculture generally can earn more money than their parents, and the disposal of this money is more under their own control. Previously, the production team head had given the earnings from all the members of a household to its official head—normally the senior male.

Not surprisingly, the net result of the changes described above has been increasing economic insecurity on the part of the older rural population. When Chinese households "divide," that is, when extended families decide to establish separate budgets for the constituent nuclear families, formal arrangements for the care of dependent parents are usually written into the division agreement. Recent investigations in Zhejiang by Yang (1989) suggest that the younger generation meets the needs of the elderly primarily through the provision of grain and only secondarily through cash. According to Yang's analysis, the nature of the sons' work is the major influence on the likelihood of their supporting their parents with money. Sons working in the agricultural sector have very limited cash incomes and tend to provide their parents with grain, whereas sons employed in the industrial or commercial sector, with higher cash incomes, tend to provide their parents with cash. Not surprisingly, Yang's informants thought that the "perfect arrangement" for support in old age was to have one son working in the fields and one working outside the village.

In March 1987, to help deal with this problem as well as with increasing disparities in income between villages, the State Council approved a plan of the Ministry of Civil Affairs to establish a social security system in the villages (Chow, 1988). Various types of programs were to be introduced depending on the level of economic development of the locality. Thus, underdeveloped and "hardship" regions were to operate the Five Guarantees system and provide relief for "hardship" households with funding coming from state relief funds as well as local subsidies. Developing regions were to undertake additional welfare responsibilities and set up savings cooperatives. Funding would come from state relief funds as well as contributions from collectives (village-run enterprises) and individuals. Developed and affluent regions were to introduce social insurance schemes which would be funded by contributions from insured parties.

Bright Moon Village in Hunan province responded promptly to the proposal from the Ministry of Civil Affairs and had its regulations in place by May 1987. Jia (1988) reports that, as prescribed, the funding for the old-age security program comes from personal contributions of participants (3 yuan a month—less than $1 US) and from contributions from the collective sector (9 yuan a month per participant).[2] Monthly benefits up to a maximum of 40 yuan will depend upon the length of time the retiree has contributed to the program. For those individuals already 60 years of age or older, the village will pay out 18 yuan monthly—this sum is totally inadequate to support a living, but it does address the issue of pocket money. Significantly, Jia (1988, p. 145) adds:

> At the present stage, the social security system in the rural areas is far from comprehensive and can only serve as a supplement to family care. The family still plays a vital role in supporting the elderly both financially and physically. Bright Moon Village has written in its village agreement for taking care of the elderly that if the living standard of any elderly is below the minimum their children have to pay the rest to meet the standard.

Another change associated with the reforms—though not intended by them—has been that with the shift from a collective to a private orientation many villages found that it was difficult to sustain their voluntary medical insurance programs as wealthier households, confident that they could pay for their own care should the occasion arise, ceased to participate. In 1975, according to Liang and Whitelaw (1987), 85% of the production brigades had such insurance; but by 1981, this figure had already shrunk to 58%. Thus, nearly half of the rural population was already facing full responsibility for medical expenses; and this proportion can be expected to grow.

To summarize, the recent rural reforms and their aftermath have jeopardized the security of the elderly even as they have raised the general standard of living. Families are now able to afford the construction of new dwellings which are set aside for the use of newly married couples. The separation of residence, in turn, facilitates the practice of budgetary separation with mixed results for the dependent elderly. Furthermore, employment opportunities outside of the village frequently remove the younger generation from the daily life of the elderly and result in the elderly having to perform not only ordinary household tasks but heavy fieldwork as well. Should health fail, not only are caregivers less likely to be immediately available, but the costs of medical care are likely to be beyond the reach of most elderly. The recommendation that rural areas develop social insurance schemes in accordance with local resources only reproduces regional inequalities, providing pocket money at best, and doing nothing to deal with the problem of increasing health care costs.

Urban Reforms: Employment, Housing, and Health Care

The elderly in the urban areas have been less dramatically affected by the urban economic reforms which did not begin to take effect until around 1983. One of the major urban reforms was to restructure the financial relationship between state enterprises and the central ministries to which they are responsible. Instead of relying on the ministry to even out the profits and losses of its set of enterprises, state enterprises became individually responsible for their own profits and losses. In theory, instead of having its losses covered by the following year's budget, an enterprise could go bankrupt. The objective of the new policy was to increase efficiency, and the hope was that since successful enterprises would now be allowed to retain their profits they would use them for investment and expansion. Once their budgets were relatively freed of central direction, however, managers disproportionately funneled their profits into fringe benefits for their workers. Since the primary felt need of the workers was for housing, an unprecedented construction boom (the very one providing so many employment opportunities to rural youth) began.

Much of the new housing construction is occurring in the outskirts of the cities, where land acquisition costs are less. While older people welcome new housing that makes it possible for their children to marry and establish households, they themselves are less enthusiastic about moving out of their familiar, even if congested, neighborhoods. Now, for the first time in decades, more and more urban Chinese families have to make decisions about both their living arrangements and the desirablity of their consequences rather than simply resigning themselves to years of doubling up. Judging from the preferences cited earlier, it is clear that we can expect the proportion of elderly living alone or only with a spouse to increase. Furthermore, since the new housing is often located miles away from the urban core, distance poses a real problem for caregivers living separately from the elderly.

Another reform intended to increase efficiency in urban enterprises has been wage reform. Prior to the middle 1980s, wages were based essentially on technical grade and seniority. Performance had no noticeable affect on income or job security, and state workers referred to their jobs as "iron rice bowls." Now, however, a worker's base wage, still determined by type of work and seniority, makes up only part of the monthly paycheck. Another hefty chunk—sometimes as much as 100% of the base wage—is made up of bonuses based (at least in theory) on performance. Pensions, however, are still calculated on the basis of the last wage earned before retirement. Consequently, the situation described by Davis-Friedmann (1985), in which the retiree's income exceeded that of the younger members of the household, is likely to become less frequent.

As in the rural areas, another significant reform primarily affecting young people entering the labor force has been an increase in job opportunities and geographic mobility. Although college and university students continue to be subject to "unified assignment" upon graduation, middle school graduates may seek jobs anywhere within their particular metropolitan area as well as in certain designated areas, such as the coastal Special Economic Zones. Both the new wage system and the possibility of employment outside of one's immediate neighborhood have the effect of increasing the younger people's autonomy and control over their own income.

A further reform, implemented in 1987, affects the medical insurance systems. With the general inflation that has followed in the footsteps of earlier reforms, health care costs have escalated—in at least one province quadrupling between 1980 and 1986—and the Chinese government has sought ways to reduce the burden on the state of these costs. Previously, state employees and retirees had all their normal medical expenses covered as fringe benefits by their units. All they were responsible for was a nominal registration fee whenever they saw a doctor as an outpatient, and the costs of their meals when they were hospital inpatients. Now, however, they are additionally responsible for small copayments on the order of 5% to 10% for medications and hospitalization, and some expensive medications and procedures are entirely the patient's responsibility. Those working in the collective sector have always had less generous coverage, but recently some financially strapped workunits have cut contributions to their workers' medical costs to only a few yuan a month. Workers in the private sector are entirely responsible for their own health care.

To summarize, though less drastic overall, the combined impact of these reforms on the urban elderly is similar to that experienced by the rural elderly. More and more families are likely to have to negotiate future living arrangements as more housing becomes available. Increased freedom of choice in job selection and in job location provides young people with legitimate reasons for moving away from their parents. Changes in the wage structure and in responsibility for meeting health care costs work—at least temporarily—to the advantage of the young and the disadvantage of the old. Thus, just as older people may need to rely on the financial resources of the family, more younger people are less likely to be immediately available to meet their needs.

Perhaps even more pressing than financial issues are service issues. Specifically, who will meet the service needs of the elderly who do not live in extended families? Currently, services such as the Five Guarantees in the rural areas or free assistance from a neighbor who is paid by the street committee are options reserved for the childless elderly. Similarly, candidates for homes for the aged must be without family and capable of self-care. As Olson (1987) points out, the decision to limit services to those elderly without families serves the interests of current policymakers' intent on modernization of the economy. Focusing on the childless elderly serves two purposes: overall costs are kept down while, at the same time, younger people are assured that if their one child does not survive to adulthood they nevertheless will be cared for in old age.

The emphasis on filial obligation also serves to obscure the plight of caregivers who themselves are elderly, such as spouse caregivers, whose numbers are likely to increase as more young people live independently. Currently, families are very much on their own when it comes to providing care to the chronically ill or impaired. Some rely on domestic help, but the women prepared to accept this kind of work demand wages most families cannot easily meet and tend to move on to higher paying factory work as soon as they can. Though there is a home physician program in the urban areas, there are no equivalents of home health aides, homemakers, day care facilities, or respite care programs to alleviate the constant pressure on family caregivers. Given the absence of support programs for family caregivers, it seems reasonable to conclude that the topic of caregiver burden will become an important popular—if not official—topic in the near future.

There is a precedent to suggest directions the Chinese government may take to deal with these problems. Fifteen years ago, the people and the government of Hong Kong faced a situation very similar to that currently facing China. A glimpse at how Hong Kong dealt with the transition from a rhetoric of filial piety to the realities of family caregiving may prove instructive.

A Glimpse into the Future

The population of Hong Kong is nearly 99% ethnic Chinese, and almost the entire older population was reared in China. In Hong Kong, the British colonial government long subscribed to the view that the existence of a family obviated any need for the development of special services for the elderly, and into the 1970s, provided minimal services despite the fact that many elderly were separated from their families who had remained in China. Up until the early 1970s, when the Hong Kong government and private welfare organizations began to reconsider the nature of the services available to the elderly, institutionalization had been the preferred mode of resolving their housing and financial problems (Tao, 1981). In order to be admitted to a home for the aged or a hostel (facilities located in public housing blocks), a candidate had to be destitute and capable of self-care, as these institutions were, with only two or three exceptions, primarily homes for the well elderly and not nursing homes—the same criteria currently used in China. Applicants had to be without family members in the Colony or, in a small minority of cases, estranged from them. However, by the early 1980s, the populations in these homes for the aged were by and large no longer capable of "self-care." Furthermore, there was a substantial noninstitutionalized population looking for the kind of care that was only likely to be available in nursing homes. While the government was slow to acknowledge this need, the private sector was not; and scores of unlicensed nursing homes run as businesses were set up to meet it.

In Hong Kong, unlike China, pensions were scarce (a 1977 study revealed that less than 3% of the elderly claimed to have pensions) and public assistance extremely limited. In 1973, out of a total elderly population of 288,688, only 10,043 individuals were receiving public assistance (Ikels, 1975). With no money of their own, the elderly were totally dependent on their children, even for pocket money. Advocates for the elderly argued that their inability to contribute to the household budget was responsible for severe strain in many families. Economic difficulties were predicted to force more and more elderly out of their families and onto the public assistance rolls. Thus, in 1973, the Hong Kong government took its first step toward alleviating the burden of financial support by instituting an extremely modest financial grant program known as the Infirmity Allowance. Under this program, all people who had attained the age of 75, regardless of their family or personal financial situation, were entitled to receive a fixed monthly grant. The size of the grant was such that it was not in itself sufficient to enable a recipient to establish an independent household, but enough to enable the recipient to have some financial independence so that he or she would not have to beg family members for tea or snack money.[3] Again, this is the same philosophy inherent in the Bright Moon Village pension scheme.

At the same time, the Hong Kong government was advised by its own Working Party on the Future Needs of the Elderly to abandon the institutionalization approach to problem solving and to make "care in the community" its guiding principle. As Chow (1983) points out, this type of policy is especially appropriate for developing countries with severe budgetary constraints; but in the case of Hong Kong, its implementation was hampered by a lack of support services to make such care feasible. Furthermore, the assumption that so long as they lived with their families the elderly would be satisfied continued to guide service provision, and little attention was directed to issues of family dynamics or to alternative choices for the elderly who might wish to live apart from their families.

In reality, many elderly already lived apart from their families. Ikels (1983) found that so long as a married couple remained intact, there was an increasing likelihood of a period of independent living in late middle age as adult children married and moved out. Later, upon the death of one of the parents, the other usually moved in with a married child. Joining a married child's household in old age has very different implications for power and authority than remaining in one's own home and allowing one's son to bring in a wife. Despite the potential for intergenerational conflict due to differences in education and exposure to foreign ways, Ikels found that most elderly could—or had to—rely on their families when need made independent living impossible. Thus, the current increase in the availability of housing in China may temporarily lead to an increase in separate living of the generations; but when parental need becomes problematic, it is likely to result in the resumption of shared living.

In terms of long-term care, if we can judge from the experience of Hong Kong, we can expect family caregivers in China to continue to carry the main burden of providing services to the elderly—either directly, or indirectly by hiring others. Alternatively, the legitimation and expansion of China's new private sector may facilitate the emergence of nursing homes for those able to pay for them. In the interests of avoiding having to play a role in providing such services from its own budget, the state is likely to continue to invoke the Chinese tradition as an adequate assurance of care for the elderly.

Notes

1. Female workers may retire at 50 and female office staff and professionals at 55 with full retirement benefits—pensions, health coverage, and housing (if their workplace provides it). Their male equivalents, however, may not retire until 60.
2. According to the Statistical Yearbook of China (Chinese Statistics Bureau, 1988, p. 799), peasant annual net per capita income in China in 1987 was 463 yuan or 38.5 yuan per month. Presumably, peasant incomes in Bright Moon Village were above this average since contributory social insurance schemes were deemed appropriate only for developed and affluent regions.
3. Since its inception in 1973, the monthly payment under the Infirmity Allowance (and successor programs) has been steadily increased, and the threshold for eligibility has been lowered.

References

Chen, T., & Chen, W. (1959). Changing attitudes toward parents in Communist China. *Sociology and Social Research, 43*, 175-182.
Chinese Statistics Bureau. (1988). *Statistical yearbook of China (Zhongguo Tunggaai Nianjian)*. Beijing: China Statistics Press.

Chow, N. (1983). The Chinese family and support of the elderly in Hong Kong. *The Gerontologist, 23*, 584-588.

Chow, N. (1988). *The administration and financing of social security in China.* Hong Kong:
University of Hong Kong.

Davis-Friedmann, D. (1983). *Long lives: Chinese elderly and the Communist revolution.* Cambridge, MA: Harvard University Press.

Davis-Friedmann, D. (1985). Intergenerational inequalities and the Chinese revolution. *Modern China, 11*, 177-201.

Fei, H. et al. (1986). *Small towns in China—functions, problems & prospects.* Beijing: New
World Press.

Hareven, T. (1987). Reflections on family research in the People's Republic of China. *Social
Research, 54*, 663-689.

Hsu, F. (1953). *Americans and Chinese: Two ways of life.* New York: Henry Schuman.

Ikels, C. (1975). Old age in Hong Kong. *The Gerontologist, 15*, 230-235.

Ikels, C. (1983). *Aging and adaptation: Chinese in Hong Kong and the United States.* Hamden,
CT: Archon Books.

Ikels, C. (1988, May 14). *New options for Chinese elders.* Paper presented at the Conference on
Social Consequences of the Chinese Economic Reforms, Harvard University, Cambridge,
MA.

Jia, A. (1988). New experiments with elderly care in rural China. *Journal of Cross-Cultural
Gerontology, 3*(2), 139-148.

Liang, J., & Whitelaw, N. (1987). Long-term care in the United States: Some implications for
China. In J. Schulz & D. Davis-Friedmann (Eds.), *Aging China: Family, economics, and
government policies in transition* (pp. 294-311). Washington, DC: The Gerontological Society of America.

Olson, P. (1987). A model of eldercare in the People's Republic of China. *International Journal
of Aging and Human Development, 24*, 279-300.

Tao, J. (1981). Growing old in Hong Kong: Problems and programmes. In J. Jones (Ed.), *The
common welfare: Hong Kong's social services* (pp.107-115). Hong Kong: Chinese University Press.

Wei, H. (1987). Growth of the aged population in China: Trends and policies. In J. Schulz & D.
Davis-Friedmann (Eds.), *Aging China: Family, economics, and government policies in transition* (pp.10-18). Washington, DC: The Gerontological Society of America.

Yang, H. (1989, March 17). *The future family support system for the rural elderly: The conse-
quences of the one-child policy and the latent impacts of the current rural economic reform.*
Paper presented at the 41st annual meeting of the Association for Asian Studies, Washington,
DC.

Zeng, S. (1983). China's senior citizens. In *The elderly in China* (pp.2-12). Beijing: China Re-
constructs.

About the Editors

DAVID E. BIEGEL, Ph.D., is the Henry L. Zucker Professor of Social Work Practice, and, Director, Practice Demonstration Program, Mandel School of Applied Social Sciences, Case Western Reserve University. Dr. Biegel has been involved in research, scholarship, and practice pertaining to the delivery of services to hard to reach population groups and the relationship between informal and formal care for the past ten years. He is the author of a number of books and articles about caregiving, self-help, social networks, and social support. Current research activities include serving as Co-Investigator of a four year NIA funded longitudinal study of caregivers of dementia patients, and Principal Investigator of a cross-sectional study of black and white family caregivers of mentally ill persons funded by the Ohio Department of Mental Health. Dr. Biegel is the author of over fifty publications.

ARTHUR BLUM is the Grace Longwell Coyle Professor of Social Work at the Mandel School of Applied Social Sciences, Case Western Reserve University. During his career he has served as Director of the Center on Juvenile Delinquency, the Mandel Center for NonProfit Organization, and the Practice Demonstration Programs, Case Western Reserve University. He has published widely in the field of social work on group work and group therapy, delinquency, residential treatment, mental health, aging, service delivery, and the value base of social work. He serves on a number of journal editorial committees. Dr. Blum has served as a consultant in Israel to the School of Social Work, Tel Aviv University and to the Israeli government, and in Sweden and Norway. His current areas of concentration are the design of service delivery systems, which includes an emphasis on support networks and self-help activities, and the value dilemmas underlying social work practice and policy.

About the Contributors

LINDA BOISE, Ph.D., received her degree in Urban Studies at Portland State University in June, 1989. Her current research involves a comparison of the impact of caregiving for children and caregiving for parents on job stress and absenteeism. Her research interests include the relationships between employment and family responsibilities, the effects of social and health policies on women, and family caregiving.

EDGAR F. BORGATTA is Professor, Department of Sociology, at the University of Washington. Author and editor of numerous publications in the fields of aging, social psychology, and research methodology, his recent works include *Critical Issues in Aging Policies* (with Rhonda Montgomery) and *The Future of Sociology* (with Karen Cook). In addition, he was a founding editor for the journals *Sociological Methods & Research* and *Research on Aging,* the latter of which he still serves as editor. His current research interests include studies on the relationship between life expectancy and population change, and the relationship of these to periods of dependency in the population.

NANCY J. CHAPMAN, Ph.D., is a Professor in the Department of Urban Studies and Planning at Portland State University. She has been involved in research on informal helping networks and caregivers of the elderly for more than 10 years. Her related publications include: *Helping Networks and Human Services* (Sage, 1981) with Charles Froland, Diane Pancoast, and Priscilla Kimboko; and an information synthesis of the literature, "Gender, marital status, and childlessness of older persons and the availability of informal assistance," in *Health Care for the Elderly: An Information Sourcebook* (Sage, 1989), edited by Marilyn Petersen and Diana White.

TAMY S. CHELST is a Research Assistant Professor at the Institute of Gerontology of Wayne State University. As a doctoral candidate in Audiology at the University of Michigan, she developed a conversational passage design to study the impact of the hearing loss of a conversational partner on communication. She has focused clinical and research interests on the diagnostic and rehabilitative audiological treatment of institutionalized and independently living elderly individuals. Dr. Chelst is presently the principal investigator of a one year grant from the AARP Andrus Foundation to study the impact of conversational behavior between drivers and passengers within the automobile on driver performance for normally hearing and hearing impaired elderly drivers. Other current research interests focus on changes in student sensitivity toward the hearing impaired elderly after an extended hearing loss simulation experience. To complement traditional in-service training for front line staff in long-term care facilities for the elderly, Dr. Chelst plans to study the impact of hearing loss simulation on nurses and nurses' aides. Specifically, she will investigate syntactic and pragmatic strategies in conversational behavior addressed to hearing impaired residents.

DAVID A. CHIRIBOGA is an Associate Professor and the Chair of the Department of Graduate Studies at the School of Allied Health Sciences of the University of Texas Medical Branch at Galveston. For over seventeen years, he was on the faculty of the Department of Psychiatry at the University of California, San Francisco, where, with Marjorie Fiske and Majda Thurnher, he conducted a series of longitudinal studies on the impact of normative and nonnormative transitions across the life course. His principal research interest lies in the domain of stress and coping. Dr. Chiriboga's current research focuses on the stresses experienced by middle-aged men and women who act as caregivers to parents afflicted with Alzheimer's disease.

ARTHUR C. EMLEN, Ph.D., has been Director of the Regional Research Institute for Human Services for 16 years and Professor of Social Work at the

Graduate School of Social Work at Portland State University for 24 years. For the past seven years, Dr. Emlen's research interests have centered around child care and work–family issues, specifically the impact of employees' child care needs on the workplace. Prior to that, he conducted research on informal family day care arrangements, neighborhood referral services, family permanency, and planning for children who are in foster care or at risk of unnecessary placement. In 1987, Dr. Emlen was awarded the Branford Price Millar Award for Faculty Excellence by his peers. Also in 1987, at the 75th anniversary of the United States Children's Bureau, Dr. Emlen received the Secretary of Health and Human Services Award for pioneering work that assisted states to plan toward a permanent family status for children who receive public child welfare services.

TANYA M. GALLAGHER is a professor of speech language pathology and the Director of the School of Human Communication Disorders, Faculty of Medicine at McGill University, Montreal, Quebec. She was formerly an associate professor of speech language pathology at the University of Michigan (1972–87). She obtained her Ph.D. in speech language pathology in 1972 from the University of Illinois.

NANCY GILLILAND, Ph.D., is an Associate Professor of Sociology at Moorhead State University, Moorhead, MN, where she teaches courses in aging, medical sociology, and gender. She has published in the areas of dual career families, women's health, aging policy, and has coauthored an ethnography of a nursing home. Current research interests include conceptualizations of gender in regression models and energy conservation by older householders.

ROMA S. HANKS is Project Coordinator for Interactive Planning for Family Futures. She holds a B.A. in psychology from David Lipscomb College, an M.A. in clinical psychology from George Peabody College of Vanderbilt University, and is a candidate for the Ph.D. in family studies at the University of Delaware. She is a member of the American Sociological Association, the National Council on Family Relations, Phi Kappa Phi and Omicron Nu. She has presented scholarly papers nationally and internationally in the areas of family and organization ethics, corporate mobility, and family/organization interaction. She is currently coediting a special issue of *Marriage and Family Review* on "Corporations, Businesses and Families."

LINDA HAVIR, Ph.D., is an Associate Professor of Sociology at St. Cloud State University, St. Cloud, MN, where she teaches courses in statistics, research methods, aging, and medical sociology. She also supervises sociology internships. She has conducted applied research on rural elderly and was just awarded a 1989 Gerontological Society of America postdoctoral applied research fellowship to study rural senior centers in Central Minnesota. She has published research on working mothers, elderly volunteers, and the professional careers of sociology graduates. Current research interests include the role and functions of senior centers in rural areas, the theoretical integration of the research on the rural elderly, the impact of internships on the careers of sociology graduates, ethical issues involving informed consent, and the volunteer roles of older women.

MERL C. "TERRY" HOKENSTAD is the Ralph S. and Dorothy P. Schmitt Professor at the Mandel School of Applied Social Sciences, Case Western Reserve University. Professor Hokenstad's publications include three books and numerous monographs and journal articles in the areas of social welfare policy, service provision for the elderly, and human services education. He has been the principal investigator or participant in a number of studies on community services and home care for the elderly. In recent years, Professor Hokenstad's academic interest has centered on international social welfare. He has traveled and lectured extensively in industrialized nations and has studied the provision and coordination of health care and social services in different national contexts. He has served as a Fulbright Lecturer and Visiting Professor in Comparative Social Policy at Stockholm University in Sweden and as a Fulbright Research Scholar at the Institute for Applied Social Research in Oslo, Norway. His current research is focused on comparative approaches to care of the elderly in Scandinavia and the United States.

NANCY R. HOOYMAN is Professor and Dean at the School of Social Work at the University of Washington. Nationally recognized for her scholarship in aging, issues related to caregiving of dependents, feminist social work practice, and administration and community organization, she has authored or coauthored numerous publications, including two books—*Social Gerontology: A Multidisciplinary Perspective*, and *Taking Care: Supporting Older People and Their Families*. Dean Hooyman lives in Seattle with her husband and two sons.

CHARLOTTE IKELS is Assistant Professor of Anthropology at Case Western Reserve University. She has conducted research on the elderly and family caregiving in Hong Kong, the United States, and, most recently, in the People's Republic of China. Her publications include *Aging and Adaptation: Chinese in Hong Kong and the United States*, articles in *The Gerontologist*,

Journal of Family History, Research on Aging, Journal of Marriage and the Family, Journal of Cross-Cultural Gerontology, and the *Journal of Comparative Family Studies,* as well as several invited chapters.

BERIT INGERSOLL-DAYTON, Ph.D., is an Associate Professor in the Graduate School of Social Work and Department of Psychology at Portland State University. Much of her research has focused on the social supports of the elderly. She has recently published two articles in this area: "Reciprocal and Non-reciprocal Social Support: Contrasting Sides of Intimate Relationships," coauthored with Toni Antonucci and published in the *Journal of Gerontology;* and "Supportive Relationships in Later Life," coauthored with Charlene Depner and published in *Psychology and Aging.* Another research focus is directed toward interventions with the elderly and their families. An article, "Intergenerational Family Therapy: Theory, Practice and Research," coauthored with Bonnie Arndt and Dixie Stevens, recently appeared in *Social Casework.*

LENNARTH JOHANSSON, M. Sc., is formerly a clinical psychologist working in psychiatric care. For nine years he was Senior Research Officer at Spri (The Swedish Planning and Rationalization Institute for the Health and Social Services, Stockholm), specializing in care for the elderly. Since 1987 he has been affiliated with the Department of Social Medicine at the University of Uppsala. He is working on a doctoral dissertation in the field of informal care for the elderly.

EVA KAHANA, Ph.D., is Professor and Chair of the Department of Sociology at Case Western Reserve University and Director of the Elderly Care Research Center. She is past Chair of the Behavioral and Social Sciences section of the Gerontological Society of America and currently serves on the executive committee of the Sociology of Age section of the American Sociological Association. Dr. Kahana has published extensively in the area of stress and adaptation of the aged and is coauthor of two forthcoming books dealing with stress, aging and health, and altruism among the elderly.

T. MICHAEL KASHNER, Ph.D., J.D., M.P.H., is an economist and an Assistant Professor in the Department of Psychiatry and Behavioral Sciences at the University of Arkansas for Medical Sciences. A University of Michigan graduate, he is currently pursuing research on the legal and economic aspects of the relationship between use of care, health outcomes, and costs for patients with disabling psychiatric disorders.

KARL KOSLOSKI received his Ph.D. in Social Psychology from the University of Nevada, Reno, where he was an NIMH Predoctoral Fellow. He completed an NIMH Postdoctoral Fellowship in Mental Health and Aging at the University of Washington. He is presently an Assistant Professor (Research) at the Institute of Gerontology at Wayne State University. Dr. Kosloski has studied and published in the areas of retirement, health care planning, utilization of mental health services, and developmental methodology.

JAY MAGAZINER, Ph.D., M.S. Hyg., is Director of the Division of Gerontology in the Department of Epidemiology and Preventive Medicine at the University of Maryland Medical School. He received his doctoral degree from the Committee on Human Development at the University of Chicago and his M.S. Hyg. from the Graduate School of Public Health at the University of Pittsburgh. His research focuses on the relationship between psychosocial and environmental factors and health, functioning, and long-term care utilization in the aged.

RHONDA J.V. MONTGOMERY is currently Director of the Institute of Gerontology at Wayne State University. Her recent work has focused on factors associated with caregiving and the causes and consequences of caregiver burden. She is also interested in health service utilization among, and social policy for, the elderly. In addition, she is coeditor of the journal *Research on Aging*.

MARGARET B. NEAL, Ph.D., is an Assistant Professor in the Department of Urban Studies and Planning and a Research Associate of both the Institute on Aging and the Regional Research Institute for Human Services at Portland State University. She has conducted research related to the development and evaluation of social and health programs and policies for the elderly and their families for the past 14 years. Her particular interests are in informal caregiving, terminal care, and assessment of quality of care. She was the Principal Investigator of the Work and Elder Care Project, through which the data described here were gathered.

KAREN NIELSEN, B.A., B.S.W., M.A., is a doctoral candidate with the Fielding Institute. Her prior experience includes ten years with the Texas Research Institute of Mental Sciences (TRIMS), where she was project director on several studies examining family dynamics and depression in older populations. Her doctoral thesis examines the range of stressors experienced by adult child caregivers to parents afflicted with Alzheimer's Disease.

SHERI PRUITT, M Ed., is a doctoral candidate in the clinical psychology program at the University of New Mexico where she is pursuing studies in the areas of behavioral medicine and health psychology. She has published several articles on pain and coping with medical procedures. Her research efforts include laboratory investigations of mood states and the psychological and physiological substrates of pain.

VICTORIA H. RAVEIS, Ph.D., is Assistant Director of Research in the Department of Social Work at Memorial Sloan-Kettering Cancer Center and an Adjunct Faculty Member in the School of Public Health, Division of Sociomedical Sciences, Columbia University. She is a sociologist who has published in the areas of stress, strain, coping and psychological well-being, adolescent suicide, developmental changes in licit and illicit drug use, research methodology, and survey research.

RICHARD SCHULZ, Ph.D., is Director of Gerontology and Professor of Psychiatry at the University of Pittsburgh. His interests include psychosocial aspects of aging, death, and dying, and the psychosocial impact of disabling physical illness on patient and caregiver. He is currently directing three longitudinal studies focused on caregivers of Alzheimer's patients, stroke patients, and elderly outpatients. Dr. Schulz is the author of two books, *The Psychology of Death, Dying and Bereavement* (1978) and *Adult Development and Aging* (1988), as well as over fifty research papers in professional journals.

BARBARA H. SETTLES is Professor of Family Studies at the University of Delaware and is Principal Investigator for "interactive planning for family futures." She holds a B.A., an M.S., and a Ph.D. from the Ohio State University. She is a member of the National Council on Family Relations, American Sociological Association, Groves Conference on Marriage and the Family, and the American Home Economics Association.

KAROLYNN SIEGEL, Ph.D., is Director of Research in the Department of Social Work at Memorial Sloan-Kettering Cancer Center, and Associate Clinical Professor of Public Health at Cornell University Medical College. She has received research grants to study the caretakers of cancer and AIDS patients, childhood bereavement, AIDS risk-reduction behavior, and cancer survivorship. Dr. Siegel has published numerous articles on research methodology, cancer survivors, suicide, and AIDS.

MYRIAM SUDIT, Ph.D., is a postdoctoral fellow in the Rutgers-Princeton Program in Mental Health Research at the Institute for Health, Health Care Policy, and Aging Research, Rutgers University, New Brunswick, NJ. She received her Ph.D. in Sociomedical Sciences from Columbia University. Dr. Sudit has published in the areas of determinants of medical professionals' attitudes and behavior, substance use and the relationship between income, job insecurity, and mental and physical health.

CHARLES A. TAIT received his Ph.D. in Audiology from Stanford University in 1965, and was a faculty member at the University of Wisconsin, Madison, until 1971. He then served as Program Director For Speech Pathology and Audiology at the University of Michigan Institute for the Study of Mental Retardation and Related Disabilities until 1983. His publications include articles on electrophysiological aspects of hearing, learning and language problems in children, and hearing aids. He is presently on the faculty of the University of Michigan, Speech and Language Pathology program.

PHILIP G. WEILER, M.D., is Professor of Community Health and Director of the Center for Aging and Health at the University of California, Davis. He is formerly Chief Deputy Director, State of California, Department of Health Services. In 1970, he worked on President Nixon's Nursing Home Reform Program and started one of the first Adult Day Health Care Programs in the country in 1972. His book, *Adult Day Care: Community Work with the Elderly*, highlighted the need for expanding this form on noninstitutional care for the elderly. While Chief Deputy Director of the California Department of Health Services, he greatly expanded the Preventive Services for the Elderly Program. Dr. Weiler was also responsible for the establishment of the Office of Long-Term Care and Aging in the Department and promoted the establishment of a variety of programs, pilot projects, and research activities to extend health services to the frail elderly in California. He received a commendation from the California State Assembly in 1981 for this outstanding effort. He attended the 1981 White House Conference on Aging and has been actively involved in promoting legislation to meet the needs of the elderly. He significantly contributed to the passage of a bill in California which established and funds Academic Geriatric Resource Centers at the medical schools. Dr. Weiler received the 1985 Key Award from the American Public Health Association Gerontological Health Section and the 1987 Research Award from the American College of Health Care Administrators. Dr. Weiler holds an M.D. from Tulane University and an M.P.H. and M.P.A.

from Harvard University. He did his preventive medicine training in the U.S. Public Health Service.

ROSALIE YOUNG is Assistant Professor of Community Medicine at the Wayne State University School of Medicine. Dr. Young has conducted research and taught in the areas of gerontology, medical sociology, and health service research for ten years. Publications and presentations have focused on these areas and also on effects of chronic disease on families and caregivers. Several publications in medical, social science, and gerontological journals have resulted from her recent study of older heart patients and their family caregivers after hospital discharge for a heart attack.

NOTES

NOTES